BEING A MAN

A GUIDE TO THE NEW MASCULINITY

PATRICK FANNING
MATTHEW McKAY, PH.D.

NEW HARBINGER PUBLICATIONS, INC.

Publisher's Note

This publication is designed to provide accurate and authoritative information in regard to the subject matter covered. It is sold with the understanding that the publisher is not engaged in rendering psychological, financial, legal, or other professional services. If expert assistance or counseling is needed, the services of a competent professional should be sought.

Copyright © 1993 New Harbinger Publications, Inc.
5674 Shattuck Avenue
Oakland, CA 94609

Edited by Kirk Johnson
Cover design by SHELBY DESIGNS & ILLUSTRATES

Library of Congress Catalog Card Number: 92-062206

ISBN 1-879237-40-7 Paperback
ISBN 1-879237-41-5 Hardcover

Printed in the United States of America on recycled paper.

First printing 1993, 10,000 copies

To Kirk Johnson

Contents

I

A Starting Place

You start with two facts about yourself that you can't change: gender and genes. Your basic identity is determined by whether you were born a boy or a girl, and by who your parents were.

You can't change these circumstances, but you can ponder them and understand them better. In the first chapter you can examine what it means to be a man instead of a woman, and determine the strengths, weaknesses, challenges, and opportunities that make up your unique masculinity.

The first step in being a man is being a son. In the second chapter, you can come to terms with your father, the most important parent for boys.

1

Being a Man: Appreciating Gender Differences

This is a book for men who reject outdated ideas of masculinity and want to create a new masculinity.

The old masculine stereotype describes a tough, lonely man who works hard and suffers in silence. The dark side of this stereotype is the man about whom women complain so much—the man who is violent, abusive, lustful, and untrustworthy. This typical man is a kind of zombie: uncommunicative, dead inside, apparently incapable of an inner life. He is friendless, unavailable to his children, and estranged from his own father. He is almost completely out of touch with his feelings, unable to express any emotion except anger. He drinks and works too much.

You've found the right book if you reject that stereotype as a description of your unique masculinity. You're reading the right book if you want to clear up your relationship to your father, come to terms with your work, and make the kind of close male friends you may remember from childhood or school days. This is the book for you if you want to develop a daily spiritual or meditative practice to nurture your inner life. This book can help you form and foster a meaningful love relationship, control your anger, and be a good father to your children. You can learn how to identify your feelings and express them openly and accurately.

Basic Assumptions

We'll go into greater detail later, but there are a few basic assumptions that inform this book. It will help to know from the start that this book assumes that:

Men Are Good—Just as Good as Women

It's good to be a man. You should be proud to be a man. This simple point can be very difficult to grasp these days. Male pride has been obscured and eroded by the rise of feminism in the last three decades. Many men feel vaguely guilty about their masculinity. They agree with some radical feminists that men are the sole beneficiaries of a "patriarchal" society. They accept it that men are to blame for war, injustice, pollution, and most of the other problems on the planet—and that women are the powerless, persecuted victims. It follows that the only hope to heal the planet is to empower women, switch to a matriarchy, and let these kinder, gentler creatures run things on a nurturing, preserving, cooperative model.

But it's not that simple. The emerging men's movement and some members of the women's movement have begun to notice that it takes two genders, working actively together, to keep the so-called patriarchy going. Women vote just as eagerly as men for war-mongering politicians. Polls taken during the Persian Gulf War showed that just as many women as men were in favor of the war (and just as many women as men were opposed to the war). Women share in the economic benefits of strip mining and clear-cutting. Women are largely in charge of raising children in whom patriarchal values persist. And so on.

Our society harms men as well as women, in different but equally devastating ways. Men feel an incredible pressure to earn money. Where women are too often considered sex objects, men are just as often considered to be wage objects or success objects—an equally dehumanizing experience. Much has been made of the fact that working wives are usually still expected to assume nearly all the psychological responsibility for their family's emotional well-being. But working husbands, even those whose wives outearn them, still assume all the psychological responsibility for their family's financial well-being. It's a heavy worry. It's been said that in these liberated times a woman has three options: full-time career, full-time family, or some combination of the two. On the other hand, most men have these three options: work full-time, work full-time, or work full-time.

Men are cannon fodder. In all modern wars, it is the young men who are expected to leave home, fight, kill, and be killed. What does this say about the relative value of the genders? Society's message to men is that we are expendable. Male life is held cheap, and millions more men than women have been slaughtered in war.

Men are expected to stifle their emotions, ignore inner qualms and misgivings, and keep working, keep marching. Men aren't really expected to take good care of their cheap, expendable bodies, or pay much attention to their inner yearnings, lest either of these distractions interfere with their earning capacity or fighting efficiency.

Men can expect to live shorter lives than women.

Although the cliché is that "men have all the power," the average man feels powerless in the face of economic and political events.

Men Are Different from Women

Obviously, sexual equipment and certain hormones are different. As a rule, men are taller, stronger, hairier, and deeper of voice than women. Nobody can deny these traits. But there are more subtle and profound differences that have been listed and debated for centuries. Men are more rational, linear, and aggressive while women are more emotional, intuitive, and passive. Men are objective, product-oriented, competitive builders while women are subjective, process-oriented, cooperative growers.

It's fun to speculate about whether these gender differences are inherent or learned—in our genes or in our child-rearing practices. Either way, how did gender differences come about? What shaped our physical and cultural evolution?

Gender Differences Have Survival Value

To survive, a species must have a wide range of traits to draw on in hard times. For example, when the climate cools, the species will survive only if it has some members who can tolerate cold a little longer, who will survive long enough to reproduce and pass on their cold tolerance to their young.

As organisms get more complex, they need more and more traits to survive. Some traits are almost self-canceling. For example, it's hard to imagine a single individual capable of being both very aggressive and very nurturing, or good at both rational thought and intuitive leaps, or simultaneously decisive and flexible.

Higher life-forms, by reproducing sexually and having innate gender differences, greatly deepen the pool of traits available to them to draw upon to meet changing times. Thus it seems reasonable that humans need both intellect and intuition to survive, and that at some time, millions of years ago, one trait became the specialty of males and the other became the specialty of females. Whether this division of traits took place at the cellular level or the cultural level isn't important. What's important is the realization that men and women are necessarily different, that both genders have their strengths and specialties, and that all the traits are necessary for the survival of the human race.

A funny thing has happened in the last thirty years. The female set of traits has risen in popularity. They have become virtues. At the same time, many of the male traits have fallen into disfavor. They have become vices. For example, women are good because they enter into relationships easily and like to collaborate with others. But men are bad because they are more autonomous and prefer to work alone. In fact, neither approach is inherently better than the other. Both the male and the female style can accomplish great things and be accounted a virtue. But either style can be carried too far and become a vice. Men can become so independent and autonomous that they become isolated and friendless. Women can become so overextended in their commitments to relationships that they become completely engulfed.

You can be proud of your "typically male" behavior. In a wide range of circumstances, traits such as emotional reserve, strong commitment to work, or fierce independence can actually be virtues with high survival value. They are not necessarily vices to eradicate and feel guilty about. You don't have to become less male or more female in order to be a better person. Men have within them the seeds of their own perfection. They don't want and don't have to become more like women to improve, thrive, and prosper.

Of course, these gender differences are generalizations. They hold up only on the average. When you start looking at yourself or particular individuals you find plenty of intuitive men, autonomous women, passive men, workaholic women, and so on.

Men and Women Are also very Similar

The similarities are more important than the differences. In fact, the very complexity and diversity of human experience shows that the chances for cooperation and collaboration between the genders are more numerous and powerful than the chances for conflict.

Men Aren't any Better than Women

This isn't a backlash book. It seeks to take nothing away from women or put them down. Rather, this book seeks to do for men some of the things feminism has done for women: empower them, show them cause for pride, teach them the skills they need for growth and satisfaction.

"Men" Includes Gays

This book assumes that some men prefer sex with women, some men prefer sex with men, and both preferences are natural, moral, and legitimate. We have tried to make chapters such as "Being Two: Making Partnership Work" and "Being Sexual: Enjoying Responsible Sex" apply to both straight and gay couples. If you feel uncomfortable reading the occasional example of two men loving one another, please stay with the feeling, examine your underlying prejudices, and consider the exercise good practice in overcoming homophobia.

How This Book Is Different

This is a different kind of book from others you may have read. This book is more like a shop manual or a workbook in that its main purpose is to teach skills rather than to entertain, inspire, or inform. It tells you what to do instead of what to think. It fills a gap in the growing literature about men by providing step-by-step instructions for accomplishing the goals that other books merely describe as desirable.

Read this book with a pencil in your hand, ready to do some work. Just skimming or browsing won't do much for you. The whole idea is to learn new skills by doing the exercises. To gain anything lasting from this book, you need to make a commitment, right now, to follow the instructions and do the exercises.

This is not a mythopoetic book like Robert Bly's *Iron John* or Joseph Campbell's *The Hero With a Thousand Faces*. It's not a speculative, philosophical work like Sam Keen's excellent *Fire in the Belly*. This book is not an anecdotal account of personal healing like John Lee's *Flying Boy*. This book is not merely a political statement about men's rights or a moral exhortation to eschew sexism.

This book is not based on Jungian psychology, as much of men's literature is. The psychological theory that underlies this book is cognitive and behavioral. The emphasis is on making long-term changes in thoughts, feelings, and behaviors to increase your enjoyment of life and decrease your pain.

To get the most out of this book, you need to be sincere, clear-minded, and have good impulse control. In other words, this is not a book for anyone actively addicted to drugs or alcohol or for anyone who has problems with physical or sexual abuse. If you are struggling with alcohol, drugs, violence, or inappropriate sexual urges, you probably need another kind of help. Consider seeking a twelve-step group, a therapist, or both. In the jargon of the twelve-step programs, this is a post-recovery or thirteenth step book.

Your Gendergraph

This is the first exercise. If you haven't got a pencil yet, go get one. This also goes for women who are reading this book—the exercise works for both genders.

Your Gendergraph

This is the first exercise. If you haven't got a pencil yet, go get one. This also goes for women who are reading this book—the exercise works for both genders.

Below are thirteen "gendergraphs." Each covers an important skill, activity, or character trait in which men and women are commonly thought to differ greatly.

The words and phrases in each gendergraph describe a continuum of behavior or traits, going from one extreme on the left to another, opposite extreme on the right.

To do the exercise, circle the word or phrase that best describes how you operate, most of the time. If none of the choices seems right, just make a dot on the continuum line that feels right for you, most of the time. You can also circle two words or make two dots, to indicate a range of behavior or traits that best describes you. If a word or phrase occurs to you that you find more appropriate, write it in where it fits best.

There are no right or wrong answers in this exercise. It will not be scored or graded. It's for your information only. You don't have to show it to anyone if you don't want to. So be as honest and accurate as you can, and you will get the maximum benefit possible from the exercise.

Relationship to Your Father

completely alienated — antagonistic — strained — respectful, cordial — warm, close — interfering — enmeshed — dependent

Quality of Inner Life

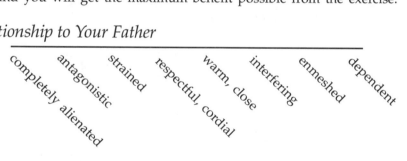

empty, dead — shallow, blank — unaware, unconcerned — vital, interesting — rich, deep — distracting, dreamy — obsessive, spacey — alarming, haunting

Integrity

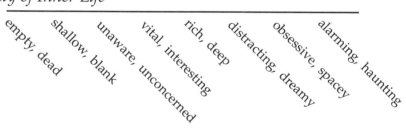

unethical, ruthless — lax — expedient — dependable — honest — scrupulous — judgmental — puritanical

Dedication to Work

workaholic · obsessed · driven · committed · steady · part-time · dabbler · no real work

Friendship

isolated · lonely · independent, autonomous · one good friend · a few close relationships · many good friends · overextended · engulfed

Sex

limp, frustrated, bored · seldom aroused, apathetic · ready, satisfied · turned on, excited · tuned-in, fulfilled · in touch, interested · out of touch, indifferent · turned off, empty

Intimate Relationships

retreating · withdrawn · reserved · close · intimate · engaged · yearning · pursuing

Closeness to Children

absent · detached · available · close · connected · enmeshed · engulfing · smothering

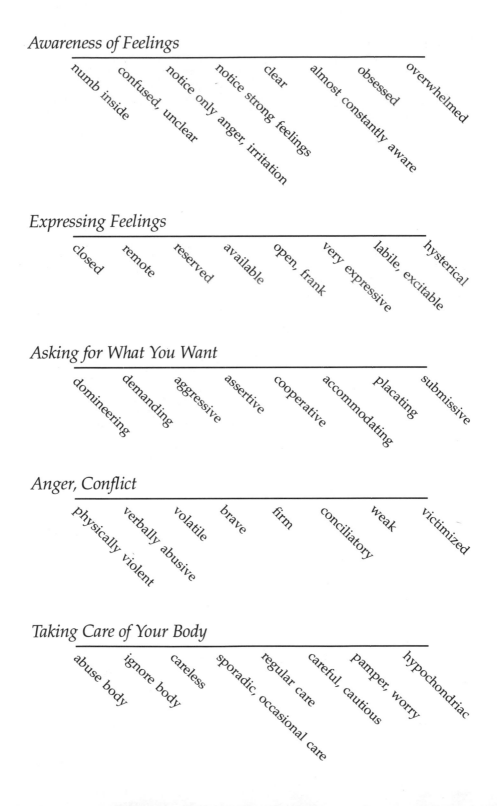

Awareness of Feelings

numb inside   confused, unclear   notice only anger, irritation   notice strong feelings   clear   almost constantly aware   obsessed   overwhelmed

Expressing Feelings

closed   remote   reserved   available   open, frank   very expressive   labile, excitable   hysterical

Asking for What You Want

domineering   demanding   aggressive   assertive   cooperative   accommodating   placating   submissive

Anger, Conflict

physically violent   verbally abusive   volatile   brave   firm   conciliatory   weak   victimized

Taking Care of Your Body

abuse body   ignore body   careless   sporadic, occasional care   regular care   careful, cautious   pamper, worry   hypochondriac

Evaluating Your Gendergraphs

The first word or phrase on the extreme left describes what some people consider "typical male" problems. The words and phrases on the extreme right describe what some people consider "typical female" problems. As you read toward the center from each end, the meanings become progressively more positive, or neutral. By the time you reach the center, the words describe male and female virtues or qualities that are neither "good" nor "bad."

The perfectly balanced man, if such a glorious creature actually existed, would probably fall slightly left of center on each scale. The perfectly balanced woman, if such a glorious creature actually existed, would probably fall slightly right of center on each scale. Of course, these two points of perfect balance assume that just the right words have been selected for each position on each scale—a big assumption.

In reality, nobody has all virtues and no vices. And nobody is typically male or female in every aspect. Men typically find that in some areas they are nearer to the "feminine" end of the scale. And women typically find that they are sometimes nearer to the "masculine" end.

The purpose of this exercise is to identify those typically male traits you have that work well for you and that you can be proud of. Also, it will identify areas in which you need to moderate your behavior—to be a little less stereotypical.

Carefully consider your response to each gendergraph. They will guide you to the chapters in this book that will be of most interest and value for you.

Relationship to Your Father

Evolution, society, culture, and education conspire to make it difficult for fathers and sons to get along. A vast majority of men report strained or antagonistic relationships with their fathers, and better relationships with their mothers. The "father wound" is the most common theme in the growing literature of men's issues.

Women tend to report the opposite pattern, having more conflict with their mothers than their fathers. When their relationships with Dad become problematic, it's more likely that they have become too dependent on their fathers, rather than estranged from them.

If you're like most men, your relationship to your father could be much better. The next chapter, "Being a Son: Relating to Your Father," contains powerful exercises for resolving old business with your father. It will help even if your dad is dead, comatose, senile, unknown, or otherwise unreachable. Even if you are one of the rare men who are on good terms with their fathers or have only fond memories of being a son, work through chapter 2 as a way of clarifying and acknowledging your paternal legacy.

Quality of Inner Life

Man does not live by paychecks alone (or woman either, for that matter). Both genders need a rich, vital inner life in order to thrive. They need to be aware of, but not dominated by, their dreams, intuitions, feelings, ideas, desires, fantasies, prayers, and visions. Men tend to fall short of this ideal through neglect. They focus so obsessively on external reality that their inner world dims and withers. Women tend toward the opposite extreme, focusing on the inner world to the point of obsession, sometimes losing the ability to effectively meet everyday needs.

These are very broad generalities. There are some dreamy, ineffective men and some hardheaded, practical women. But, as a general rule, most men will benefit from more introspection. If you suspect this is true of yourself, go to chapter 3, "Being Whole: Enriching Your Inner Life." It shows you how to enliven your spirit through a daily practice of solitude such as meditation, running, keeping a dream journal, visualization, art, yoga, martial arts, and so on.

Integrity

In their rush to get the job done, to cope, and to survive, many men cut ethical corners. Women tend to worry more about doing the right thing, sometimes going to extremes and becoming too judgmental or puritanical about correct behavior. Both deviations from the golden mean of honesty and dependability can cause a lot of pain in your life.

Even if you are not beset by obvious moral dilemmas, you may feel fragmented or pulled in several directions at once by the demands of home life, job, friends, sex, kids, parents, school, church, and all the rest. Working on your integrity as a man can help. The root meaning of integrity is "wholeness." When you have integrity, it means that you have a clear set of values that you have worked out, prioritized, and tested over time. These values help you allocate your time and money and energy and love in a way that binds the fragments of your life together into a meaningful and satisfying whole.

Chapter 4, "Being Trustworthy: Achieving Male Integrity," will teach you how to clarify, rank, affirm, and act on your values.

Dedication to Work

When it comes to work outside the home, men historically have been the workaholics and women have been the part-timers. This pattern holds true today, but it's changing fast. Social and economic trends increasingly allow (or force) women to enjoy the dubious pleasures of overwork.

You may not be a workaholic, but still find work a big problem in your life. You may be out of work, underpaid, or stuck in a job that is not satisfying. Worse yet, your work may be in conflict with your values. You may be doing something that you increasingly suspect is wrong, something that takes advantage of people, hurts the environment, or simply fails to make a positive contribution to the world.

If your work life is a problem, do the exercises in chapter 5, "Being Useful: Finding Meaningful Work." It will show you how to control workaholic tendencies or find your right livelihood.

Friendship

Men are rewarded all their lives for being competitive, independent, and hard-working. They aren't expected to have many close male friends much after high school or college. They are supposed to meet their scant needs for affiliation within their own families, with their wife and children. If you're a typical man in this regard, you don't have much time, energy, or permission to relate to other men outside of work. If your natural tendency to be autonomous has gone too far, you may feel isolated and lonely.

Women have more permission, inclination, and skill for friendship within their gender. If you want to know how to be friends, watch women. When women have problems with friendship, the cause isn't usually a scarcity of friends. The problem is more likely to be the result of a conflict with or among friends, or due to feeling overwhelmed by the demands of many friends.

If you want to make new friends and deepen your existing friendships, see chapter 6, "Being a Friend: Making and Keeping Male Friends."

Sex

This was a difficult scale to concoct. The words chosen reflect both the physical and emotional realities of sex for men and women. Generally speaking, men are more interested in visual stimulation, physical details, and release through orgasm. Women are more interested in tactile sensations, emotional overtones, and intimacy. In long-term relationships, men most often complain about not enough sex, while women complain of not enough love and affection.

The idea of species survival helps explain why men want more sex and women want more security. Wandering males who feel an urge to impregnate every young healthy female they see are nature's way of spreading genes around and getting a lot of females pregnant. Nurturing females who want to settle down in a secure family are nature's way of making sure that the pregnancies come to term and that children are raised until an age where they can reproduce in turn. (It has been said that human civilization is an egg's way of making more eggs.)

Sex is the area in which many gender differences meet head on. Sex can be a playground where differences are enjoyed, an altar where differences become a spiritual unity, or a battlefield where differences divide and wound. If sex is sometimes a problem for you, read chapter 7, "Being Responsible: Enjoying Responsible Sex." It shows how to dispel male sexual myths, assess your current sex life, add passion to your pairing, chose a sexual partner wisely, come to terms with monogamy, and stay turned on to the same partner year after year.

Intimate Relationships

This gendergraph describes the most common difference that causes problems in love relationships: one partner, usually a woman, wants more closeness. The other partner, usually a man, wants more distance. Both needs are legitimate. Men often need to reinforce their autonomy, to stand alone, to be by themselves to focus clearly on a task or a problem or just a relaxing game. Women often need to reaffirm their primary relationship, to stand together, to be united in common feeling. Problems arise when these needs are in conflict, you don't realize it, and one or both of you begins using manipulative tactics to get your needs met.

Family therapists refer to this as the "pursuer-distancer" system. If this dynamic sounds familiar, you should definitely learn what chapter 8, "Being Two: Making Partnership Work," has to teach.

But there are many other ways that intimate relationships can go wrong: communication problems, conflicts over money or childrearing, differing beliefs and expectations, and so on. It's safe to say that anyone who is (or wants to be) in an intimate relationship should read chapter 8.

Closeness to Children

Raising children is one of the biggest challenges that anyone, man or woman, can face. This gendergraph reflects the fact that men are most likely to err by being too detached and aloof from their children, if not actually absent from their lives. And women are more likely to err by becoming enmeshed in their children's lives, smothering them with too much attention.

But there are many other variables involved in raising children. Anger and abuse—emotional, physical, and sexual—are a huge problem. Discipline and setting limits are an ongoing, daily struggle. Fostering self-esteem and teaching values are important tasks that often get neglected in the hassles of family life.

If you struggle with raising your kids, read and study chapter 9, "Being a Father: Raising Your Children."

Awareness of Feelings

Men in general pay less attention to their feelings than women. This trait has survival value in that men can continue to think and function in the face of strong emotions such as fear, grief, or anger. Men often specialize in taking care of business regardless of the emotional storms around them. The problem comes when the storms abate and you cannot turn your feelings back on. Suppressing feelings and taking care of business can become a habit that is difficult to kick, like an addiction to downers.

For some women, the problem is an overawareness of feelings, a characteristic that can lead to obsession or being overwhelmed and unable to function effectively.

If you identified yourself as numb inside or find yourself confused in emotional situations, not sure of what you really feel, work through chapter 10, "Being Aware: Clarifying Your Feelings."

Expressing Feelings

Even men who are aware of their feelings tend to express them less freely than women. Again, this practice has some survival value in that you can be cool and reserved in a dangerous situation. You can negotiate and prevaricate with the enemy. But here's the rub: what's good for diplomacy is bad for intimacy.

Women tend to be much more expressive of their feelings. This trait also has survival value in that shared feelings are essential for love and true communication. Also, women traditionally have been assigned the job of teaching children how to feel.

Even if you have a pretty good handle on what you feel, do the exercises in chapter 11, "Being Open: Expressing Your Feelings." All your relationships will be the better for it.

Asking for What You Want

As a general rule, men tend to be more assertive than women. Women tend to be more cooperative than men. If the differences stopped there, we would be in good shape. There are times when both tendencies are necessary and appropriate. Problems arise when masculine assertion becomes domination and feminine cooperation becomes submission. To complicate matters, there are also significant numbers of domineering women and submissive men.

So everybody, regardless of gender, needs to know the skills taught in chapter 12, "Being Assertive: Asking for What You Want."

Anger, Conflict

For a primitive people in a harsh environment, volatility is an important survival trait. The man who can jump up, ready to fight at the first sign of threat or danger, is a real asset. The woman who can jump up quickly, grab the kids, and run or hide is likewise valuable. Modern society still values quick reactions, righteous anger, and a willingness to engage in conflict, especially for soldiers and leaders. These qualities are dignified by the names bravery or courage. And most societies still would prefer women to devote themselves to the care of home and children.

But we don't live in caves anymore. For the average person, neither rage nor withdrawal is the best strategy for handling conflict. Evolution and culture predispose men to anger, so they most often become the verbal and physical abusers. Evolution and culture predispose women to avoid anger, so they most often become the victims.

If you have a problem with anger, read and work through chapter 13, "Being Strong: Controlling Your Anger." For many men, anger is the fatal flaw that ruins their chances for happiness and satisfaction in life.

Taking Care of Your Body

In animal kingdom, the females of most species are more important to survival than the males. The females bear and nurse the young, while the males merely contribute a little sperm once in a while. Thus to the males fall the more dangerous roles of bringing down big game and fighting off predators. In lean times, the males are more likely to starve. In primitive human societies, men are praised for toughness, for a willingness to risk their bodies or ignore pain. Women are given most of the responsibility for care of their own and others' health.

Even though we *Homo sapiens* now live in a technological society much more complex than a troop of baboons or clan of hunter-gatherers, it is still true that men's bodies don't get as much care as women's bodies. This is perfectly consistent with our evolution, with the old stereotype of tough men who can take it, and with the economy's and the government's need for expendable men's bodies to burn up in work and war.

The opposite end of this scale is hypochondria—taking too much care of your body, to the point where you seek treatment for ailments you don't actually have. Although there are plenty of male hypochondriacs, it is more typically a female problem.

If you tend to ignore your body or abuse it, read chapter 14, "Being Healthy: Taking Care of Your Body." Even if you are in decent shape, read chapter 14 to make sure you know about the physical problems that are of particular concern to men: stress, heart disease, testicular cancer, and prostate cancer.

2

Being a Son:
Relating to Your Father

Start at the beginning. Start where you first learned how to be a man. Start with your father.

In your family of origin, your first, best, and most enduring relationship was probably with your mother. Your second, worst, and most troubling relationship over the years was probably with your father.

In her *Hite Report: A Study of Male Sexuality*, Shere Hite relates that almost *none* of the 7,239 men she surveyed said that they were close or had been close to their fathers. Almost all the men reported having a better or at least less problematical relationship with their mothers.

Why is this such a persistent pattern? To answer that question, it helps to look at what developmental psychologists have to say about the ideal pattern of psychosocial development for boys. Most theories of developmental psychology agree on some basic stages of development that must by negotiated by males in our society:

1. Early childhood: Separate from and grieve the loss of your mother.

2. Boyhood: Identify and bond with your father.

3. Adolescence: Weaken the bond with your father in order to gain autonomy.

4. Young adulthood (twenties, early thirties): Establish your own identity as an adult.

5. Later adulthood (late thirties, forties): Reconnect with your father as a peer.

Most men accomplish the first stage—breaking with their mothers—in some fashion. Our social, economic, and educational systems make this separation somewhat automatic.

The same social, economic, and educational systems make the second stage—bonding and identifying with your father—very difficult to accomplish for most boys. To bond and identify with your father, he has to be present, he has to have time for you, he has to be interested in you, he has to be warm and accepting, and he has to be patient and peaceful.

These kinds of dads are rare. One study of men in therapy showed that:

- 23 percent had physically absent dads—gone from the home most of the time.

- 29 percent had psychologically absent dads—too busy, uninterested, or passive.

- 18 percent had disapproving dads—cold or moralistic father.

- 15 percent had dangerous dads—yelling and hitting.

- 15 percent had nurturing dads.

Statistics like this show that the "ideal" pattern of development is far from the "typical" pattern of development. The typical pattern is incomplete and runs like this:

1. Early childhood: Separate from and grieve the loss of your mother.

2. Boyhood: Never fully bond and identify with your father.

3. Adolescence: Active rebellion, extreme alienation.

4. Young adulthood: Immaturity, insecurity; feel like a boy masquerading as a man and experience continued alienation from your father.

5. Later adulthood: Natural urge to reconnect frustrated by original failure to bond and remnants of unresolved adolescent resentment.

So what can you do about it? What can you do if you're now in your thirties or forties, after decades of lousy communication, fumbled connections, and missed opportunities with your father? What can you do if your dad is dead or senile or refuses to have any contact whatsoever with you?

You can turn your attention toward your boyhood, perhaps to some memories you would rather forget. You can re-create your early relationship with your father and maybe learn some things that you were too young to notice at the time. You can identify your unspoken anger and fear and sadness. Even if your dad is dead, you can formulate and write down all the things you never said to him that needed saying. You can find some peace and understanding within yourself.

If your father is alive and approachable, you may be able to write or talk to him about your memories and feelings. You may actually be able to improve your relationship with your father.

Work through the exercises in this chapter. Even if your father is dead—especially if he died with a lot unresolved and unsaid between you—do the exercises. Even if you have a fairly friendly relationship with your father, do the exercises. They will be helpful to you at whatever stage you are in your relationship with your father.

Types of Fathers

Write down your boyhood memories of your father. What kind of father was he? How often did you see him? What did you talk about? Where did you go together? What did you do with him?

Put the memories into the appropriate categories that follow to get an idea of what type of father he was to you.

Memories of times when he was absent or seldom home:

Memories of times when he was too busy or disinterested:

Memories of times when he was cold, aloof, or critical:

Memories of times when he was dangerous or violent:

Memories of times when he was loving or nurturing:

After writing down the memories that seem most emblematic of your relationship with your father, take a look at the categories that most of them fall into. If you were able to talk to your father about this exercise, how would you complete these statements?

"When I was little, you seemed _____."
(*dangerous, absent, cold,* and so on)

"I wanted you to _____."
(*hold me, play with me, listen to me,* and so on)

"Here's how I thought you felt about me: _____."
(*angry, indifferent, loving,* and so on)

"What I most wanted to know was _____."
(*that you loved me, that I was okay, why you drank,* and so on)

What else could you say to your father to explain and amplify this exercise?

Here's how Randy, a 38-year-old grammar school teacher, completed this exercise.

Memories of times when he was absent or seldom home:
He was always there. I wish he hadn't been.

Memories of times when he was too busy or disinterested:
He ignored my successes in sports and making models.

Memories of times when he was cold, aloof, or critical:
He called me stupid and dumb and lazy.
He hassled me for hours over a D on my report card.
He complained about my messy room, clothes, homework.
He insisted on respect, never gave it himself.

Memories of times when he was dangerous or violent:
He scooped the candles off my birthday cake and threw them on the floor.
He threw a block at me on Easter morning.
He "cleaned up" my room by throwing my rocks and shells away.

Memories of times when he was loving or nurturing:
None: He gave very few hugs, kisses, touches. He gave no positive strokes, just criticism.

When I was little, you seemed *cold and critical.*

I wanted you to *approve of me, hold me, tell me I was a good kid.*

Here's how I thought you felt about me: *disappointed, critical, unloving.*

What I most wanted to know was *what it took to please you—I've never figured out how to please you.*

I think now that you must have been stressed out during holidays. You always got pissed off during birthdays and Christmas. Were you drinking more then? What was it about family gatherings that you found so hard to take?

Adolescence

For each of these common problem areas, write down the memories that stand out as typical of the way you interacted with your father when you were a teenager.

Driving

Staying out late

Chores, household duties

Language

School

Friends

Girls, dating, sex

Alcohol, drugs

Money

Food

Hair, clothes, grooming

Music

Politics

Other

What would you say to your father about your adolescent years, if you could have a safe, meaningful conversation with him?

What I most regret about my teenage years with you is

What you never understood was

I really wanted you to

I'm sorry about

If I had it to do over, I would

You were right about

You were wrong about

Other:

Here is how Reuben, a 31-year-old musician, completed this exercise.

Driving
I wrecked his car.

Staying out late
I always did it, he always complained. I'm a night person.

Chores, household duties
I hated doing the lawn, the garbage, shining his bohunk shoes.
Stopped doing any at about age 15.

Language
He called my band foul-mouthed punks.

School
A disaster.

Friends
Same foul-mouthed punks. Especially Larry.

Girls, dating, sex
Not an issue; more into my guitar than my dick.

Alcohol, drugs
Threatened to kick me out if he ever caught me smoking dope.
Almost caught me once.

Money
He said his biggest mistake was buying me a guitar at 13.
Never wanted to spend on my real interests, always willing to spend
     for shit like pharmacy school or a three-piece suit.

Food
Not an issue, hardly ever ate together.

Hair, clothes, grooming
If it was cool, he hated it.

Music
After I was 15 he never came to hear me play. Complained about
     rehearsals in the garage. Wanted me to go to trade school, become a
     bootlegger, kite checks...anything but play music. Our biggest,
     darkest cloud—comes between us like a wall of smoke. Neither of us
     can see through it.

Politics
Not sure either of us have any.

Other
Being constantly disapproved of just wore me down. Like walking
     around with an anchor dragging.

What I most regret about my teenage years with you is *that you never came to hear me play after I was 15.*

What you never understood was *how much music meant to me. It was the air I breathed. I couldn't just stop breathing to please you.*

I really wanted you to *support me instead of trying to change my direction.*

I'm sorry about *how I taunted you with weird styles, raunchy lyrics, stories about my spaced-out friends.*

If I had it to do over, I would *understand that you honestly wanted the best for me, but didn't see how music could possibly work out.*

You were right about *the car. I was too immature and reckless.*

You were wrong about *music being an automatic path to destruction.*

Other: *I'm sorry. Let's make the best of the time we've got left.*

Your Paternal Heritage

In this exercise, you will explore what you may have learned or inherited from your father. You'll begin to reconnect with him by finding out what you two have in common, how you are alike and different.

In the four squares that follow, list the character traits, habits, virtues, vices, interests, opinions, and so on that you like and dislike about yourself. As you think of each positive or negative characteristic, consider whether you are similar to or different from your father in that regard, and put the characteristic in the appropriate box.

When you are finished, look especially at the top square on the left. These are your good qualities that you share with your father. It makes a lot of sense to say to your father, "Thanks for teaching me how to be this way. Thanks for passing these good things on to me."

Then look at the top square on the right. These are problems you have that your father also had. This is an area in which you can exercise empathy. Whatever disappointment and pain you may suffer because of these traits you dislike about yourself, you probably share that discomfort and pain with your father. Rather than blame your father for making you this way, say instead, "I understand your pain. I have that problem too."

Now look at the bottom square on the left. These are your own personal accomplishments: the good things about you that you somehow acquired on your own, for which your father provided no example or maybe a negative example. These are your legitimate bragging points.

	Things I like about myself	Things I dislike about myself
Ways I am similar to my father		
Ways I am different from my father		

You can say to your father, "Look, I am a valuable person in my own right. I have learned to do this on my own. I have added this to our family's repertoire of gifts."

Finally, look at the bottom square on the right. These are your grounds for humility. These are your failings or shortcomings or blind spots for which you cannot blame your father. This square reminds you that you too are human, you too are prone to weakness and mistakes. This square is also a gold mine of opportunity because it probably contains stuff that you can still learn from your father.

Here is how Pete, a 45-year-old architect, completed this exercise.

	Things I like about myself	Things I dislike about myself
Ways I am similar to my father	*Strong family values* *Good with my hands* *Good with my hands* *Excellent design sense* *Like to camp, hike, fish* *Easygoing, reasonable* *Helpful* *Good neighbor, citizen*	*Tend to drink and eat too much* *Get preoccupied with work projects* *Color blind* *Poor driver*
Ways I am different from my father	*Willing to take chances* *Can delegate authority and supervise others well* *Sensitive to emotional overtones* *Good with words, ideas*	*Have a hard time making friends* *Prone to depression* *Not very spiritual* *Have lost my curiosity about life* *Bad at golf, though I enjoy it*

Soap Opera

This questionnaire gets at the family traumas, misunderstandings, secrets, and so on that can keep you apart and prevent you from improving or resolving your relationship with your father. This is the stuff of soap opera: the affairs, the drinking, the abuse, the violence, the lies, the cover-ups, the betrayals, the conspiracies, the resentments that bind families into a dense web of silence or a vicious circle of bickering.

Put aside for a moment the question of whether it is even *possible* for you to resolve your relationship with your father. Just ask yourself:

What you would have to do?

What would you have to forgive?

What would you have to forget?

What feelings would you have to reveal?

What secrets would you have to tell?

What secrets would have to be told to you?

What unspoken facts or events would have to be acknowledged?

What ongoing conflicts would interfere?

What questions would you have to ask?

What would you have to apologize for?

What would you want to demand or insist on?

And the big question: How much of this could you accomplish on your own, unilaterally, without the cooperation of your father or the rest of your family?

The answer to this last question will determine whether it's worth it for you to actually make the effort to clean up a relationship gone badly wrong. But don't let pessimism stop you from continuing with the exercises in this chapter. Getting the situation clear in your own mind is of great benefit, whether you can ever effectively share your thoughts and feelings with your father or not.

Don is a 25-year-old house painter who completed this exercise as follows:

What would you have to do? *Open up a twenty-year-old can of worms.*

What would you have to forgive? *My father's abuse of me and my sister.*

What would you have to forget? *The pain.*

What feelings would you have to reveal? *Hatred, fear, shame.*

What secrets would you have to tell? *That he beat me and molested my sister.*

What secrets would have to be told to you? *Whether he ever felt guilt or tried to get help.*

What unspoken facts or events would have to be acknowledged? *Both my mother and father would have to acknowledge the abuse.*

What ongoing conflicts would interfere? *My sister's lawsuit against our father.*

What questions would you have to ask? *Why did he do it? Why did my mother let it continue?*

What would you have to apologize for? *Apologize to my sister for not taking part in the lawsuit, apologize to parents for the help I did give my sister.*

What would you want to demand or insist on? *I want my childhood back.*

And the big question: How much of this could you accomplish on your own, unilaterally, without the cooperation of your father or the rest of your family? *Not enough.*

Don comes from a family that is so dysfunctional that it is impossible for him to make peace with his father. Doing this exercise helped him to see that. It helped him give up his vague fantasies that somehow they could be one big happy family. It helped him see that there was no way he could give everyone what they wanted.

A Letter to Your Father

One of the purposes of all the exercises to this point is to generate material for a long letter to your father. A letter is best. Better than a heart-to-heart talk. Much better than a phone call. In a letter, you can take your time, you can be sure to cover all the important issues, you won't get sidetracked or interrupted, you can get the wording just right, you can avoid being overwhelmed by your emotions, and you don't have to be there when he reads it.

Even if your father is dead or incapacitated, write the letter anyway. You will get enormous value out of just writing the letter. A lot of healing will take place as you decide just what you need and want to communicate to your father.

Whether you mail the letter or whether your father is alive to receive and respond to it are questions you can deal with later.

A good way to get started is to include the material you have written in the other exercises.

- From your boyhood memories, include what it was like for you as a boy, being his son, what kind of father he was, what you felt then, what you wanted to tell him then but couldn't.

- Use your adolescent memories to summarize your teenage years and include all the pertinent messages that you couldn't communicate then or that you have recently realized you want to convey.

- From the exercise on your paternal heritage, thank him for the good things you learned from him. Commiserate about the failings and problems you share. Tell him what you're proud of accomplishing on your own. And acknowledge your shortcomings and the things that you can still learn from him.

- Include the "soap opera" material that you have been too silent or too hostile about before this. Be honest but not brutal. Ask the questions you need to ask.

In addition, here are some things that are true for almost all sons and fathers that you might want to include in your own words:

I love you.
I know that you love me.
I know that you were doing the best you could at the time.
I accept you the way you are.
I am sorry for everything I ever did that hurt you.
I have learned a lot from you.
Thanks for everything you've done for me.

Some useful questions are:

What was going on for you in those days?
What were the pressures, the pleasures?
What was it like being my father?
What did you want me to understand that I never seemed to get?

What do you like and dislike about yourself?
How do you see us as being alike and different?
What would you do differently, if you knew then what you know now?

Here is Pete the architect's letter to his father.

Dear Dad:

I have been thinking about you and me a lot lately, so I decided to put my thoughts on paper and share them with you.

I remember when I was a little boy, you were a great father. We did little league and boy scouts. You explained stuff to me and let me "help" in building the old house and on various remodeling projects.

Sometimes you seemed preoccupied, too busy for me. I wonder, what was going on for you when I was six or seven? There must have been pressures, problems, hopes, and dreams that I knew nothing about. How was it for you being my dad? When you were preoccupied, what were you thinking about that I was too young to understand?

I guess you'd agree that things started to fall apart for us when I hit my teens. I remember one summer day when I had been walking on the beach all afternoon, looking at girls' bodies and feeling strange yearnings I couldn't identify. That night I told you I didn't feel like going to the Scout meeting, that I wanted to quit the Scouts because it wasn't fun anymore. The real reason was that I wanted to stay home and think about girls. I don't know why I could never just ask you about sex, or why you found it hard to volunteer information. It's hard to even write about it now, and I'm 45 years old, for Christ's sake!

Anyway, that was the start, for me, of the split between us. After a while it seemed like we couldn't agree on anything: where to go to college, religion, Vietnam, music, beards, career. In those days I thought you were a complete dinosaur, and you must have thought I was an insufferable smart aleck and know-it-all. I know I hurt your feelings and was a real pain in the ass. I'm sorry about all that now.

It's amazing to me that when I was 18 I thought we were as different as black and white. Now I notice every day how similar we are. We both like to work with our hands and get totally wrapped up in a building project. We're both committed to our wives and kids. We love the outdoors, we both have a good eye for design, and we like to help our neighbors. These are all things you taught me, and I'm very grateful for your good example.

Of course, we are also similar in some ways that aren't so great. Let's face it, we both love red wine and salami more than is strictly good for us. We can get so tied up in our projects that we don't notice what else is going on around us. But even these shared failings make me feel closer to you. It reminds me that your life has not been a bed of roses, anymore than mine has been.

In some ways, I have taken a different road than you. You opted for the security of jobs with public utilities, while I started my own business. I have been more willing to take financial risks than you, maybe because I didn't grow up during the Depression like you did.

But there are still some areas where I think I've got some things to learn from you: I wish I had your golf swing and your putting eye. I'm still impressed with how easily you make friends wherever you go, how you stay cheerful in the face of adversity, and how at your age, you're more interested in and turned on by life than I often am. I really admire you for these things.

The one thing (besides sex) that I've always had a hard time talking about with you is religion and God. When I was a kid, you sent me to parochial school and I swallowed the party line. That's the last time we were in agreement. In my late teens I thought about the existence of God a lot, but I never told you much about my doubts. I decided that it didn't seem like there was any kind of supreme being running things, and that religion did more harm than good in the world. So I chucked the whole thing. And to this day I don't go to church, I don't pray, I don't practice anything that you would recognize as a legitimate religion. I often wonder what goes through your mind when you go to mass week after week. Sometimes you casually mention that you remember me and Janice and the kids in your prayers. Do you really? What is it like for you to believe, to pray? I'm not about to change my agnostic-leaning-toward-atheist position, but I do sometimes miss having a regular spiritual practice to fall back on. I'd like to talk about this with you some time. Maybe we are both old enough now to reopen this subject. It would be nice not to have to tiptoe around the subject of religion, being so careful not to say anything that might appear critical or challenging.

I see I've gone on for a couple of pages already. It's amazing how much there actually is to say, when you get beyond the weather and the news and start talking about real thoughts and feelings.

Anyway, I'll close with what I really want you to know: I love you, I like you, and I really appreciate everything you have done for me in my life.

Love,

Pete

Mailing the Letter

Even if your letter is mostly positive and complimentary like Pete's, you still may find it very difficult to actually mail it. What will your dad think? Men don't write this kind of letter to each other, especially if they are father and son.

What if you have a lot of harsh, unpleasant stuff to write about? What if you know for a fact that your father won't take it the right way, that his reaction will be anger or ridicule? What if you are afraid of hurting your dad's feelings or upsetting some other member of your family? What if you feel like this is a last-ditch effort on your part and that you'll be devastated if your father doesn't react in just the right way?

You know your father and how he reacts to you better than anyone else does. The final decision is up to you. But consider this: feeling better about your relationship with your father depends mostly on your making the appropriate declarations to him, not on his making the desired response back to you. Saying "I love you" is more important than hearing "I love you, too." Saying "Thank you" is more healing than hearing "You're welcome." Saying "I have a right to my own opinions" is more empowering than hearing, "Yes, you're right." Saying "I've always felt you deserted me" is more liberating than hearing "I'm sorry." Saying "I'm sorry" is more cleansing than hearing "That's okay."

Regardless of your father's reaction, you will have made an honest attempt to communicate on your part. You will reap some benefit in the form of pride and integrity, whether you get any positive response from your father or not.

If you still have too many doubts, test the water first. Pick the most simple, nonthreatening statement from your letter and communicate that to your father. Send him a short note, call him up, or work it into conversation the next time you see him. If that trial balloon isn't shot down, try another one. Confront him with something else from your letter that is a little more risky. Ease into it, one topic at a time.

It might take two or three years to tell your father everything you have to say in this piecemeal fashion. And you may give it up as a hopeless task after the first blank looks of incomprehension or the ritual explosions of rage or derision. But you will at least have gotten all the issues clear in your own mind. You will have made an attempt, and you'll feel better about yourself for having made it.

If Your Father Is Dead or Otherwise Unresponsive

If your father is dead, senile, in a coma, unknown, or completely estranged from you, you can still resolve much of your unfinished business by working through this chapter and writing your letter to him. Then you can use the following visualization exercise to simulate the experience of communicating with your father and receiving a satisfying response.

If you don't plan to mail your letter, for whatever reason, don't skip past this exercise. It may seem a waste of time or a flaky new-age thing to do. But give it a try. It's free, it's easy, and it will only take fifteen minutes. That's not much time to invest in a possible easing of the pain of a lifetime.

Read through these instructions a couple of times, then lie down on the couch and try it.

Choose a time when no one will bother you for fifteen minutes. Lie down on your back and close your eyes. Keep your legs uncrossed and your arms at your side or resting on your stomach.

Take a deep breath, hold it a moment, and let it out slowly. This visualization works best if you are physically relaxed. So take a minute or two to consciously clear your mind of daily hassles. Scan your body for any tension and let your muscles relax. Pay attention to your breathing and keep it slow and deep. Tell yourself that you are getting more and more relaxed with every breath.

Imagine that you are in a familiar room. It can be a room in your home where you live now, your home as a child, the place you last saw your father—anyplace that feels familiar and comfortable. Imagine that there are two armchairs in this room. Notice their color, their texture, and how they are placed one across from the other.

Imagine that you are sitting in one of the chairs. Your father is sitting across from you in the other chair. Focus on how he looks, the way he always sat, crossed his arms, tapped his foot, scratched his ear, and so on. Imagine that he is looking calm and receptive, even if he seldom looked that way in reality.

Imagine speaking slowly and calmly to your father. Say all the things you have written in your letter: your childhood memories and feelings, the leftover wounds from your adolescence, the things you have learned from him about how to be and how not to be a man. Tell him all the secrets and withheld feelings that you never got a chance to tell him or that he would not normally have allowed himself to hear.

While you are talking, imagine that your father is still looking calm and receptive. He is nodding and smiling at the right places. He is hearing you. In the painful, angry parts, he may look sad or frown a little. But he is taking it all in like an ideal father would.

Even if you had a terrible relationship with your father all your life, experiment with telling him that you love him, that you accept him in all his failings, that you know he was doing his best, that you thank him for giving you life, and that you want to let go of the resentments and pain of the past.

When you are finished talking, imagine that your father responds in the way that you would most like him to. You may both stand and embrace. He may tell you he loves you, that he is sorry, or that he's glad you turned out okay.

When your father is through, tell him goodbye. If your father is dead, tell him that you are sorry he died too soon for you to have this talk in reality. Tell him you are ready to let him go now, without undue anger or grief.

Watch your father leave the room. Tell yourself that you have done a good thing, a healing thing. Congratulate yourself on taking the time and having the guts to work on your relationship with your father.

When you are ready, open your eyes and get up. Think for a while about what you have experienced. You may have found yourself saying or doing something in the visualization that you didn't write in your letter or didn't plan to include in the visualization. Or maybe your father did or said something that you didn't plan to have him say or do. It's possible that these variations come from your unconscious. They may reflect feelings or attitudes about your father that you have not been aware of, even after working through this whole chapter. Pay attention to all these things. You might learn something.

Larry was a political activist in his early forties. His father died in an auto accident when Larry was 21. At that time Larry and his father were not speaking to each other. Larry had been arrested several times while demonstrating against the Vietnam war, and his father was furious at him.

When Larry decided to do the visualization exercise, he planned to tell his father, "I was doing what I believed in. At that time, I had to protest and even get arrested in order to feel like a real person, in order to be a man in my own eyes." He planned to have his father say back to him, "I'm sorry I got so upset. I'm sure we would have worked it out if we had time."

But when he got to that part of his visualization, Larry was surprised to suddenly notice that his father was sitting in the armchair wearing Viet Cong black pajamas. He was further surprised when his imagined father told him, "Thank you for fighting for me. I wasn't really angry. I was frightened. I didn't want them to kill my baby. I was proud of you, but I couldn't tell you that."

Larry found that his inner father's response was more loving, accepting, and comforting than the response he had planned. Was it true? Had his father really felt this way? Had Larry picked up this feeling on some unconscious level that hadn't surfaced for him until now? As Larry says, "Who knows? Who cares? There's no way to find out, so I chose to interpret it the way that makes me feel best: my dad was secretly proud of me, and if he had lived, he would have told me so."

Mentors

Much writing and discussion in the men's movement concerns mentors— older men who serve as guides and models for younger men. In many ways, a mentor is a father figure and functions as a substitute father in your life. Knowing this may help you deal with the ups and downs of the mentor relationship.

Since mentors are like fathers, there is a natural evolution to the relationship that parallels the developmental stages you went through from childhood to manhood: identifying and bonding with the mentor, idealizing him, then rebelling against him as a restrictive authority figure, continuing through separation and denigration, and perhaps reconnecting at a later time on a peer level.

In the course of this evolution, you may need to say the same things to a mentor that you needed to say to your father:

I love you.
I need your approval.
Please help me.
I value your attention.
I know you're doing your best.
No offense, but I need to do things on my own now.
I'm sorry for whatever I did that hurt you.
I'm grown up now.
Thank you.
Goodbye.
Hello again.

II

Where Are You Going?

This question is borrowed from Sam Keen. In *Fire in the Belly*, he tells how his friend Howard Thurman gave him the most important bit of advice he ever got about being a man:

"There are two questions a man must ask himself: The first is 'Where am I going?' The second is 'Who will go with me?' *If you ever get these questions in the wrong order, you are in trouble.*"

The three chapters in this section concentrate on first things first—where *you* want to go from here on in *your* life. For the moment, set aside considerations of family, friends, and all the other people in your life who have an opinion about where you should be going.

In this section you will take a close look inside at the contents and quality of your inner life. You will examine your values in search of a basis for personal integrity as a man. And you will consider your vocation—what kind of meaningful work you will do and it's proper place in your life.

3

Being Whole: Enriching Your Inner Life

Your inner life is sort of a soup with many ingredients: thoughts, feelings, memories, observations, insights, hopes, fears, worries, wonderings, attitudes, value judgments, fantasies, prayers, philosophical musings, aesthetic appreciations, meditations, images, predictions, inspirations.

If you're like many men, there is a tendency for the soup to get a little thin. Your inner experience of life can become dominated by the mundane considerations of your outer life: money, possessions, work, errands, chores—the daily grind of survival that can so easily steal all your time and attention. When this happens, your inner life becomes a watery and unsatisfying gruel rather than a hearty source of nourishment. It may seem like you have no inner life at all. Your life seems to consist of things and actions. You seldom have the time or the inclination to look inward.

This chapter is an invitation to introspection. It invites you to look inward and to add spice to your inner life on a regular basis.

A warning: You may experience some resistance from yourself or others when you try to do the exercises in this chapter. Men in our society are not encouraged to look within. In fact, they are discouraged from too much introspection. If you pay heed to your inner life, you might find doubts about the quality of your life as a modern male. You might be seduced away from your nine-to-five responsibilities into something impractical like art or philanthropy. You may allow your hopes and fears to take your nose away from the grindstone or jostle your aim as you draw a bead on the enemy.

Men with rich inner lives are often suspect in our day. They tend to be too individualistic to be reliable cogs in the great social machine. Society needs a large stock of stolid, dependable, interchangeable men to keep the fires stoked and the hive of consumerism humming. The ideal drone has no inner life at all.

Nevertheless, to be a complete man you need to go against the grain. You need to notice and tend to your inner life. When you engage in the daily practice of introspection, you benefit in many ways:

- You stay in touch with your feelings.

- You know quickly when your life is getting out of balance, when you need to rest, or when you need to concentrate on a neglected relationship.

- You grow in self-knowledge.

- You become aware of your subconscious life.

- You're more creative.

- You stay open to intuition.

- You can better survive the boring, tedious parts of your life.

If you ignore or deny your inner life, you become blind to the interior view. You don't know yourself. You don't know what you really want or need. Relationships wither and life becomes a meaningless parade of money and things. You can sink into dull depression lit only occasionally by flickers of irritation. You can become a dull fellow, stodgy and literalistic, with no wit, no conversation—just the kind of "typical man" women complain about.

Warm-Up Exercises

Here are four exercises you can do right now to turn your awareness inward.

Body Awareness

A good path for getting into your head winds through your body. Lie down on your back and get comfortable. Close your eyes gently. Take a deep breath, hold it for a moment, and let it out slowly. Continue to breathe slowly and deeply. As much as possible, let your mind go blank. Whatever you have been thinking about today, just set it aside for a while.

Turn your awareness inward. Become aware of your feet. Starting at your feet, scan up your body. Notice any sensations of tension or pain. Don't try to do anything about the sensations. Just notice them. Move your attention up your legs and notice any feelings of warmth or coolness. Does anything itch or feel numb or tight?

Continue to let your awareness move up into your trunk. Notice how your belly and chest move up and down as you breathe. Listen to the sound of your breath flowing in and out. Try breathing a little slower and more deeply. Think about how the oxygen is going into your body and how the carbon dioxide is being breathed out.

Notice the pressure of your back against the floor or bed or couch. Can you also feel the pressure and beat of your heart?

If you have any thoughts such as "This is stupid" or "I'm not getting anything out of this," that's okay. Those are normal thoughts. Notice them and let them drift out of your mind.

Allow your attention to drift into your arms, your neck, and then your head. Notice all your physical sensations: aches, pains, hot, cold, pressure, itching, numbness, pins and needles...whatever there is to feel.

Listen carefully now and catalog all the sounds you can hear. What you thought of as a quiet room is probably full of sounds: listen for the refrigerator motor, horns and traffic outside, kids yelling and dogs barking, a power tool in the distance, airplanes overhead, the furnace, creaks in the frame of the house...all the background noises that make up modern silence. If it really is pretty quiet where you are, listen for the sound of your own heartbeat and the faint rushing noise your blood makes in your ears.

Keep doing this exercise until you feel slowed down and very aware of what it feels like to be inside your body. Open your eyes and get up when you are ready.

Inner Inventory

Fill in the blanks. Take your time and ponder. Don't rush through and don't feel compelled to put something in each blank. Any one of these items could provoke a good long bout of introspection. If that happens, indulge yourself. Stop the exercise and daydream.

Right now, I feel

More than anything, I wish

I wonder

If I could right now, I'd

I believe in

The most beautiful thing I ever saw was

I especially like _____ because

I love _____ because

I'm worried about

I'm angry about

I'm sad about

I'm guilty about

I think

I'm jealous of

I envy

I'm afraid of

I've noticed that

I resent

I appreciate

I approve of

I trust

I hope

I expect

God is

Life is mostly a matter of

The most important thing in my life is

The Mirror

Go in the bathroom right now and stare at yourself in the mirror for a full minute. Lean in really close and try to maintain eye contact with yourself for a full minute.

This is a weird experience. You probably found it very difficult to keep eye contact. You may have had the unsettling experience of looking like a stranger to yourself. Or you may have resolved to trim your nose hairs more frequently or thought about hair weaving or plastic surgery. Did you have the urge to say something to yourself? Did you think you looked angry or scared or phony?

Whatever comes up, this is an instructive and interesting exercise, especially if you don't usually pay a lot of attention to your appearance.

Observing Nature

Go outside right now. Go into the backyard, a field, a park, even the shoulder of a road. Find someplace where you can observe things growing out of the ground. Sit down or squat down close to the ground and just observe a few square feet of ground. Notice the colors and textures, the plants growing and the bits of dead plant matter. Catalog the litter. Review what you know about plants growing, dying, decaying, feeding new generations of plants. Remind yourself that this natural process goes on and will continue to go on whether you get the storm windows up or not.

Soon, human nature being what it is, you will be thrown back to thoughts of yourself. Think of how you are also a child of nature, basically an animal that has a niche in the natural world and needs to breathe, drink, eat, move, sleep, reproduce, and so on. As you see the shadows shifting or the sun setting, reflect on passing time and your own mortality. Indulge in a little melancholy if that is what comes up for you.

This and the other warm-up exercises require that you spend at least a few moments by yourself, away from other people and away from your usual activities. Solitude is essential to your inner life. If you are surrounded by people from waking to bedtime, you need to change your schedule so that you can spend time alone. The best way to do this is to take up some daily practice of solitude.

Daily Practices

Put up a sign on your refrigerator that says: "A rich inner life requires the daily practice of solitude."

Daily practice is important because introspection doesn't give dramatic results every time. It's like fishing. If you go down to the lake every morning and spend five minutes fishing, you may get skunked on any given day. But over time, you will catch lots of fish.

So it is with a daily practice of introspection, such as keeping a dream journal. Most mornings you may just yawn your way through an incoherent sentence or two and toss the notebook back on the night stand. But the practice puts you in the right place and frame of mind to remember, record, and savor a rare and comforting dream in which your long-dead father tells you, "You were right all the time, I always loved you."

Daily practice is also comforting in that it provides a routine to fall back on, a structure of discipline, and a mental health barometer. It's good to be able to count on yourself to do your meditation or go jogging or do a Tai Chi set. And if you miss your practice several days in a row, it's an early warning signal that your life is getting too stressful, that a relationship is out of tune, or that you are not acknowledging something painful or scary that's happening to you.

Following are some daily practices that have worked for many others in fostering a rich inner life. Try them. Find what appeals to you and resolve to do it daily for a month.

(By making plans to do something daily, you have a better chance of doing it three or four times a week than if you start out planning to do it every other day. It's not actually important that you do your practice daily. What counts is that you do it regularly enough to get the benefit.)

Dream Journal

1. Before you go to sleep, tell yourself, "I will dream and remember my dreams."

2. Keep a notebook and a pencil or a tape recorder next to your bed.

3. When you awake at any time, night or morning, don't move. Stay in the position in which you were sleeping. Think back to your dreams and relive them. Get them clear in your mind.

4. Reach over very slowly, turn on the light, get your glasses, get your notebook and pencil or tape recorder. Write or record all the details you can remember about your dream. Don't worry about trying to make sense of them at this time or trying to write in complete sentences. Just get down as much as you can.

5. Don't worry if your dream characters and settings seem to keep shifting so that it's impossible to write down all the nuances and changes. Just pick one character and setting that seem interesting and put those into your journal. Completeness and accuracy are less important than just capturing as much detail as possible before the dream fades from memory.

6. Don't worry if you can't remember any dreams at first. Everybody dreams, every night. Keep your notebook handy and keep telling yourself, "I will remember my dreams." The more you pay attention to your dreams, the more dreams you will remember, and the more vivid and interesting your dreams will seem.

7. You might want to draw pictures of your dreams as well as writing them or recording them.

8. As the day goes by, stop now and then and remember the dreams you wrote down. Ask yourself what the dreams might mean. Some dreams will be very obvious and others will be more mysterious.

9. Don't worry about occasional sex, violence, or bizarre behavior in your dreams. Dreams are not under your conscious control. Just because you dream about doing something doesn't mean that you will do it or that you should blame yourself for dreaming about it.

However, if you do have frequent, recurring nightmares or dreams of bloody violence that continue to haunt you during the day, talk them over with a therapist.

10. If you get interested in analyzing your dreams, there are many books you can consult. They will suggest meanings for symbols, characters, and actions that commonly occur in dreams. For starters, you can thoroughly enjoy and benefit from your dream journal by applying common-sense analysis and considering one principle common to many systems of dream analysis: that you should consider everyone in your dream to be a version of yourself. This won't always make sense, but more often than not this approach will provide interesting insights.

For example, Brett wrote in his dream journal: "Driving in a pickup truck with cousin Carl. I wanted to go fishing because the bass were biting, but Carl said no, we have to make the state line by noon so we can deliver some important papers. I agreed to keep driving. Felt very sad and frustrated at not getting to fish."

On the surface, this was a pretty dull dream, especially since Brett hadn't been fishing or seen his cousin for years. But the dream seemed very vivid and Brett remembered it for days after writing it down. Finally he realized that his cousin Carl represented himself in his "take care of business" mode. Fishing represented spontaneity and self-indulgence—kicking back and enjoying life. Deciding to deliver the papers at the state line represented responsibility and devotion to duty—parts of Brett's waking life that were weighing him down. He concluded from this dream that he needed to take a day off and do something fun and frivolous.

Is the dream journal for you? Try it tonight and see. Mark this page and put the book and a pencil next to your bed tonight. Tomorrow morning, write whatever you recall of your dreams.

My dream:

Meditation

Meditation need not be a mysterious or complicated practice. It is just a matter of focusing your attention on one thing at a time, without passing judgment on that thing or on your own ability to stay focused. This can be difficult, but the basic idea is very simple.

What you focus on isn't important. In the exercise that follows, you'll focus on your breath and on an imaginary riverbank. The heart of meditation lies not in the object, but in your attempt to focus on the object. Your mind doesn't like to stay concentrated on one thing. Many thoughts will distract you. Each time you notice that you have become distracted, and refocus your attention on your breath or on the riverbank, you are successfully meditating. This experience of refocusing your attention will eventually teach you several liberating truths about yourself:

- It is impossible to fear, hate, or worry when your attention is focused away from the objects of your fear, hate, or worry.

- You don't have to think about everything that pops into your mind. You can choose what to think about.

- You will become aware of habitual patterns of thought, paths you have wandered down many times. As you become aware, the habitual thoughts lose their power over you.

- Thoughts and feelings aren't permanent. They pass through your mind and body. Your essence is something other than these thoughts and feelings.

- The daily practice of meditation will train you to attend closely to what is happening right now. This has the effect of smoothing out the emotional highs and lows of your life, since the regrets of the past and the worries about the future have less power over you. It's called serenity.

Meditation has a proven and measurable effect on your body. In 1968 Dr. Herbert Benson of the Harvard Medical School studied volunteer meditators to see what happened in their bodies. He found that during and after meditation:

- Pulse and breathing rates slow down.

- Oxygen consumption drops an average of 20 percent.

- Lactic acid levels in the blood, an indicator of stress, decline.

- Galvanic skin resistance to electric current, a sign of relaxation, increases 400 percent.

- EEG readings show increased alpha brain waves, a sign of deep relaxation.

Benson went on to determine just what it is about meditation that produces relaxation. He identified four key elements: a quiet setting, a comfortable position, a consistent mental focus, and a passive attitude. With that in mind, here is all you have to do.

1. Find a quiet, comfortable place where you won't be disturbed for about twenty minutes.

2. Get in a comfortable position. You can sit in a chair, sit cross-legged on the floor, or kneel Japanese fashion with your toes together, your heels apart, sitting on your feet. A little cushion on your feet will help a lot. Forget about the full lotus position for now.

   Sit with your back straight but not rigid, with your chin pulled in and the small of your back arched slightly so that the weight of your head falls straight down your spinal column. Close your mouth and breathe through your nose if you can.

3. Close your eyes. Get centered by rocking from side to side and front to back, shifting your weight around until you feel comfortable. Find a comfortable way to rest your hands in your lap or on your knees. Get grounded by feeling how your weight flows from your head down into the chair or floor. Feel the pressure in your feet and seat.

4. Keep your eyes closed gently and take several deep breaths. Notice the quality of your breath. Is it fast or slow, deep or shallow? Does your stomach or your chest move out farther when you inhale? Practice moving your breath into your belly and up into your chest. Try to breathe more into your belly.

5. When your breath has settled down, start counting your breaths by fours. As you exhale, say "One." Continue counting each exhalation by saying "Two...three...four." Then begin again with "One." If you lose count, simply start over with "One."

6. When you find that your attention has wandered, as it will, simply note it, and start counting again.

7. If a particular sensation arises in some part of your body, pay attention to it until it recedes, then resume counting your breaths by fours.

8. If you get tired of counting, try a variation. Put your attention on the sensations of breathing instead. Focus on your abdomen as it rises and falls. Tune into your breathing and sense how the size of the empty space in your abdomen grows and shrinks as your breath goes in and out.

If you have stopped counting, you may notice that you experience more distracting thoughts. The counting was keeping your mind going around a small circle of numbers, which left less room for distractions. Don't be disturbed by distractions. Remind yourself that the essence of meditation lies in the refocusing of your mind after a distraction.

You may come across a thought that is very enticing, and want to pursue it instead of continuing your meditation. When this happens, promise yourself that you will entertain the thought fully after your meditation. Imagine the thought as a bubble rising in a deep pool. Watch it coming up, watch it hit the surface and disappear. Then refocus your mind and concentrate on your breathing or on counting your breaths by fours.

One meditation technique to learn more about yourself is called *thought labeling*. While breath counting, simply notice and label each thought that comes up: "Anger...Sandra...Sandra...anxiety...work... anxiety...Sandra...anxiety...work." You may find it interesting to notice the themes that emerge.

If this taste of meditation pleases you, continue it as a daily practice. There are many excellent books on meditation that can guide you as you become more adept. A good one for modern Western men is *The New Three Minute Meditator* by David Harp.

When you learn more about meditation, you will discover that many simple activities can be done as a meditation: folding laundry, stacking firewood, doing dishes, walking the dog, painting a fence, and so on.

Visualization

Everybody visualizes. You visualize whenever you daydream, remember a past experience, or think of someone you know. Visualization is a natural, largely automatic activity like breathing or walking. But you can consciously direct your existing powers of visualization to enrich your inner life.

Like keeping a dream journal, visualization is a way of accessing your unconscious. But it's better in some ways, since you are awake and can choose the time, place, and general content of your visualization.

To give you a taste of visualization, here are two typical visualization exercises. Record these instructions on tape and play them back while lying on your back with your eyes closed. Speak slowly and pause between sentences.

Special Place Visualization Script. Lie down and close your eyes. Take a deep breath, hold it a moment, and exhale. Take another breath and really fill your lungs. Exhale with a sigh and empty your lungs completely. Continue breathing deeply and slowly, breathing down into your belly, so that your stomach rises more than your chest.

As you breathe, scan your body for tension and allow yourself to relax. If any part of your body is tight, try tensing the muscles in that part and then relaxing the muscles.

You are getting more and more relaxed. Your breathing and heart rate are slowing down. If any thoughts occur to you that you aren't doing it right or that it isn't working, that's okay. Just notice the thoughts and let them drift away. It doesn't matter. All you have to do is listen to the tape and accept whatever happens.

Imagine that you are walking down a path in the woods. These woods can be a place you have been or a place you would like to be. Look down and notice the surface of the path: the dirt or sand or grass. Notice what kinds of plants and rocks there are on both sides of the path. Look up and imagine the trees and bushes. The sky is a clear blue and the sun is shining. Feel the sun on your face. As you walk along, look around and fill in all the details of color, texture, light, and shadow.

Feel the breeze against your face. Hear the sounds of the wind in the trees, birds singing, water running in a stream somewhere in the distance.

Continue down the path until you come to a sort of enclosed area. It can be a small meadow surrounded by trees, a hollow at the foot of a hill, or even a shallow cave. Imagine a comfortable, special place where you would like to stop and rest for a while. Stand in the center of this special place and look around.

Notice its shape and general layout. Take in the sights, sounds, and smells. Notice the rocks, grass, flowers, water, and so on. Are there any birds or squirrels around? Is there water nearby that you can see and hear? Look off in the distance as far as you can see. You can create any kind of view you want.

This is your place, special for you alone. You can come here any time you want. No one else can come unless you invite them. It's safe and secure, a quiet place of relaxation and peace.

Walk around your special place and notice the quality of light. Make it comfortable—not too bright or too dim. You are in control. You can make the temperature warmer or cooler, make the wind stronger or cause it to die away entirely, make the sun shine or clouds come or turn day into night.

Notice what you are wearing—the colors and style
and how it feels against your skin. Change to something
else if you want. You can dress any way you choose here.

Find a comfortable place to sit or lie down. It can be a
bed of dry moss, a patch of sunny grass, a flat rock, or
even a real chair or bed. Sit or lie down and relax. No one
can bother you here. You can come here any time you want
and escape all pressures. This is a place where you can
come to rest, to be with yourself, to explore your inner self.

Time doesn't exist here. Deadlines are suspended, the
past can't haunt you, the future can't worry you. You can
travel effortlessly in time—back to your boyhood or forward to your old age. You can bring your adult resources
to bear on problems you couldn't handle very well as a
boy. You can tap into an age-old wisdom that transcends
your everyday experience.

This is a special place where you can see things that
you normally don't see. Here you can lift the lid of your unconscious a crack and shine a little light down where it's
usually dark.

Logic doesn't count for much here. You can answer
questions and solve problems that have stumped your logical, rational mind. You can hear answers to which you are
normally deaf.

Look around you and find a place where a small object about the size of a book could be hidden. If you don't
see a hiding place, make one up. The hiding place can be inside a treasure chest, under a rock, behind a tree, inside a
clump of bushes, or within a hollow tree—any place that
feels right to you.

This will be a place to discover messages from your
unconscious. The messages you receive in the hiding place
can take many forms. They might be as obvious as a written note or as ambiguous as a small white stone or a glow
of light. Often the message will be symbolic. Sometimes
there will be nothing there at all.

Get up and approach the hiding place. Clear your
mind of all expectation and desire. Tell yourself, I am ready
to accept whatever I find, even emptiness. Look inside the
hiding place and observe whatever you see there. Notice
your thoughts at this instance—whether you are interested,
scared, excited, disappointed. If the message is something
you can pick up, do so and explore it with your hands.

Put the message back in the hiding place. Don't decide
right away what it means. Plan to ponder it over the next

day or so. Tell yourself that you are going to stay open to messages from your inner self.

Prepare to leave your special place. Get up and take a last look around. Remember this place so that you can return again. Walk back along the same path until you can't see your special place any more.

When you're ready, open your eyes and get up slowly. As you go about your daily routine, remember from time to time that you have a special place that you can go to in your imagination whenever you need rest or refreshment.

Inner Guide Visualization Script. Lie down and close your eyes. Take a deep breath, hold it a moment, and exhale. Take another breath and really fill your lungs. Exhale with a sigh and empty your lungs completely. Continue breathing deeply and slowly, breathing down into your belly, so that your stomach rises more than your chest.

As you breathe, scan your body for tension and allow yourself to relax. If any part of your body is tight, try tensing the muscles in that part and then relaxing the muscles.

You are getting more and more relaxed. Your breathing and heart rate are slowing down. If any thoughts occur to you that you aren't doing it right or that it isn't working, that's okay. Just notice the thoughts and let them drift away. It doesn't matter. All you have to do is listen until the end of the tape and accept whatever happens.

Walk down the path to your special place. Notice all the sights, sounds, smells, feelings, tastes, and so on, as before. Imagining details that appeal to all the senses is a way of deepening your relaxation and making your visualization more vivid, enjoyable, and effective.

Enter your special place and make yourself comfortable. Sit or stand somewhere that gives you a view into the distance. Imagine that there is another path, different from the one you entered by, that comes from far away. This is the path that your inner guide will use. If necessary, alter the arrangement of your special place to make room for this path. Make sure that you can see down the path for a considerable distance.

Soon your inner guide will come down that path. Your inner guide is an imaginary person, animal, or other being that you create to help you explore your inner life. Your guide is your own best self, your unconscious all-knowing mind given a form and a voice. Your inner guide is the personification of your own inner wisdom. Your inner guide will answer questions and give you advice. He or she will serve as a channel for messages from your unconscious. Consulting your inner guide is a way of clarifying what you really need or want and uncovering feelings that you may not be fully aware of.

You may already have an idea of what your inner guide will look like. You may expect a man or a woman, an old person or a child. But don't be alarmed if your inner guide takes an unexpected form. Your inner guide may appear as a wizard, a priestess, an angel, a circus ringleader, a Greek god or goddess, an animal such as a lion or a stag, a space alien, your own grandfather, a childhood friend, a movie star—the possibilities are endless.

Remain open to whatever form your inner guide will take. Look down the path and see a tiny dot in the distance. This is your inner guide, far away, approaching you slowly. Watch as the dot expands and you just start to be able to make out some details.

By now you can see the general shape of the figure. Is it a person or an animal? Is it a man or a woman?

As the figure gets closer, see more and more details. How is this figure dressed? In regular clothes, in robes, not dressed at all? Any hats, staffs, bags? What colors and textures do you see?

You can see small details now: the color of the eyes, the texture of skin, the shape of the nose and chin and brow. You can hear the figure's steps. Let this being get closer, right up to the edge of your special place, then stop.

Does this figure look friendly? This is an important question. If the figure you've called up looks angry or dangerous, there's no need to invite it into your special place. Turn it around and have it walk away into the distance and disappear. Imagine another, friendlier figure approaching you.

Don't send away a possible guide just because it doesn't meet your expectations. You may find that the same unexpected, weird figure returns over and over. This is an indication that you have conjured up the correct figure, even though it seems odd to your conscious, critical mind.

Ask the figure, "Are you my guide?" If the answer is no or is ambiguous, send the figure away with the instruction "Please send me my guide." Then wait for another figure to approach.

When you are satisfied that your guide is friendly and authentic, invite your guide into your special place. You can speak out loud and say, "Come in," or gesture or use mental telepathy to communicate with your guide. Greet your guide in a way that feels appropriate. Say hello or shake hands or embrace.

Welcome your guide. Show your inner guide your special place, as if you were showing off a new house or garden. Tell your guide that you are glad to have him or her there and that you trust your guide to help you explore your inner life.

Now grasp hands or stare into your guide's eyes. Ask your guide these questions:

"What is my greatest gift?"

"What is my greatest challenge?"

"Where should I put my energies?"

"What do I need to know about my inner life right now?"

Accept whatever answers you receive. The answers may come in the form of words, gestures, or feelings. Your guide may give you a symbolic object by way of an answer. Don't worry if some questions aren't answered or if you don't fully understand the answers.

Finally, say goodbye. Promise to keep in touch. Have your guide promise to visit you whenever he or she is invited. Suggest to your guide that he or she should "drop in" on you whenever there is something important for you to know. Watch your guide leave your special place.

Rest for a moment alone in your special place. Know that you have an inner guide that you can trust. Your guide can come to you whenever you need a visit. Your guide is wise, all knowing, and has only your best interests at heart.

When you are ready, remind yourself of your actual surroundings. Open your eyes and end the session. Get up slowly, feeling refreshed and invigorated.

In the next day or two, ponder what your guide told you. Meditate on the meaning, and make note of any further questions that occur to you. Then do the exercise again and ask the new questions.

Over time, your guide may change gradually or suddenly take on a new form. This can happen as your inner life changes or as you work on different parts of yourself.

Jack's special place was a meadow similar to one in the Sierras where he had often gone camping. There he met his inner guide, an old indian chief. His guide told him that his greatest gift in life was his openness to change and his greatest challenge was also his openness to change.

Jack took this to mean that he had a tendency to leap on any new information or philosophy, entertain it for a while, and then cast it aside in favor of the next interesting idea he encountered. This interpretation was reinforced by another of his guide's comments: "Work on faithfulness and perseverance."

Gordon's special place was a dock by a slow moving river, under a weeping willow. It reminded him of an illustration in an old edition of *Huckleberry Finn*, a book he loved as a boy. His guide first came to him as a black panther that communicated with him by telepathy. When Gordon asked the panther, "What do I need to know about my inner life?" the panther looked him in the eyes and Gordon heard a voice in his head say, "Wake up." Sometimes the panther would only answer yes by purring or no by looking away—and when this happened Gordon had to phrase his questions carefully. In later visualizations, the panther became a sort of cat woman who came to the dock in a canoe. She spoke to Gordon directly about how he could work on his chronic depression by "waking up" to possibility in his life.

Art

Paint, draw, sculpt, write, dance, sing, play an instrument, design buildings, throw pots, carve soap. For the purpose of nourishing your inner life, "art" is a broad term, embracing any activity in which you are making, changing, or arranging something. It can also include pastimes that some professional artists denigrate as mere crafts or hobbies, such as cabinetmaking or gardening.

Art can be an important doorway into your inner life. Writing a poem, playing your guitar, or even painting your front door allows you time by yourself, puts you in touch with your intuitive mind, and brings beauty and order into your life.

The creative act also tends to focus your attention on one thing at a time, an experience that has been called the heart of meditation. This takes you out of your immediate concerns and reminds you that you are more than your immediate circumstances.

If you decide to try art as a path to your inner self, there are many approaches you can take. If you have some creative activity that you already enjoy, you can simply make a time each day in which you will enjoy it. If you want to learn something new, call up your local community college or look in the Yellow Pages under "Art Instruction," "Music Instruction," "Craft Instruction," "Dancing Instruction," and so on.

As you do your art, take frequent breaks. Take your time so that you can focus on the process of creation rather than the finished product. Ask yourself how it feels to be creating something new and beautiful. See if you feel different before and after working on an art project.

Notice the thoughts that run through your mind: "This looks good... I'm making a botch of it...People will think I'm so creative...They'll hate it...I'm wasting my time...This is fun." Remind yourself that it is the creative process that is important, not the quality of the finished product.

Pay attention to how your body feels. Does singing make the tight muscles in your back loosen? Does your ulcer leave you alone when you are watering your bonsai trees?

Body-Centered Practices

For many men, the path out of the head and into the spirit is through the body. During physical exercise your attention is pulled away from your habitual thoughts and centered in your body. From there, it is easier to identify feelings, indulge in fantasy, and exercise your creative faculties.

Walking and running. These require no special training. Just take a walk or go jogging. Settle into a comfortable pace and breathing rhythm. Notice your surroundings—the houses, trees, cars, other people. Let your mind drift. Entertain whatever fragments of memory or fantasy come to mind. Take what you get.

Yoga. Yoga is a centuries-old practice of quieting the mind, controlling the breath, stretching and strengthening the body—all with an eye toward greater serenity and self-knowledge. Taking a class with a good yoga master can be a very enlightening experience.

Martial arts. Karate, Tai Chi, Aikido, and many other martial arts can be pathways to your inner self, especially when approached as meditative, daily practices of self-discipline and understanding—not just a collection of aggressive and defensive techniques.

Day Trips

Here are some illuminating experiences you can enjoy from time to time that will enrich your inner life:

Wilderness. This is an extension of the "observing nature" warm-up exercise. Get into nature, as remote and wild as possible. There's nothing like the natural world, with little trace of humankind in it, to put your problems into perspective and let your spirit expand. Remind yourself that you are, at bottom, an animal, a creature of nature, subject to all natural laws.

Think about the earth as Gaia, a vast living being made up of all the living and nonliving beings of the planet. Think of the planet as one organism, with all the parts, including yourself, working together to make up the whole.

Put a few rocks in a circle or stick some feathers in the dirt to mark the spot. Make it a little shrine to Mother Earth or a commemoration of your experience here. An offering. A prayer of willingness to be connected.

Church. This one works best if you don't usually go to church at all. Regardless of your beliefs about a higher power in the universe, creation, soul, morality, religion, and so on...go into a church. Old Catholic churches are good for this, but any convenient church will do. Sit or kneel there. If there are candles, light one. Put some change in the poor box. Whether you believe or not, say a prayer. Sit silently until you get bored. Then sit awhile longer. How do you feel? The point here is not necessarily to have a religious experience, but to have an uncommon experience.

Listening to music. Put on a favorite piece of music. Ideally, use headphones. Just listen. Don't read or tidy your desk or do the dishes. Let the music carry you away to yourself.

Museum. Go into a museum or art gallery. Get beyond passing judgment or a shopper's mentality. Try to see the beauty or meaning in each piece you observe. Don't' look at too many items. Try to see what the artist saw and wants you to see.

Poetry. Read a poem--just one. Think about it.

Parting Thoughts

Make a Refuge

A refuge is a place to be alone with yourself. For Thoreau it was his cabin on Walden Pond. For you it can be an actual cabin you build, a room with a door you can shut, a bench in the garden, a special spot in the park—someplace you can retire to, away from the cares of your workaday world, and attend to your inner life.

Sharing

Tell someone about your inner life exercises. Talking about them will make your experiences come alive for you in a new way. You are also likely to find that your inner adventures give you new things to say to those around you who share your outer life.

4

Being Trustworthy: Achieving Male Integrity

The search for a new definition of masculinity is a search for integrity. Above all, the ideal new man has integrity. He is solid, whole, consistent. He is dependable. He tells the truth. He keeps his promises. He is honest, fair, and just. He lives his life according to a consistent set of values that he has worked out for himself over a period of time. Others may not always agree with a man of integrity, but they have to respect him for speaking out and acting according to his convictions.

Integrity isn't something that just happens to you. It's a skill that you can acquire with practice. This chapter will guide you through the four essential steps to integrity:

1. Clarifying your values

2. Ranking your values

3. Affirming your values

4. Acting on your values

Clarifying Your Values

Life can be seen as a continuous series of decisions. Many are virtually unconscious choices made according to habit: when to go to bed, which cereal to have for breakfast, which part of the Sunday paper to read first. Other decisions are more significant and require more thought: whether to buy a new stereo, where to go on vacation, what classes to take, whom to invite to a party. Once in a while you are faced with a really important decision that has far-reaching consequences: whom to marry, when to change careers, how you should discipline your children, whether you should blow the whistle on someone who has done something illegal, what to do about someone who has harmed you, whether you should own up to a serious mistake.

All decisions are based on values. Values are the rules you live by. They run along a continuum from arbitrary preferences such as "Big cars should be painted black" to moral commandments such as "Thou shalt not kill." Even if you are not consciously aware of all of your values, you have a long list of rules that guide your minute-to-minute decisions.

There are basically two kinds of values: moral and nonmoral. Moral values have to do with right and wrong, good and evil. They guide your behavior with the force of obligation. Moral values determine such ethical behaviors as telling the truth, keeping agreements, and not injuring others. Associated with moral values are such character traits as honesty, loyalty, and fairness. Moral statements often contain words like *must*, *ought*, *should*, *never*, and *always*.

Nonmoral values have to do with tastes, preferences, and styles. They relate to what is desirable and undesirable, as opposed to what is right and wrong or good and evil. Nonmoral values usually carry no sense of obligation. They are associated with personality traits like charm, shyness, or cheerfulness, as opposed to character traits like honesty or fairness. The behavior resulting from nonmoral values is preferred, not dictated: you choose to go to the ballgame instead of to a movie or to read a book instead of watch television. Nonmoral values are more plentiful than moral values, since they are expressions of your attitudes toward all sorts of people, places, things, concepts, and experiences. Statements of nonmoral value often contain the same words as statements of moral value: "I *never* run on asphalt or concrete." But examination shows that the words are not meant as a guide to ethical action.

How Values Are Formed

As an infant, your only "value" is self-preservation. As you grow up you become more socialized and take on a more complex system of values. You draw first from the conventions of your family: "Nice boys say please and thank you...Don't hit...Watch out for your sister." Then your peers contribute some values: "Cool guys wear chinos and penny loafers...You gotta have team spirit." Finally, some of your values are inspired by law: "Stop at red lights...You have to pay your taxes."

At any point in your moral development, you may have all of the following reasons for acting in a certain way: because it's essential to survival, because it's what your family taught you to do, because it's the conventional thing to do, because it's the law, and because you have decided that it's the right thing for you to do morally.

In the final analysis, the last reason is the only one that counts. Mere self-preservation won't get you very far. Most crises of judgment are social in nature. They have to do with your relationships to others, not your physical survival. Wholesale adoption of your parents' code of behavior won't do either. They are different people who grew up in different times. Even if you come to agree with all of their values eventually, you need to go through the evaluation process on your own.

Forget about laws as guidelines for behavior. They are often too literal, negative, and limited. For example, the rules about not parking on the north side of the street on Wednesday mornings will tell you nothing about what beliefs you should have about urban sanitation, crowding, or appropriate kinds of public services. Whatever the Supreme Court decides about access to abortion, you are still going to have to figure out your own stand on your own terms.

And don't rely on conventional wisdom. The prevailing rules of society are often imprecise, contradictory, and subject to exceptions and change. For example, it was once considered very nasty for a woman to show a bare ankle in public, while at the same time it was considered perfectly legal and moral to own slaves.

The best guide to action is your personal value system, based on your independent observations and carefully worked out over time. In your growth toward integrity, you need to examine your values and your reasons for holding them. You need to decide for yourself what is right, regardless of what your parents, your friends, your teacher, your lover, the majority, or the government thinks.

Why Values Matter

Why is it so important to have a personal value system that you have thought out and are committed to putting into action? Because if you don't, you are inevitably headed for pain. Here's how faulty value systems cause stress and painful emotions:

Arrested development. This occurs when you are stuck between the two stages of moral development. When you're young, you decide what to do by an unthinking adherence to the customs of your family, your social class, and your peer group. As you grow older, there should be a natural shift toward basing your behavior on thought-out, personal, internalized values. If you are trying to make adult decisions with an adolescent value system, you are in for some trouble.

For example, Ben grew up in a devout Jewish family that judged the value of his male cousins' and brothers' marriages by whether they married nice Jewish girls. Ben fell in love with a nice Irish girl, who loved him and hinted about getting married. Every time he thought of asking her to marry him and setting a date for the wedding, he felt very anxious about what his family would think. In order to reduce this anxiety and proceed into married life, he had to work out a more mature value system. He gave up the externally imposed notion that a particular heritage is the most important consideration in choosing a wife. He replaced it with an internalized, personal value that love and compatibility are more important considerations.

Conflicting nonmoral values. Conflicting nonmoral values are major contributors to stress. For example, Tony was a high school teacher who placed a very high value on leisure time, but also held the belief that a man must provide a certain high standard of living for his family. This second value led him to take a moonlighting job as a security guard to earn extra money, which virtually eliminated his leisure time. He was chronically tired, irritable, and unable to function well either at his job or at home. He had to examine his values in order to reveal this conflict to himself. He was finally able to explain his values to his wife and son and to take action to eliminate the conflict. Tony decided to give up the security guard job, accept a lower standard of living with less income, and have more leisure time at home. Another man might have decided to pursue a better paying second job or an entirely different career. The point is that conflicting values cause distress and will continue to do so until you resolve them somehow.

Moral dilemmas. Most of the time, you are only aware of your nonmoral values, since there are so many of them and since they guide so many of your daily decisions. However, when there is a decision to be made and both kinds of values are in direct conflict, you can become painfully aware of your moral values.

For example, Scott was a bright guy, a high school graduate with a couple of years of junior college credit, working in Buffalo, New York, for a big computer firm. He really wanted to move to a warmer climate. He heard that the Los Angeles division of his company had an opening, but it required a college degree. Scott thought he could handle the work, and he knew that if he just lied and said he had a college degree, the company would probably never check it out.

However, Scott was an honest person who believed in telling the truth. His moral value about telling the truth was in direct conflict with his nonmoral value of wanting to live where it's warm.

Scott came up with the rationalization that the lie wasn't so bad because it wouldn't really hurt anybody and the benefit of living in a warmer climate justified a little lie. He sent in the fraudulent application, got the job, moved west, and almost immediately began sabotaging his own chances of success at the new job. He came in late. He made stupid mistakes. He was nervous and apprehensive all the time. He thought that others could tell he was a fraud. He was punishing himself for having violated his own moral code. He finally quit and found another job at less pay, but on his own true merits.

Perhaps Scott was overscrupulous. The point of this example is that if you hold a value to be morally binding on yourself and you run counter to it in pursuit of one of your nonmoral values, you will experience conflict. And you will often find some way to blame or punish yourself.

The whim of iron. This happens when you give mere tastes and preferences the status of moral values. If you apply nonmoral values like "people should stay in shape" with the same strictness as truly moral values like "People should not murder each other," your unreasonable expectations will make life miserable for you. You will see every flabby person you meet as the moral equivalent of a murderer and punish yourself unfairly for any deviation from your own fitness regime.

The will of water. Conversely, you'll experience considerable discomfort if you regard moral values like keeping your promises with the same casual attitude you take when deciding if this weekend is a good time to till the garden. The nature of moral values is that they demand consistent action, regardless of the dictates of expediency. On a practical level, if you don't keep your promises or respect others' rights consistently, few people will trust you or want to associate with you in any serious relationship or enterprise. Also, your self-esteem will suffer because you will be lacking any experience of personal integrity.

Double standards. The flip side of duties is rights. If you have a moral duty to treat others justly, that means that you also have a right to be treated justly yourself. If you insist on your right to be heard, you have a duty to hear others out. Double standards arise when you claim a right without acknowledging your corresponding duty, or when you claim a right for yourself while denying it to others, or when you claim a duty for others without acknowledging it for yourself.

The classic example of a double standard is the idea that it's all right for you to have had premarital sexual relations, but any woman who expects to marry you had better be a virgin. Trying to operate according to a double standard breeds emotional pain because it flies in the face of justice. You are constantly bombarded from within by suspicions of your own hypocrisy and from without by cries of "Foul!"

Value Inventory

Under each of the topics that follow, write one or more of your personal values—the rules you follow most of the time, your strongest preferences, your usual attitudes. Put down whatever comes to mind without judging it or wondering what others would think about it. This is your list. There are no absolutely right or wrong answers. In the extra spaces at the end, list things you like to do, things you approve of, things you disapprove of, and any other kinds of values that occur to you.

Politics

Religion

Work

Leisure

Education

Family

Aging, death

War, peace

Style in clothes, grooming

Material possessions

Friends

Health

Rules, laws, authority

Love

Sex

Truth

Art, music, literature

Money

Power

Race

Gender

Ecology

Other

Now go over what you have written and put an M next to the items that express a moral value—the rules that have the force of obligation for you, the rules that determine right and wrong actions for you.

Here's how Peter filled out his value inventory:

Politics—*Vote on the issues.*

Religion—*Avoid. Has nothing to do with spiritual life. Respect others' religious choices. (M)*

Work—*Make a contribution to the world.*

Leisure—*Use time wisely.*

Education—*Important. Owe it to the young.*

Family—*My highest priority. (M)*

Aging, death—*Just the last part of life, a natural process.*

War, peace—*No such thing as a just war. (M)*

Style in clothes, grooming—*Basically unimportant. Just keep clean.*

Material possessions—*Best to have just a few treasures, not a lot of junk. But I have a lot of junk.*

Friends—*Stand by them, be loyal. Treat according to golden rule.*

Health—*?*

Rules, laws, authority—*Necessary, but not to be followed blindly.*

Love—*Conquers all. Seriously, it's what is behind the golden rule, treating others as you want to be treated. (M)*

Sex—*Trust is important. Natural expression of love. Anything goes between consenting adults. (M)*

Truth—*Necessary for trust and love. Difficult. (M)*

Art, music, literature—*Not that important to me.*

Money—*Root of most evil. Greed corrupts.*

Power—*Worse than money. Hard to use for good, easy to misuse.*

Race—*Believe in absolute equality. (M) South Africa makes me sad and furious. Still lots of discrimination here too.*

Gender—*Confused about being a man. Genders should be absolutely equal too. (M) But it's hard to change stereotypes.*

Ecology—*Golden rule applied to the planet. (M) Most crucial issue in the world today. More important than war, starvation, etc. I don't do enough locally.*

Other—*Also important values: keeping promises, (M) loyalty, freedom of choice in abortion, constitutional rights like free speech, stubbornly sticking to your guns, not lying to yourself.*

Ranking Your Values

From the M items in the list above, select the most important and write them in the space provided on the next page. You can combine several values into one, or divide one general value into several more specific values. Work on this list until you have at least five value statements that sum up your most important moral values.

Here is how Peter summarized his most important value statements:

Treat others the way I want to be treated.

Respect others' religious beliefs and sexual preferences.

Take care of my family.

Pacifist.

Tell the truth even when it's hard. Especially to myself.

Don't discriminate against other races, women, etc.

Take care of the planet.

Keep promises.

This is a very difficult exercise. You are engaged in "hard thought about right action"—Socrates' definition of moral philosophy. Plato's *Republic, Crito,* and *Apology,* written in the fourth century B.C., are about the same questions of right and wrong that probably appear on your list: When, if ever, is it right to tell a lie? Under what circumstances should one break a promise? Is law, convention, personal morality, religion, or self-preservation the final arbiter of right action?

Early moral philosophers argued that right action is motivated by cardinal virtues. Cardinal virtues were like primary colors—they were the essential traits of good moral character from which all other moral virtues could be derived. Plato held that the cardinal virtues were wisdom, courage, temperance, and justice.

Later moralists abandoned the word "virtue." Since the beginning of the modern age moralists have tended to speak of ethical principles instead. A common first principle that is mentioned or implied by most ethicians is benevolence: the principle that you should do good and avoid or prevent evil. To this is usually added the principle of beneficence or utility: that you should seek the greatest balance of good over evil in the universe. Derived from or related to beneficence is the principle of justice: that you should distribute good equally. From these basic principles are derived all sorts of more specific principles such as not injuring anyone, telling the truth, keeping agreements, not interfering with another's liberty, and so on.

Have you spotted the real question yet? After you ponder basic ethical principles for a while, you realize that it all hinges on this question: What is the "good"?

Hedonists would say that the good is pleasure, perhaps going on to define pleasure as including intellectual and spiritual as well as physical pleasure. Others would say that pleasure is just a side effect of achieving or experiencing other desirable goods such as wisdom, intimacy, beauty, and so on.

Here is a list of important "goods" that have been discussed by philosophers and other thinkers over the last thirty centuries. They are ranked roughly in order by how much importance they have been given, with the values that have been traditionally regarded as most important near the top and those traditionally accorded less importance near the bottom. Go ahead and rerank them yourself from 1 to 20 according to your own values.

1___ Life

2___ Consciousness

___ Activity

6___ Health, strength

___ Pleasures and satisfactions

___ Happiness, contentment

3___ Truth

7___ Knowledge, understanding, wisdom

___ Beauty, harmony, aesthetic experience

___ Love

___ Friendship, affection

14 Cooperation, community

4 Just distribution of goods and evils

13 Achievement, progress, growth

9 Power

10 Self-expression

5 Freedom, liberty, independence

8 Peace, security

20 Adventure, novelty

15 Good reputation, honor, esteem

This is not idle speculation. How you rank the "goods" of life has serious and far-reaching implications. When Peter did this exercise, he put "life" at the top. This made sense because, as a pacifist, he held life sacred. For Peter, there could be no other "good" so important as to require him to take a life. But then he thought about the time his grandfather was in the hospital in a coma. After several weeks, his family decided to discontinue life support and his grandfather died. Was this not choosing "consciousness" as a higher good than life? He also asked himself what the high value he placed on life implied about his own belief in a woman's right to choose to have an abortion. Peter had to do some long, hard thinking before he was satisfied that his values were clear and consistent. It made him a lot less eager to judge others who held differing values.

In the light of this ranking exercise, how would you revise your own list of personal and moral values from the previous exercise?

Here is Peter's revised list:

Protect life—Control anger, protest violence, work for peace, preserve the planet, take care of my family.

Respect rights: women, all races, religions, sexual preferences, etc.

Tell the truth, face facts about myself.

Keep promises.

Peter found that all his values fit under four themes: life, rights, truth, and promises. These words had very personal, exact meanings to him that they don't necessarily have to other people. The words you choose will be different, reflecting your unique history and beliefs.

Affirming Your Values

A complete man, a man with integrity, is willing to go on record with his beliefs. He publicly affirms his values and sticks by them, even in the face of disagreement or disapproval. He also knows when the circumstances are appropriate for taking a stand, and when to remain silent.

The following exercise will help you explore your patterns of self-disclosure in regard to your values. It will help you decide what you are willing to affirm and to whom. It may show you where you are ineffective in life through being too open or too closed.

The concentric circles below indicate the different "audiences" to which you are willing to reveal your values.

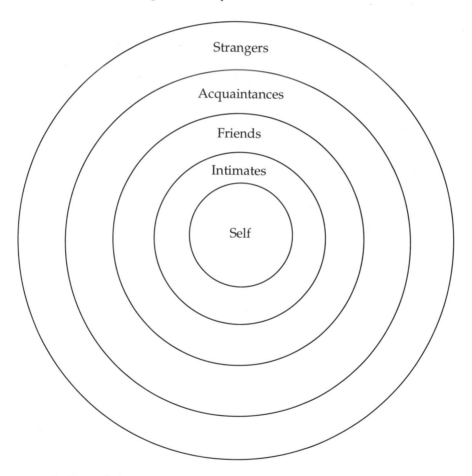

1. In each band, write a key word that will remind you of a value you would be willing to affirm to the audience represented by the band. For example, if you wouldn't mind telling a stranger

your position on war, write "war" in the outside band. If there is only one person in the world that you are willing to tell about your sexual preferences, write "sex" in the intimates band.

2. Write the word "love" in the band representing whom you would be willing to tell about a love affair and how it affected your values concerning love.

3. Write "extra" in the band representing the person you are willing to tell your values concerning extramarital sex, including your own experiences or temptations in this area.

4. Write "money" in the band representing whom you would tell about the money you make, the money you owe, and what you would and wouldn't do for money.

5. Write "spirit" in the band representing those with whom you would discuss your spiritual beliefs and practices.

6. Write "anger" in the band representing whom you would tell about your struggles with anger and violence.

7. Write "family" in the band representing the person to whom you would reveal your values about family life, including your childhood traumas and problems in your current family situation.

8. Write "politics" in the band representing those with whom you would discuss your political views.

9. Write "lie" in the band representing the people to whom it would be okay for you to tell a lie.

10. Write "promise" in the band representing those to whom you would consider breaking a promise.

11. Continue, writing key words representing your other important values in the relevant bands.

At this point you may begin to see a pattern. If you are only willing to affirm your values to yourself and one or two intimates, it suggests that you need to go on record with a wider audience. If you don't express your values to friends and acquaintances, you will have trouble acting on your values consistently. And you won't have very deep relationships with people, because they will be lacking some important information about you.

On the other hand, you may be too willing to tell all. Simply talking too much about your values to strangers and casual acquaintances who don't need to know every detail of your moral code isn't a big problem— unless you find yourself using your values as a weapon to judge, condemn, and dominate others. If this is the case, you may need to consider adding "Respect for others' opinions and autonomy" to your list of values. Try being quiet and just listening to what your son or daughter or wife have to say about their own values and beliefs. Listen and learn for a change. Can you remember occasions when sharing your value system may have meant that you were either overly judgmental or guilty of butting in with unwelcome advice?

There may be one or two values that you aren't willing to disclose to anyone. If this is the case, ask yourself if you really do cherish and prize this value. Is it in conflict with some other value? Is it a leftover from your early childhood or religious training that you don't really believe in, deep down? Is it a preference that you are actually ashamed of? A value that can't be affirmed to someone is not a real value. It's more likely to be a rationalized vice, a prejudice, or a vestigial piece of received wisdom that you are ready to jettison.

You may find a pattern in which there are topics you are willing to discuss with friends or acquaintances, but not with intimates. For instance, you may be willing to tell a friend or a therapist about an extramarital affair you had, but not want to tell your wife about it. Or you might find it easy to tell your friend that you disapprove of your daughter's sex life, but find it very difficult to tell your daughter herself. This is a deadly pattern because the more information you withhold from an intimate, the less intimate your relationship becomes. You end up relating on a shallow, surface level, or fighting about side issues, or retreating into silence and separate lives.

Finally, you should look for people to whom you are willing to affirm your values, but have not yet done so. Take a moment right now to identify these people and what you need to tell them:

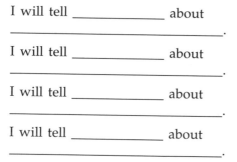

I will tell _____ about
_____.

I will tell _____ about
_____.

I will tell _____ about
_____.

I will tell _____ about
_____.

When Peter did this exercise, he discovered two things. First, he found that he never talked to anyone about certain "monkey wrenching" tactics used by radical pollution protesters that he admired. He had always liked to hear stories about people sabotaging developers' bulldozers, introducing computer viruses into multinational corporate data bases, and so on. Upon examination, he realized that such tactics were actually in violation of his values regarding nonviolence and respecting others' rights. He saw that he was indulging in violent fantasies about such tactics, but didn't really approve of them.

The other thing Peter discovered was that he needed to speak up about recycling at work. He had kept quiet for too long about the quantities of paper that were wasted in his office building.

Other Ways to Affirm Values

Is there a bumper sticker that sums up one of your important values? Get one and put it on your car. Is there a political candidate who embodies some of your values? Wear his or her button, pass out campaign literature, or volunteer at election headquarters. At least be sure to register and vote. Is there an organization that fights for something you believe in? Join it, go to the meetings, volunteer, or make a financial contribution. Is there any local or national legislation pending that supports or runs counter to your values? Write a letter to your representative or sign a petition.

Acting on Your Values

You make hundreds of decisions every day of your life. Most are governed by habit or simple preferences. The moral stakes are low and you act on your values almost automatically.

But some decisions require careful value judgments. Different courses of action may involve different values. For example, suppose you had promised a friend that you would come over on Saturday to help him clean out his garage. But as the week progresses, you get overscheduled, very tired, and feel like you may be coming down with a cold. You have conflicting values. You want to make good on your commitment and not disappoint your friend. But you also have made a commitment to reduce stress in your life and take better care of yourself.

If you are a man of integrity, you will carefully consider the values involved and choose to act on the values you consider most important. If you decide that it's more important to keep your date, you will show up on time on Saturday and work with a will. If you decide it's more important to take care of yourself, you will call up your friend right away. You will clearly and honestly tell him your reasons for canceling.

If you lack integrity, you may put off the decision until the last minute, then call your friend with a phony excuse. Or you might show up late on Saturday, grumbling about your cold and your schedule and feeling resentful all the time you are providing listless, grudging help.

The important thing in this example is not which action you choose, but that you choose consciously, carefully, and with responsibility.

Exercise

Possible actions	Values	Rank

Right action:

Desired outcome:

Feared consequences:

When and how I will act:

1. Choose a particular situation in which you need to take some action. Write down each possible action you could take. There might be three or four possible actions—not all moral dilemmas resolve themselves neatly into a pair of black and white possibilities.

2. Under each action, write the values you hold which tend to support that choice.

3. Rank the values, assigning the number one to the value that seems most important in this situation, assigning the number two to the value that is next in importance, and so on until all the values are numbered. In assigning rank, refer to the work you have done in the earlier parts of this chapter to identify and rank your values.

4. Under "right action," rewrite the course of action that grows out of your highest values. Write each step of the action in detail. Anticipate any barriers to the action and write how you will overcome them.

5. List the desired outcome of the right action.

6. List possible negative consequences of the right action: what you are afraid will happen if you do the right thing.

7. Write out when and how you will act. Make a plan that maximizes your chances of achieving the desired outcome and minimizes the chances of the feared consequences.

Examples

Rob. Rob supervised an office of mostly white, male claims adjusters. He needed to hire another experienced claims adjuster. He had interviewed ten different applicants and narrowed the field to two strong contenders. One was a white man who had all the qualifications for the job. The other was a black woman who had even better qualifications. Here is how he set up his value judgment:

Possible actions	Values	Rank
Hire the qualified white man	*Competence—he'll do a good job*	3
	Comfort	5
	He'll fit in well with the other guys	4
Hire the more qualified black woman	*Justice—equal opportunity*	1
	Competence—she'll do a better job	2

Right action: *Hire the black woman.*

Desired outcome: *She'll do a good job and come to be accepted and respected by the rest of the staff.*

Feared consequences: *The other guys will ostracize her and consider me some kind of gender or race traitor.*

When and how I will act: *I'll offer the job to the black woman this afternoon. If she accepts, I'll notify the other applicants that the job has been filled. I'll speak privately to each claims adjuster and tell him that I've hired the person who's the most qualified for the job and that I expect him to welcome her and treat her professionally.*

This is a true moral dilemma. Rob's higher moral values of justice and equal opportunity are in conflict with his lower nonmoral values of comfort and preserving the "good old boy" atmosphere in the office. It would have been easier for Rob to hire the white man, and nobody would have to know that he had chosen the less qualified applicant. But he would have violated his own integrity. And he would have had to compound the violation by lying to the black woman about why she didn't get the job.

Rob wisely chose to make the more difficult choice, to take the high road, to follow his higher values and act with integrity.

Blake. Blake was a draughtsman and surveyor's helper who wanted to return to school and get a degree that would allow him to eventually change careers. He was interested in engineering and environmental studies. Here is how he analyzed his options:

Possible actions	Values	Rank
Major in engineering	*Earn more money*	2
Major in environmental studies	*Help preserve the environment*	1

Right action: *Go for environmental studies.*

Desired outcome: *Enjoy studies, graduate, get a job in resource management or doing environmental impact studies.*

Feared consequences: *I may regret not going for the higher paid field. I may end up just as dissatisfied as I am now.*

When and how I will act: *I'll register in environmental studies, but I'll make an appointment right away with a guidance counselor and gather all the facts about possible careers. I need more information to be comfortable sticking with environmental studies.*

Blake's analysis turned out to be oversimplified. He discovered that he didn't need to make such a black-and-white choice. He was able to major in environmental studies with a minor in engineering. He eventually landed an interesting job at a decent salary with a water district in a rural county. He got to make a worthwhile contribution to protecting the environment in a position that also required engineering know-how and drafting skills.

Carl. Carl had been married for six years. He had been sleeping with another woman off and on for six months, feeling guilty and anxious, and coming to realize that he needed to make some basic decisions about his marriage, his relationship to his mistress, sex, communication, and so on. Here is how he analyzed the situation:

Possible actions	Values	Rank
Separate from wife and live with mistress	*Sexual pleasure*	5
	Intimacy	4
	Novelty	6
Preserve status quo— keep seeing mistress, say nothing to wife	*Security, routine*	7

Break off with mistress, say nothing to wife	*Fidelity*	*3*
Break off with mistress, come clean with wife	*Truth*	*1*
	Honesty	*2*
	Restored intimacy	*4*
	Fidelity, keeping marriage vows	*3*

Right action: *Break off with mistress. Tell wife the truth, ask to work on reaffirming our commitment.*

Desired outcome: *Wife is upset, but forgives me. Agrees to get into couples therapy, work on more satisfying sex life, stay in communication.*

Feared consequences: *Both women are very upset, neither wants anything to do with me, I end up with nobody.*

When and how I will tell mistress: *Over coffee Thursday morning. I'll say I value her, the intimacy, the good talks, the sex—but I can't go on living a lie. I'm sorry.*

When and how I will tell wife: *After dinner Monday night. I'll say I made a mistake, took the easy way out. I want to recommit to our relationship. I want a second chance. I think our love is deep and strong enough to face up to the truth and make a new beginning. I'd like to start therapy and work on rebuilding trust, openness, and passion in our life together.*

In this case, Carl decided that he valued telling the truth and honoring his marriage vows over the pleasure and novelty of continuing to see his mistress. It's interesting to note that the value of increased intimacy shows up under two possible options: he could look forward to chances for increased intimacy with his mistress if he separated from his wife, or with his wife if he gave up his mistress. The value of intimacy is notably missing from the option of continuing with the status quo and living a lie.

The right action was obvious to Carl, but very frightening: to break up with his mistress and tell the truth to his wife. The feared consequences were daunting. There was a real possibility that his chosen course of action would end not only his affair but also his marriage. He finally decided to go ahead with the right action when he realized that he wouldn't want to remain in a marriage where he couldn't tell the truth and be given a chance to repair his mistakes.

Key Values for Men

Courses in Values Clarification are offered in some high schools. The teachers encourage free discussion and try not to steer the class toward a particular moral code. They adopt a stance of moral relativism and refuse to say that one principle is more important or ought to have more weight than another.

That stance is not appropriate for this book. If you're trying to be a man of integrity in the late twentieth century, there are definitely some key values that you need to integrate into your life.

Benevolence. This is the basic principle that you should do good and prevent or avoid evil. Your most difficult applications of this principle are likely to be made in the work arena. In relation to what you do for money, the principle of benevolence is summed up by the saying "you're either part of the solution or you're part of the problem." A Buddhist would talk about benevolence in work as "right livelihood."

Many men are caught in a career trap. They need to make money, so they enter a field that seems lucrative and that they have some aptitude for. It can be almost anything—banking or geology or making electronic components. Somewhere along the line they realize that their chosen profession involves foreclosing on poor families' homes or drilling for oil in fragile ecosystems or making parts for weapons. Their values centered around making money and being a productive citizen and a good provider come into conflict with other values about justice, equality, preserving the environment, peace, and so on. They start to wonder if they are doing more harm than good, if they are more a part of the problem than part of the solution. If this kind of moral dilemma is raising its head in your life, you should carefully read the chapter on work (chapter 5) and resolve to do something about bringing your work more in line with your most important values.

Justice. This principle states that the good things of life should be distributed equally. For a man of integrity, this is the principle that should determine how you treat women. To the extent that it is in your power to "distribute the goods," whether they be love, respect, attention, approval, power, jobs, money, opportunity—you need to distribute these goods equally to women and men. In less abstract terms, this means that you need to learn to listen to your girlfriend or your wife or your women colleagues carefully and respectfully. It means that you can't deny a promotion or an apartment or a loan to someone just because she's a woman. It means that you can't just assume that women are going to do the dishes and change the diapers.

Not hurting. The meaning of this principle is obvious, and for modern men so is its application. A man of integrity simply doesn't abuse anyone: not kids, not women, not other men; not verbally, not physically, and not sexually. If you have serious trouble controlling your anger, see the chapter on anger (chapter 13) and see a therapist.

Telling the truth. This value has several implications for modern men. Telling the truth is good for your relationships. Telling the truth in a relationship means that you should tell not only the facts, but your feelings as well. Your feelings are part of the deepest truth about yourself. Sharing them deepens the relationship and keeps it alive and satisfying. That's why there are two whole chapters on feelings in this book (chapters 10 and 11).

Telling the truth means no manipulation. It means being frank and open about your motives, your expectations, your needs, and your wants. That's why there is a chapter in this book on simply asking for what you want responsibly (chapter 12).

Telling the truth means self-disclosure in general. The more you tell people about yourself, the richer your interactions become. When you keep secrets or withhold relevant bits of information about yourself, you impoverish your interactions and make them shallow and superficial.

Keeping promises and commitments. For men, the toughest application of this principle is monogamy. Making and keeping a promise of sexual and emotional fidelity is a challenging and recurring moral choice.

Freedom. This principle is related to justice. For modern men, it frequently means letting go of control issues, not trying to dominate or influence the decisions and actions of others, allowing them their own autonomy.

Preservation of your own health and well-being. Many modern men need to adopt, affirm, and act on this value. See the appropriate chapters if you tend to focus exclusively on work or other interests (chapter 5), ignore your physical health (chapter 14), or pay no attention to your psychological well-being and inner life (chapter 3).

Protecting the weak, educating the young. This has to do with your responsibilities as a man to younger generations in general, and as a father to your own children in particular. A complete man, a man with integrity, passes his knowledge, his love, and his values on to his children...mostly by example, not by precept. If you know you need to concentrate on your role as a father, see the chapter on parenting (chapter 9) for further work.

The golden rule principle. When you're considering a possible action, ask yourself what the world would be like if everybody did it. For example, Gerald was remodeling his house, which involved removing some old asbestos shingles. He pried them off and filled a wheelbarrow with the scraps. Now, according to the rules at his local landfill, asbestos is a hazardous waste. You have to keep things like discarded asbestos shingles separate, transport them to a separate part of the dump, and pay quite a bit extra in disposal fees. Gerald knew that if he just mixed the shingles with his other debris, they would never be noticed when he went to the dump.

Then Gerald applied the golden rule principle: "What if everybody dumped their asbestos in the wrong spot? Then we'd have more of the same mess we have now: landfills that are such a stew of toxics that the land is poisoned and useless for hundreds of years." Gerald acted as a man of integrity and put the shingles in a separate garbage can and paid the extra dumping fees.

This is a difficult principle to follow. But there's nothing like it for cutting through rationalizations to show you the unpleasant but ethical thing to do.

Husbandry. Many of these principles could be summed up in the term "husbandry." The word husband comes from old English and Norse roots. It refers to a house dweller, someone who is deeply bonded to his house and land. A husband is the opposite of a nomad or wanderer. The term has long been associated with farming and caring for the soil. Good husbandry implies a commitment to wife, children, community, and land.

Today, few men are farmers. But you can still practice husbandry. You can thoughtfully allocate your time and money and energy in ways that preserve family relationships, nurture children, and care for the world around you. This suggests such values as thrift, recycling, conservation, learning to do things for yourself, and becoming involved in community action. Moving in the direction of husbandry is a step away from the alienation and isolation that men have increasingly felt since the beginning of the industrial revolution.

Special Considerations

Consistency. A man of integrity not only makes value judgments carefully and consciously, he also makes them consistently. He applies the same hierarchy of values to similar situations. He doesn't avoid the decision one time and act another. He doesn't base his actions on fairness one time, expediency the next time, and comfort a third time.

Transgression. Sometimes you know what the right action is, but you choose the wrong one anyway. For example, you believe in truth, but you cheat on your income tax. Or you believe in equal opportunity for all, but you exaggerate your experience on a job application to get a job you want desperately. Or you believe in honesty, but you falsify a loan application so you can buy a great house.

In cases like these, it's best to just admit to yourself that you are transgressing against your values. Don't make matters worse by rationalizing that "everybody does it." Don't try to make it okay by some complicated moral juggling. Just admit that you are acting according to a lower value and accept the fact that you will feel some guilt as a consequence. It's better to say "I'm wrong, but I'm going to do it anyway" than to distort and confuse your value system with a lot of self-deluding rationalizations.

5

Being Useful:
Finding Meaningful Work

For most men, the hardest part of the question "Where are you going?" is "What will you do for a living?"

In our society, you are what you do. More than anything else about you, your occupation determines how others see you and how you see yourself. Your job not only influences obvious things like your income, residence, and lifestyle, but also profoundly affects your self-esteem and the level of happiness and self-fulfillment you can hope to achieve.

You may argue that this is not right or fair. You may contend that what really counts is who you are inside, whom you love, what you believe, the children you raise, and the beauty you may add to the world as you pass through it. This is all true, and the rest of this book deals with those issues. But this chapter takes a hard look at work as it exists in the real world today.

There are basically three ways that work can give you trouble: you can have too much work, the wrong kind of work, or not enough work.

If you work too much, chances are you are a workaholic—someone who has an addictive relationship to work. This chapter will help you decide if you have this problem, set goals to change, and reduce work to a more reasonable force in your life.

The wrong kind of work means that you are doing something that is not satisfying or that conflicts in some way with your values. This chapter will explain the concept of right livelihood and help you discover the most meaningful vocation for you.

Not enough work means that you are unemployed or underemployed. The material in this chapter on right livelihood will help you figure out the kind of work you want to look for. But this chapter won't cover the nuts and bolts of job hunting. There are several good books that have already done that, the most popular being *What Color is Your Parachute?* by Richard Bolles.

Too Much Work

These days, the "addiction model" is very popular for explaining all sorts of behavioral problems. Regarding work, the idea is that if you work too much, if you're obsessed with your work, and it affects the rest of your life negatively, then you are a workaholic. You are addicted to work. Lots of parallels are drawn between the characteristics of workaholics and alcoholics or drug addicts.

Like alcohol, work is a socially acceptable vice. In fact, our society actually encourages workaholism. There is tremendous pressure on a man to be a good provider, to work hard, to succeed. Your identity as a man is tied to your work more firmly than to any other fact about you. You are what you do. The more you do, the better you are.

For men, work is the first line of defense for protecting and ensuring self-esteem. If you are feeling a little insecure, unsure of yourself, unworthy, a hard day at the desk or the shop can make you feel that you have a place in the world and that you are okay.

When men who want to work can't work, their self-esteem plummets. For proof you only have to look at this statistic: when unemployment goes up one percent, male suicide goes up three percent.

Besides, for many men work is fun. They are good at it and they enjoy it. Men seem to thrive—up to a point, anyway—on a challenge, on problems to solve and new ideas to create. If your work is your major outlet for your creativity and your sense of mastery in the world, no wonder it can be addicting.

For example, Hal was a 48-year-old man who owned half-interest in a medium-sized supermarket. He and his partner had built the store up over a fifteen-year period until it was the most attractive and popular market in town. Hal was a recovering alcoholic and an ex-smoker who had struggled mightily to get off booze and cigarettes, only to find that his addictive patterns had found expression in his work. He was officially the evening manager of the store, responsible for everything that went on from three in the afternoon until midnight. But you could find Hal at the store almost any time, day or night. Hal felt most secure and in control of his life when he was sitting in his little office on the mezzanine, going over the receipts and stock orders, glancing out the little window overlooking the checkout stands. The store was making enough money so that he didn't have to spend so much time there. But when he was away from the market for a day or two, Hal felt restless, uncomfortable, bored, and unsure of himself.

Are You a Workaholic?

Whether the model of addiction is strictly true or not, some fairly clear-cut symptoms of workaholism have been identified. If you exhibit more than half of these tendencies, they should serve as warning signs that you need to restore some balance to your life.

- ☐ I consistently work over 40 hours a week: going in early, staying late, working weekends and holidays, and so on.

- ☐ I think about work a lot when I'm not there.

- ☐ I take work home or take it on vacation.

- ☐ I often don't take the sick days and vacation time I have coming.

- ☐ When I'm not working, I often feel

  - ☐ restless

  - ☐ anxious

  - ☐ guilty

  - ☐ depressed

  - ☐ irritable

- ☐ I find myself doing other people's work for them to make sure it's done right or on time.

- ☐ I have trouble delegating tasks and responsibilities to others.

- ☐ I sometimes work to avoid relationship problems or thinking about other areas of my life.

- ☐ When I resolve to leave on time, take a day off, or otherwise cut back on work, I find it very difficult to accomplish my resolution.

- ☐ If I ever run out of things to do at work, I create work for myself rather than go home.

When Hal looked at this list, he checked almost every item. He spent time at home reading retail food trade magazines and plotting new in-store promotions. He was always "helping" the stock boys and baggers and clerks, even though they didn't really need the help and in fact wished he would stop breathing down their necks. When he was at home, he would call the store to check on things and encouraged the staff to call him at home if there were any problems.

The Costs

You'll never be motivated to really get control of your work life until you get a clear look at what workaholism costs you. For each of the areas below, write a brief description of any work-related limitations or problems you experience.

Mate

Children

Parents

Friends

Co-workers

Health

Leisure

Hobbies & interests

Education

Material goods

Community involvement

Spiritual life

Other

Here is how Hal assessed the costs of his devotion to his super-market.

Mate   *Wants a divorce because I'm never home.*

Children   *Hardly know my daughter Sarah.*

Parents

Friends   *Only have "couple" friends or business contacts.*

Co-workers   *Partner relies on me to be there. Staff think I meddle too much.*

Health   *Overweight (around food all the time). Out of shape (no time to exercise).*

Leisure   *Have none.*

Hobbies & interests   *Never play the guitar anymore. No time to put in orchard or garden.*

Education   *Haven't learned anything new in years that didn't have something to do with food retailing.*

Material goods   *Don't care much for things, but would like to enjoy our land more.*

Community involvement   *Partner bugs me to join Kiwanis.*

Spiritual life   *Not sure I have one. Used to meditate in the sixties, when it was cool.*

Other   *Time for a change, or my wife will leave me.*

Hal felt particularly bad about his daughter and his wife. They were essentially strangers to him, since for years he had been gone from mid-morning to midnight most days. He had made a lot of money, been a good provider. Three years ago they had moved into a big new house on five acres outside of town. Last fall his daughter Sarah had gone off to college, and his wife Jane said, "Now that Sarah's out of the house, I feel like I can concentrate on what I need for myself." One thing she thought she might need was a divorce. That's what finally prompted Hal to consider that he might have a problem with his work.

Goals for Cutting Back on Work

The first step in the treatment of workaholism is to set some goals. You need to look at the pattern of your overwork and set limits on the time and energy you will devote to your work. For starters, look at this list and check off strategies that may work for you.

☐   Stick to 40 hours per week.

☐   No weekend work.

☐   No Sundays.

☐   Don't arrive before __:__.

☐   Leave work by __:__.

☐   No taking work home.

☐   No taking work on vacation.

☐   Work at home only during certain hours: _____.

☐   Confine work at home to a certain room or area.

☐   Don't obsess about work at home.

☐   Stop doing others' work for them.

☐   Delegate more.

☐   Don't call work.

☐   Don't take work calls at home.

☐   Other goals:

Hal's goals were to be at the store only eight hours a day, stay out of the staff's business, not read trade journals at home, and cut way down on phone calls to and from the store when he was at home.

Achieving Your Goals

Just having goals is not enough. You need a twofold plan. First, you have to make changes at work that will free you to go home. Second, you have to plan what to do at home when you get the urge to return to work. For the first half of your plan, review this list and check off any ideas that you can use.

☐   Get support and agreement from bosses, partners, co-workers, subordinates, and so on.

☐   Stop doing what's not worth doing.

☐   Get someone else to do some important things.

☐   Lower standards.

☐   Raise prices to make the same income on less work.

☐ Cancel projects, products, services.

☐ Postpone projects.

☐ Schedule more time for projects.

☐ Hire more help.

☐ Use more free-lancers or subcontractors.

☐ Accept less pay if I have to.

☐ Ask for help.

☐ Set limits on being called at home.

☐ Get time-saving equipment, tools, or software.

☐ Transfer to a less stressful department or position.

☐ Quit and get a less demanding job.

☐ Insist on overtime pay—stop giving it away and they may stop asking for more time.

☐ Say no more often.

☐ Say yes less often.

☐ Delegate more responsibility.

☐ Get an assistant.

Obviously, not all these ideas are possible or appropriate for everyone, and you can probably think of several that are not on the list that pertain to your particular situation.

In order to implement his goals, Hal decided to stop doing stocking and checking unless the staff asked him to help. He canceled his "Hawaiian Days" and "Western Days" promotions for the next year. His partner and the staff were supportive of his efforts and agreed not to call him at home unless there was a genuine emergency.

The second part of achieving your goals is the most important: *What are you going to do instead of working?* In this regard, overcoming workaholism is like overcoming any addiction—you need alternative behaviors to replace the addictive behavior. Your alternative activities should be things you really like doing, not things you "should" do. If you hate doing chores around the house, it won't work to plan to paint your house on weekends instead of going into the office. The first Saturday you have to face those peeling shutters and drippy rollers, you'll find a reason why you have to go in "just for an hour." And you'll be there all day.

Look for alternative activities in your hobbies and interests, the people you like to spend time with, sports and fitness, reading, taking classes, getting involved in the community or with a church group, and so on. Plan things that you can do day or night, rain or shine. If it's too dark to take a walk, have something else on hand, like a woodworking project or a computer magazine you've been wanting to read. Combine ongoing activities like taking a course in watercolors with more spontaneous projects such as building a bird feeder with your daughter.

To write a workable plan for replacing work with a more balanced home life, use a two column format. On the left, write the danger signals—the symptoms or situations that come up that make you want to escape into work. Include typical painful feelings, relationship hassles, demands from your work, financial worries, chronic ruminations about work, and so on.

For each danger signal, write in the second column an alternative activity that you plan to engage in instead of working. You can use the space provided or work it out on a separate piece of paper.

Danger Signals	Alternative Activities

Here's how Hal did this exercise:

Danger Signals	Alternative Activities
Feel restless	*Fire up the tractor, disk and level the field.*
Jane is restless	*Suggest we go to the movies or go out for some ice cream.*
Argue with Jane or Sarah	*Ask to postpone discussion, go out and cultivate garden.*
Store calls with problem	*Ask "What do you think we should do?" Get them to solve their own problems.*
Feel anxious, guilty	*Play my guitar.*
Saturdays empty	*Take guitar lesson in afternoon, plant trees.*
Sundays empty	*Go to church with Jane, drive out to the lake.*
Partner complains he never sees me	*Join him in Kiwanis.*
Feel stressed out	*Make cup of tea, put on some music. Try meditating again.*
Remember something I forgot at the store, need to check something, get a terrific promotion idea	*Make a note to myself, take it in the next day.*

Get Support

You can't do everything on your own. That attitude may have helped trap you in your work in the first place. You need to get your loved ones on your side. Let your family know that you are determined to get out from under your workaholism. Discuss what it means to them in terms of having you around more, new family activities, the possibility of lower income, and so on.

Having you at work less and at home more may be a mixed blessing to your mate or your kids. If you get resistance, see chapter 8, "Being Two: Making Partnership Work."

The Wrong Kind of Work

This is the section for you if you are not satisfied with your work. Do you have any of these symptoms of "Wrong Livelihood"?

☐   I feel out of place at work.

☐   I avoid telling others what I do for a living.

☐   I dread going to work.

☐   I have a lot of conflict with my co-workers.

☐   I feel guilty about what I do for a living.

☐   I'm jealous of others with different jobs.

☐   My work feels meaningless to me.

☐   I'd like to make more of a contribution to the world.

☐   I feel trapped in the wrong field.

☐   When I think of doing this for the rest of my life, I get depressed.

☐   Other:

Many cultures believe that work is a virtue in itself. The kind of work doesn't matter much. What's important is that you have a good-paying job, show up on time, work hard, show loyalty to your employer, strive for advancement, don't make waves, and so on. If you do all this, you are virtuous, a good provider, a proper head of household, a pillar of the community, and a hero.

Then why do you feel so miserable, if you are performing according to the official work ethic?

To get a more balanced, thoughtful view of the place work should have in a man's life, you need to look beyond this relatively recent and narrow-minded tradition. You may find the Buddhist world view much more helpful.

According to ancient Buddhist tradition, the way to lead a decent, satisfying life is to follow the Noble Eightfold Path, a middle way between excessive austerity and outright sensuality. The Eightfold Path consists of:

Right views—seeing life as it is, recognizing truth

Right mindedness—being a friend to all life

Right speech—telling the truth kindly

Right action—acting skillfully, sympathetically, peaceably

Right livelihood—doing work that doesn't violate morality

Right endeavor—seeking self-improvement

Right mindfulness—becoming self-aware, compassionate, serene

Right contemplation—cultivating intuition, wisdom

The first thing to notice is that work—right livelihood—is only one of eight steps on the path. And it's fifth on the list, not at the top. That's a good clue for workaholics.

But even more important is the fact that work made the list at all. Whether to marry or whom to marry isn't on the list. Whether to have kids or how to raise them isn't on the list. What kind of car to buy or house to live in or clothes to wear isn't on the list. But work *is* on the list of the important steps you must follow to live a decent, satisfying life. And the quality of work that is important is not high-paying work or high-status work or high-tech work—it's *right* work, work that doesn't violate your own code of law and morality, or force others to violate their codes.

This belies any attempts to say to yourself, "Work is just a necessary evil—I have to get enough money to survive, and how I do it isn't important to the rest of my life." Not true. Finding the right livelihood for yourself is crucial to your happiness and satisfaction in life.

In sixties terms, the principle of right livelihood means "If you're not part of the solution, you're part of the problem." If you're not doing something to improve the world, you are helping harm the world, at least through inaction, ignorance, or apathy. In this view, there are no morally neutral occupations or actions. The smallest act can be seen as socially constructive or destructive. Littering is allied to clandestine dumping of nuclear waste. Recycling your newspapers is seen as a noble act.

The heroes of right livelihood are loggers who become tree planters, pulp mill supervisors who switch to managing recycling centers, soldiers reborn as peace activists, housing developers retreaded as forest rangers, and so on.

Basic Principles of Right Livelihood

The basic principles of right livelihood are the basic principles of ethics, as outlined in the previous chapter on integrity. As you read these principles, don't feel bad if your occupation is used as an example of one that is "less right" than another occupation. Making a list like this necessitates making generalities and value judgments. But when it comes to your particular experience of your particular profession, only you can judge whether it is right for you.

No harm. Medical doctors have this written into their Hippocratic Oath: "First, do no harm." At the very least, your work should not physically harm people. It's clear that mugging people for a living violates this principle. But what about working for a corporation that has a division that makes parts that end up in nuclear power plants? What about working for a chemical company that sells third world countries cancer-causing pesticides that are banned as a health hazard in the United States? What about joining or working for the military?

Honest. Your work should not be based on deception or manipulation. Obviously, you wouldn't be proud of being a professional con man who cheats bereaved widows out of their inheritances. But how far do you personally need to extend this principle in order to feel comfortable? Could you sell used cars that look better than they actually are? Could you be an advertising executive? A personal injury lawyer?

Just. This means that your work shouldn't require you to take unfair advantage of others, especially those who are weaker, poorer, less informed, or less clever than you. This obviously rules out extortion and loan sharking. But how far down this road are you willing to go? What about being a slum landlord? Shady real estate speculator? Insider stock trader?

Beneficial. This means that it's preferable to do something constructive, creative, and healing, rather than something destructive, unimaginative, or sickening. Thus, building houses is better than buying and selling them or tearing them down. Designing gardens is more rewarding than assembly line work. Being a nurse or a therapist is better than being a tobacco broker or a liquor salesman.

Useful. The principle of utility suggests that your work should provide goods or services that other people really need. Accordingly, making real furniture would be a higher calling than making doll furniture, and making sturdy chairs would be better than making flimsy ones.

Real. Some areas of endeavor such as the stock market are very abstract—mostly concepts and numbers. Other work is more real in that it involves physical goods or observable services, such as selling shoes or painting someone's house.

As you read farther down this list, you get into areas involving more preference than morality. In terms of benefits, utility, and degree of concreteness, you can only say that one job is "better" than another when you know who is holding the job, what he is required to do, and what it means to him. One solvent chemist may be happily working on a project to make more healthy and environmentally safe paints, while another solvent chemist may be working for a company that tries to circumvent and foil the new EPA regulations about safer solvents.

Changing Your Current Job for the Better

This is the approach to try first, since it involves the least disruption to your life. Write out a detailed job description below. Include as much information as you can, including the parts of your job you like, what you hate, and what is tolerable.

Current Job Assessment

Job title

Duties

Report to

Supervise

Company products, services, and policies

Now go back and cross out the parts you hate. Add notes to explain exactly what you hate about each aspect. Then go through your list again and circle the parts you actually like. Add notes to clarify what it is specifically that you like about each good point. What's left is a list of duties, products, services, policies, and so on that you find tolerable. Here is an example of how Roy filled out his assessment.

Current Job Assessment

Job title

Carpenter

Duties

~~*Unload and stack materials*~~ *(hard, boring)*

~~*Demolition*~~ *(dirty)*

Read plan

Lay out walls

Framing

(*Raise walls*)(*sastisfying*)

~~*Sheathing walls*~~ *(repetitive nailing hurts elbow)*

Mark and cut joists and rafters

Install joists and rafters

~~*Sheathing roof*~~ *(hurts elbow)*

(*Some finish carpentry*)

Coordinate with subcontractors

(*Deal with clients*)

Call for inspections, meet with inspector

~~*Clean up*~~ *(boring)*

(*Teach new carpenters*)(*fun to share skills*)

(*Do material takeoffs for bids*)(*use my mind*)

Report to

~~*Pete Baccardi, crew chief*~~ *(looks over my shoulder too much)*

(*Dan Dixon, company owner*)(*smart, fair, nice guy*)

Supervise

(*Two to four laborers, depending on job*)(*good at it, firm but fair*)

Company products, services, and policies

(*Build small houses on spec*)

(*Mostly custom house building*)

(*Some large remodels*)

(*Policies: Keep the customer happy*)

Run one crew at a time

~~*Work one job at a time*~~ *(too much down time
for carpenters at end of jobs)*

Now that you have a detailed assessment of your work, consider these questions to formulate a plan for change:

Plan for Change

How can I change my duties or transfer to another job within the same organization that will allow me to do more of what I like and less of what I hate?

How can I change the products, services, or policies of the organization to make the job more rewarding for me?

Can I create new projects or departments that would be more nourishing for me?

What additional training, degree, experience, equipment, and so on do I need to accomplish these changes?

Whose support, approval, cooperation do I need to bring this off?

How long will it take to make these changes?

Is it worth the trouble?

Can I stick it out until things get better?

What are the drawbacks to this plan?

What is my plan and schedule for change?

First step:

   Deadline:

Second step:

   Deadline:

Third step:

   Deadline:

Here is how Roy completed his plan for change:

Plan for Change

How can I change my duties or transfer to another job within the same organization that will allow me to do more of what I like and less of what I hate?

I can try to delegate the more boring, exhausting, dirty jobs to the laborers, but that won't change my job enough.

How can I change the products, services, or policies of the organization to make the job more rewarding for me?

If we ran two crews during the busy season, I could boss the second crew and get to do more of what I like.

Can I create new projects or departments that would be more nourishing for me?

I could propose a second crew.

What additional training, degree, experience, equipment, and so on do I need to accomplish these changes?

I'd need to learn how to run the scheduling and accounting programs on the computer and bone up on the plumbing and electrical parts of the building code.

Whose support, approval, cooperation do I need to bring this off?

I need to convince Dan that I can do it and that he'll make more money with a second crew. I need to win Pete over to the idea, probably by agreeing to do the less interesting remodels with the second crew.

How long will it take to make these changes?
Set it up this winter, start in spring.

Is it worth the trouble?
Yes, if it works.

Can I stick it out until things get better?
Yes.

What are the drawbacks to this plan?
It means more responsibility, more pressure, a real chance of failure.

What is my plan and schedule for change?
First step: *Mention it to Pete first, so he won't think I'm after his job or going over his head*
    Deadline: *Tomorrow.*

Second step: *Draw up plan in the form of a letter to Dan, copy to Pete.*
    Deadline: *End of the week.*

Third step: *Meet with Dan and Pete.*
    Deadline: *Two weeks.*

Changing Jobs

If you can't change your current job enough for the better, you'll have to change jobs. If you are faced with this decision, it's comforting to know that most successful men have had three different careers by the time they are sixty. In our rapidly changing society, midlife career changes are becoming more common, more acceptable, and more necessary.

Look Inside

The first place to look for a new job is inside yourself. Take a moment right now to close your eyes, take a few deep breaths, and just imagine yourself in the ideal job. Start without preconceptions. Imagine yourself getting up in the morning, ten years from now. You shower, shave, dress, eat, and head off to work. Are you working at home or going somewhere else? Are you working with others or alone? Inside or outside? Are you using your body, your hands, your mind, your eyes, your voice, your creative faculties? Are you working with objects and materials, with paper, with machines, with ideas?

Let the images come as they will, without judgment, without trying to figure things out. What you see may surprise you by being very similar to what you do now for a living, or so wildly different that it seems impossible. Don't worry about it. The images of work that come to view are just what your unconscious finds interesting or vital about work at this moment. They may change with time.

The images may be unclear or disguised in the form of symbols. For example, Benjamin was a 41-year-old real estate salesman. When he closed his eyes and imagined the perfect job, he saw himself in a quiet, vaguely Japanese room, talking softly to a weeping woman. Another time he imagined that he was walking with a strange man through a dark cave, showing the way with a flashlight. He wasn't sure what these images meant, but he was glad they had nothing to do with selling real estate.

Repeat this little eyes-closed experiment from time to time as you look for your right livelihood. Notice what details and themes repeat themselves. Recurring themes such as working outdoors or using your voice are indications of what you want to do in your heart of hearts.

Next put your conscious mind to work and do some careful self-analysis.

How are you unique? What makes you special?

What are you good at?

Go beyond the obvious categories of training and experience to consider character traits such as honesty, generosity, stubbornness, wit, empathy, and so on. If you are outgoing and funny, maybe you should be a comedian or do something involved with entertaining people. If you like to work alone, doggedly pursuing the ideal solution to a problem, perhaps computer software development is your field.

What are your interests and hobbies?

Write this stuff down here, in a diary, or just on a piece of paper that you can carry around with you. Whenever you are doing something you enjoy that you are good at, make a note. When Benjamin the real estate salesman tried this exercise, he wrote down that he was good at sizing people up, at tuning into what they really wanted, at listening between the lines. It was one of the things that made him a pretty good salesman, but it also bothered him because it involved a sort of manipulation.

Consider your interests and hobbies carefully. Chances are you would enjoy making a living doing what you are already eager to do for no pay. Actually, workaholic men are notorious for turning hobbies such as auto restoration or woodworking into money-making ventures. If you follow this route, just remember to phase out your current, unsatisfying job. The idea is to find something different and more rewarding to do, not to double your workload.

Add to your list all the values that are important to you. Include the good things of life that you want more of, and the ethical principles that you would like to express in your work. Here are some examples that other men have put on values lists:

warm family life	social commitment
health	friendship
helping others	serenity
spiritual enlightenment	financial security
prestige	artistic expression
leaving a personal monument	professional recognition
intimacy	personal growth
religious convictions	political ideals
fitness	love

Benjamin listed personal growth, serenity, and helping others as important values. His sales career hindered his growth because it involved him in the same commercial negotiations over and over and demanded a certain amount of ruthless calculation on his part. His serenity was threatened constantly by the uncertainty of the real estate market. Sometimes he felt he was helping others, but mostly he felt like he was tricking them or taking advantage of his superior expertise.

Consider Changing Jobs Without Changing Careers

At this point, you may have found that you like what you do, but you don't like where you do it. For example, you may like the intellectual challenge and the gambler's thrill of being a stock analyst. But you have qualms about recommending investments in companies that make munitions or support repressive regimes in foreign countries or have a history of discrimination in hiring. In this case, the solution is not to retrain as a social worker. The solution is to continue to do what you love doing, but do it for one of the "socially responsible" mutual funds that screen investments for clients who want their money to work for the common good.

Ask yourself if there is an alternative version of your current job that would be more meaningful for you, cause less stress, have less environmental impact, be of greater service to others, empower you and others, and so on. If you can't stand building highways any more, what about building low-income housing? If you're sick of selling printing supplies, how about selling solar heating supplies or environmentally safe cleaners? If you're burnt out teaching algebra to high shoolers, how about teaching reading and writing to migrant workers' kids?

Gather More Information

There's one nice thing about the stress that our culture puts on work: there's lots of information available about career selection, and most of it is free for the asking. Here are just a few suggestions.

Write or call for a free copy of the *Whole Work Catalog* from the new Careers Center, 1515 23rd Street, Boulder, CO 80306, (303) 447-1087. This is a terrific catalog with a strong right livelihood slant. Highlights from the "Alternative Careers" section include books on acting, art, photography, writing, music, film, accounting, teaching, journalism, careers outdoors, working with animals, health care, careers without college, internships, starting a retail business, and mail order. Other sections cover job hunting, working from home, self-employment, job satisfaction, resumés, and workaholism.

Check with your state employment agency for information or counseling services. Note that the amount and value of the help you can get varies from state to state and sometimes from office to office.

Call up your local community college or junior college and ask if they have a career counseling office. Most do. They can administer interest and aptitude tests, tell you what training and experience is typically required for different jobs, and advise you on courses to take to prepare for a new career.

Call up someone who is doing the kind of job you think you might want to do. For example, if you think you might enjoy working outdoors as a surveyor, phone several surveyors in your area. Ask them what professional organizations they belong to. Then call up the organization and ask for any career information they can send you. Many professional societies have informational packets that they send out regularly.

As you are calling people who are in a career that interests you, be on the lookout for a man who sounds enthusiastic about his work and is willing to talk about it. Make an appointment to visit him at his place of work. Look around and soak up the atmosphere. Ask what he does in a typical day, what he enjoys, and what he doesn't like about his work. Ask about money, benefits, and the outlook for the future in this kind of work. Share your own values and interests and ask if he thinks you would be happy in the work. Interviewing someone who is actually doing the work you want is a great way to penetrate the hype you will find in the little brochures from the professional organizations or the junior college counseling center.

Setting up an interview like this may feel intimidating. You might assume that men in desirable jobs are competitive and secretive. But this isn't necessarily true. If you make an "apprenticeship gesture" by asking sincere, thoughtful questions, many men these days will be glad to discuss their work. There is a new work ethic quietly blooming that stresses cooperation instead of competition. In most fields of endeavor there are older, more experienced men who are finding it more rewarding to be a mentor offering a hand up the ladder than it is to be a fossilized dinosaur who must be kicked off the ladder.

If you've narrowed your search down to one or two areas and you are willing to spend money, you might look in the Yellow Pages under "Career and Vocational Counseling." Most of the listings will be employment agencies looking for fees from you and prospective employers, so shop around to find an outfit that genuinely offers some vocational counseling.

If you are interested in a vocation that is of service to others, such as social work, counseling, teaching, or health care, there is probably ample opportunity for you to volunteer your services right now, before you have any additional training or experience. By volunteering a few hours of your spare time, you can find out what the work is like, what the people are like, how you fit in, if you really feel the fulfillment you thought you would feel, and if you have what it takes to stick it out over the long haul. Volunteering is a good reality check. The reality of working in a health clinic or a classroom hour after hour is sometimes different from your romantic vision of yourself as a great healer or wise teacher.

One of the hardest parts about gathering information is getting started. The worksheet that follows will help you organize your search efficiently. Grab the phone book and fill out your worksheet right now.

Information Gathering Worksheet
White Pages

State Employment Department

      Address _____

      Phone _____

Community College Counseling Center

      Address_____

      Phone _____

Volunteer Center

      Address _____

      Phone _____

Yellow Pages

Local people or companies doing the kind of work I'm looking at

      Name _____

      Address _____

      Phone _____

      Name _____

      Address _____

      Phone _____

      Name _____

      Address _____

      Phone _____

Schools—Business and Vocational

    Trade and Technical

Social Service Organizations

Career and Vocational Counselors

Benjamin set about gathering information in a systematic way. In the *Whole Work Catalog* he found a book on changing careers that was very inspiring. He made an appointment to talk with a counselor at the local junior college. After talking awhile, he began to take more and more interest in the counseling process itself. An aptitude test showed that he was suited for any profession requiring good social skills, empathy, and intellectual analysis.

Benjamin began seriously considering going back to school studying psychology or social work, and getting a Marriage, Family, and Child Counseling license. The requirements were daunting—a lot of course work and thousands of hours of supervised experience. But the prospect excited him. He visited a low-cost mental health clinic in a nearby town and talked with one of the counselors there and one of the interns. He ended up volunteering on Tuesday mornings at the clinic, and found that he loved the atmosphere, the commitment to helping, and the learning process that went on there.

Set Goals

After you have the information you need and you are pretty sure what work you want to pursue, set your goals.

Right Livelihood Goals

Ten years

Five years

One year

Next month

Tomorrow

Start with how you want to be earning your livelihood ten years from now. Describe what you will be doing, with whom, where, for how much money, and so on. Use your imagination and assume the best. Paint a glowing picture of your ideal work situation, with everything in place and all your work requirements met. Don't worry if your ultimate goal appears impossible to achieve at this point.

Now, in order to achieve this ten-year vision of paradise, what has to happen in the next five years? Describe the five-year goals that you will have to achieve to keep on track toward your ten-year goals.

Then back up and describe where you need to be in one year in order to make your five- and ten-year dreams come true.

Continue to bring your goals back toward the future: list what you need to do next month in order to be on the way and what you will do tomorrow as a first step.

If you follow this exercise to the end, you will see three things:

1. That even the most ambitious goals can be broken down into small daily steps.

2. That it is the size and difficulty of the daily steps that determine how hard it is to reach the ultimate goal.

3. That having the goal isn't enough. You have to take the small daily steps.

Resolve to take the first step today or tomorrow. Repeat this exercise every few months to make sure your ultimate goal remains clear. As you progress toward your goal, you'll find that it may change due to your increased experience in your chosen work. And as you gain expertise and confidence, you may find some shortcuts to your goal.

Here is how Benjamin set his goals.

Right Livelihood Goals

Ten years
Support myself and family as a therapist. Be well-established in the field, with a beautiful office outside my home, a long waiting list, a thriving practice. Be happy that I'm helping people grow, and growing myself.

Five years
Setting up my practice in a home office. Getting referrals. No longer selling real estate.

One year
Enrolled in MFCC program. Selling real estate part-time. Making ends meet with wife's salary and maybe loan from parents.

Next month
Submit school applications to two places. Talk to agency about selling part-time.

Tomorrow
Write for transcripts. Call parents about possible future loan. Talk to wife about finances.

Get Support

Your efforts toward right livelihood don't occur in a vacuum. That way lies workaholism. While evolving your new work life, you must also stay involved in your intimate relationships, family, friends, health, finances, leisure activities, community, spiritual life, and so on.

The way to achieve right livelihood without the rest of your life going down the tubes is to line up lots of support for what you are doing. Share the process, every step of the way, with those around you. Don't be the strong silent type, figuring it out on your own and then springing the fully formed plan on an unsuspecting family.

Share your doubts, your qualms, your research, your hopes, your fears, your goals, and your plans. Tell your wife, lover, parents, children, friends, and colleagues as much as possible. Ask them to bear with you when you get irritable, to adjust to lower income, to postpone purchases or vacations, to baby-sit while you attend classes, to do your chores for you—whatever you need in the way of help.

For Benjamin, getting support meant that he had to talk to his wife about her continuing to work for the next five years and about postponing buying land in the country. He had to ask his parents for a loan against his inheritance. He got his real estate agency to let him work part-time. When he got discouraged he shared his feelings with his wife and his best male friend. When he got busy and exhausted, he had to ask his wife and co-workers to take up the slack.

Benjamin will get his MFCC license next spring. He finally made it, but it would have been impossible without the support of his family and friends.

III

Who Will Go
With You?

Once you have a sense of direction in your life—when you have come
to terms with your inner self, your father, and your work—you can turn
your attention to the question of who will go with you.

This section concentrates on creating, nurturing, and healing your
relationships to the important people in your life: friends, lovers, mates,
and children.

6

Being a Friend:
Making and Keeping
Male Friends

Is this you? You used to have lots of male friends in high school or college, but it's been years since you made a new friend. The older you get, the fewer friends you have, and the less time you have to spend with them. When you do spend time with a friend, the experience may not seem as rich and satisfying as you remember from your earlier days. Making a list of the men you know, you realize that mostly you have superficial relationships with co-workers, golf buddies, or "couple friends" where the real bond is between the women, and you and the other guy are just along for the ride.

Male friendships are difficult to form and maintain, especially after age thirty. Many reasons have been advanced to explain this difficulty. Some say that men are too competitive, that they would rather dominate than relate. Others say that heterosexual men are too homophobic to risk making friendly overtures to other men, lest their expressions of interest be interpreted as seductive.

Some point out that a man's thirties and forties are the age of accomplishment and nest building, a time to focus on career and family to the exclusion of friendship. Still others point out that our culture actually ridicules and discourages male friendships. For example, TV shows and movies repeatedly depict the man who maintains friendships outside his home as an immature, selfish guy who deserts his wife and children to hang out with his juvenile, low-class pals.

Perhaps male friendship languishes because few people, male or female, really value it. Think of all the jokes about "male bonding" that imply it is a somewhat crude, primitive, silly, and perhaps dangerous thing to do. Think about the stereotypes of men who can't relate except when drinking beer, discussing sports, or playing poker.

It's too bad. Because you need male friends.

A close male friend offers a special kind of comfortable intimacy that cannot be supplied by a woman. Only another man can fully see, understand, and support you *as a man*, not as a husband, a father, a wage earner, and so on.

Only another man can understand exactly what you mean when you talk about your sexual desires, your mixed feelings toward your children, your fears about your job, your disappointment in failure, your anger at your father, your sadness at your brother's death. There are secrets you can share with a male friend that you can't share with your wife or girlfriend or mother.

Having meaningful relationships with other men validates your worth as a man. It raises your self-esteem and lets you know that you are not alone.

In this chapter, you will accomplish four things:

- List and evaluate your current male friends.

- Take a long, clear look at your relationship to your best male friend.

- Learn how to make new friends.

- Learn how to deepen and improve friendships.

This chapter won't talk about female friends because most men are in much more desperate need of male friends. It's much harder for most men to make and keep male friends, and it's male friendship they are dying for.

Your Current Male Friends

The following exercise is an opportunity for you to identify whom you consider a friend, what level of closeness you've reached, and some of the obstacles that keep you from getting closer.

In the space provided, write down the name of every man you know well enough to consider more than a casual acquaintance. Include guys you grew up with, worked with, went to school with, played sports with, know through clubs and other organizations, and so on.

In the Frequency column next to the name, write the approximate number of conversations you have with this man (more than nodding and saying hi) per month. If you speak less than once a month, write 0+ in this column. In the Closeness column, rate your degree of intimacy on a five-point scale that ranges from one (superficial, nonintimate conversation) to five (able to share deepest feelings, concerns, and hopes). Now in the next column, Commitment, rate your degree of willingness to stand by, support, and help this friend if he were in need. Again, use the five-point scale ranging from one (low commitment) to five (willing to do almost anything). The column on Satisfaction and Enjoyment requires another five-point rating from one (very little) to five (extremely satisfying). Don't worry about the last column, Obstacles, right now. That's something you'll explore later.

Friends Assessment					
Name	Frequency	Closeness	Commitment	Satisfaction and Enjoyment	Obstacles
1					
2					
3					
4					
5					
6					
7					
8					
9					
10					

Now take a look at your chart. How long is the list? Did you find yourself stretching to get even a few names down? Do you have a desire to have more male friends?

In the Frequency column, are there a lot of 0+ notations? Do you *seek* contact with male friends (either visiting or by phone), or are you passive, waiting to hear from them? Do you try to have *regular* contact (once a week, once a month), or do you wait until occasions, needs, or problems push one of you to the phone?

Take a look at the Closeness column. Do you have several close friends, or are male friends mostly in the 1-2 range? Is there someone on this list with whom you wish to feel closer? Put a star by his name.

Commitment is a funny thing with men. There are buddies you hardly ever see, but for whom you'd do anything. Sometimes there's a friend you see a lot, have little real intimacy, but there's a feeling between you. You'd go a long way for the guy. In still other cases, you might see someone a lot, share quite a bit, but lack that gut sense of comradeship and commitment.

If you have relationships with high commitment rankings but low frequency or closeness, some exploration of this phenomenon might be in order. You might be allowing the feeling of commitment to substitute for real friendship. The gut feeling is there, but it doesn't get fully realized in the form of sharing or support. This friendship could be a lot more— more open, more satisfying—but something is keeping you from being actively close. Another uncomfortable possibility is that the feeling of commitment is a shell over an otherwise hollow relationship. The only thing that binds you is old times or some long bawdy nights of beer and laughter, but nothing else at this point is real; nothing is based on an authentic sharing of who each of you are.

Satisfaction is an important consideration. If most male friendships are low in satisfaction, one of three things may be going on:

1. You're not feeling close enough to get any real nourishment from your time together. Distant, desolatory conversation isn't much fun.

2. You haven't found an enjoyable activity to share. Men need more than talk. They need to *do* things together. Low-satisfaction friendships may simply be lacking the spark of an interesting shared experience.

3. Fear. Something's making you too uncomfortable to get much out of the contact. Very often it's the fear of being judged, of losing another man's respect. More will be said about this in the section, "Obstacles to Friendship."

If you have friendships that are low in frequency but high in satisfaction and enjoyment, these may be relationships worth cultivating. Are there any high-satisfaction friendships on your list that you want to develop? Put a star by those names.

Obstacles to Friendship

The following is a list of some of the common obstacles to male friendship. At the end of the list is a space for you to add additional obstacles that you have encountered.

1. Fear of engulfment.   For many men, friendship includes the danger of being pressured to do things they don't want to do. Being asked favors, getting called or visited too often, or getting pulled into unsatisfying activities can be hard to deal with. Many men are afraid to say no. So they either get stuck doing things they don't enjoy, or they avoid the whole problem by not getting close.

2. Fear of being known.   This is the feeling that deep down you're not really acceptable. There are flaws that you've managed to hide, but would certainly be discovered if you ever let your hair down. Someone might recognize your fear, or sadness, or longing. They might see awkwardness or weakness. They might see a callowness or incompetence, hurt or inadequacy (particularly sexual inadequacy). And if they came to know your flaws, any respect for you as a man would vanish.

To cope with this fear, many men become architects of an elaborate facade, a front to help them stay in the good graces of the world. Such a front is easy to maintain for an evening of revelry, with strong liquor assisting. But the facade requires such alertness and balance that it's exhausting. You've got to escape to relax. You've got to be alone to finally feel any peace.

3. Fear of rejection.   Many men simply don't expect to be liked, at least by people that they respect. One man said it very well: "Men are so hard to reach. It seems risky to show any real interest. If you make an overture, there's usually a stiff kind of dancing around, or the outright brush-off."

4. Homophobia.   Many men fear that closeness to another man will lead to sexual intimacy, or will be seen that way by others. "A man who's fired up to get to know you ain't out for your conversation or your cooking." That's how one rancher put it in a recent magazine interview. This unfortunate belief suggests that the only reason men initiate a friendship is because of an ulterior sexual desire, or that only gay men wish to be close.

Regardless of sexual orientation, men need friendship. There's a clear line between friendship and sex, and it's up to *you* whether you cross over it.

5. Fear of competition and comparison.   Some men experience male friendship as a battleground where each guy is out to prove himself, to strut, to win respect. There's a lot of one-upmanship: comparing who makes more money, who has the better car, who has the more attractive partner, who's better at darts, who's quicker with the repartee. Many men fear friendships of measurement, that form of vulturism where one man builds his self-esteem by showing the other guy up. With no other reward in sight, an endless contest just isn't fun.

6. Fear of the reaction at home.   Some men are concerned about the reaction of a spouse or partner to the time invested in male friendships. Or they anticipate resentment for taking emotional energy out of the home, for creating intimacy that doesn't include family members.

7. Guilt.   Some men experience friendships as frivolous, an indulgence that robs time from more productive activities. It doesn't seem right to enjoy a buddy when there's work to be done, needs to be provided for, a mountain of obligations.

8. Danger to one's career.   Work friends can be problematic. It's not uncommon for a man to wonder about the wisdom of getting close to someone who might learn his weaknesses and use them against him or begin judging him as lacking qualities necessary for advancement. Some men fear that friendships will inhibit them from adequately competing against friends whom they've come to like.

In the space provided, list any other obstacles to male friendship you've encountered:

9._____

10. _____

Now go back to the Obstacles column in the Friends Assessment chart. For each friend, note the obstacle or obstacles that affect you (identify obstacles by number to save space). For some friends you may experience no obstacles at all. For others there may be two, three, or even more.

Is there a relationship between the type of man and the obstacles you list? For example, do strong, self-confident men trigger fears of rejection and competition? Do the men who really like you and seek your friendship touch off fears of engulfment? Pay attention to see if any such pattern emerges for you.

Friendship is important. Friendship gives you support, validation, acceptance. It gives you the feeling that you belong. The obstacles to friendship are mostly varieties of fear. These fears can often be overcome if you recognize the value of having men in your life whom you trust.

Your Best Friend

From your chart, pick the man you consider your best male friend. Write his name below. Fill out this questionnaire carefully. It will give you a clear idea of the kind of relationship you have with your best friend, and will suggest areas in which you can improve the relationship.

My best friend's name

Age

Appearance

Occupation

Education

How long I've known him

How we met

How often we get together

How often we talk on the phone

Who usually calls first

Ways we are alike

Ways we are different

What we do together

Plans for the near future

Secrets I've told him

Secrets he's told me

Feelings I've shared

Feelings I've withheld

Feelings I suspect he has withheld

Promises I've kept

Promises I've broken

Promises he's kept

Promises he's broken

Our biggest fight

What I get out of the friendship

What he gets out of the friendship

What I value most about the relationship

What I'd like to change about the relationship

How To Make New Friends

If you want to expand your male friendships, there are some relatively simple steps that you can take.

Pick a man. They're all around you. The problem isn't one of supply, but of demand. The lack isn't men, but men willing to make the first overture. You know a lot of men, and the chances are some of them seem like pretty nice guys. And some of the nice guys are interesting—they have a good sense of humor or share an interest with you. On the blank line below write the name of a man whom you would like to get to know.

Make time. Commit to spending time creating this new friendship. Pause for a moment to think about your week: When do you have a block of time (at least two hours) that you can regularly schedule for a new friendship? Write that time in the blank provided:

Make the first overture. Call him up or corner him and suggest an activity. Arthur called up the dad of one of his daughter's nursery school friends. He invited the whole family to a barbecue, but his real intention was to get to know the other man and see if he could spark the beginnings of a friendship. Ralph invited a male co-worker to lunch, ostensibly to discuss the new company reorganization. But his real agenda was to see if they hit it off or had mutual interests. Rinaldo asked his neighbor to join a small group of friends who were going to a comedy club. He sensed that being in the group would be nonthreatening, yet would provide a way to talk and get to know each other. The contractor who remodeled Alan's kitchen was an avid jogger. Alan himself liked to run, so he suggested they jog together one weekend morning.

If you can find a mutual interest, so much the better. But if you don't know enough about your potential friend to build on a shared interest, try the direct approach: "I very much enjoyed meeting you, would you like to get together for lunch next week?"

Look for an ongoing task or activity to do together. Men tend to be doers and often need an activity as an excuse to get together. Go with the flow and cook up a project or interest for you and your potential friend. As you get to know him, you'll recognize areas where your interests overlap: you both like to play tennis, you both like surrealist art, you're both involved in conservation activities, you're both programmers with an interest in developing computer games, you both like to fish. It doesn't matter. All that counts is your ability to find that common ground and your willingness to suggest mutual activities that build on it.

Keep appointments and promises.   And don't let it slide if your friend ducks out on an agreement. Trust is very important among men and needs to develop from the very beginning. Your willingness to keep commitments indicates your respect and interest in the other person.

Persist.   Keep calling and planning. Don't get into the "tit for tat" mindset that says, "I won't call. It's his turn to call." If you want a friend, count on doing 80 percent of the work to keep the friendship progressing. If you have to initiate four times before your friend cooks up an activity of his own, that's okay. Score keeping has nothing to do with the level of satisfaction in a friendship. If you enjoy each time you get together, that's enough.

Honor confidences and secrets.   Don't gossip with a spouse or partner or other friends about private matters that were shared with you.

Practice openness.   Let your friend in on what it feels like to be you. Don't just cover the past, but also include things that affect you in your current life. Try to reveal at least one significant thing about what you feel right now on each visit with your friend. If you're feeling sad about something, acknowledge it. If something is stressing you or making you anxious, explain something about the situation. Share some of your hopes and aspirations. Each time you make a disclosure, you have an opportunity to ask your friend if he has had similar experiences. You earn the right to pry a little when you take the risk of opening up some of your feelings.

John explained to his new friend, Al, that he was concerned about a potential layoff at work. He went even further, and talked about how a previous layoff had really affected his self-esteem and his confidence about holding a job. Al reciprocated by describing a "reign of terror" he'd experienced under an unusually cruel former boss. During that time Al began drinking heavily and was now a member of AA. John's disclosure gave Al the confidence to share one of the less positive chapters of his life. And both men experienced a stronger sense of mutual trust.

Touch and hug as it feels comfortable.   Many men shrink from physical intimacy, but they're missing something. There's nothing quite like a man hugging another man. But start slow. Hand shakes are good; sometimes it's nice to shake hands while simultaneously touching a friend's shoulder. A spontaneous shoulder touch or pat on the back conveys a warmth and affection that is very nurturing. Some male friends hug when they first see each other after a period of absence. This spontaneous gesture of appreciation can touch a very deep place where you have longed for male support and approval.

If touching is something you'd like to do but is also a little scary, try this exercise: Touch a male friend on his shoulder while saying something like, "It's really good to see you, how have you been?" Pay attention to any discomfort you may feel. Are there specific fears? Are you aware of any homophobia? It is strongly recommended that you try to push through that fear. The rewards of being able to touch or hug a male friend are very real. Touching increases the emotional warmth that men can give and receive and makes friendships richer.

Enriching an Existing Friendship

Pick a friendship that could be deeper, more fun, more satisfying, and so on. Go back to your chart and notice which men have a star next to their names. What obstacles keep you from being closer? Are you willing to commit to improving your friendship with one of these men? Write his name here:

Make your plan for enriching this relationship by working through these steps:

1. Spend More Time

In male friendships, frequency often equals quality. If you only see each other every six months, you can't build your friendship because you spend all your time getting reacquainted and caught up on the news. You need to look at your calendar and schedule time for friendship. You may need to get up earlier, plant a smaller garden, or postpone a time-consuming remodeling project. Use the time to take a short trip with your friend, learn yoga together, or take all your kids on a hike. If you both devote Saturday morning to household chores, take turns helping each other and do the chores together. You could both enroll in the same class or go to the gym at the same time to work out. In the space below, write three ways you can spend more time with your friend:

2. Check in Frequently

If you haven't talked to your friend for a week, call him up just to check in. This is very hard to do for some men. But try it. And when you do get together, spend the first minute or two answering and asking the question "How are you?" with some consciousness and thought. Really tell your friend how you are feeling, what's been on your mind, what you are glad or sad or mad or worried about. When your friend tells you how he is, don't take "Fine" for an answer. Ask for details and pay attention. In the space below, write when you will next call your friend.

3. Cook Up New Projects

Activities of some kind are implied in the first item, spending more time together. But the effort to find and schedule something more than your current ongoing activities deserves separate mention. Men are often criticized as being incapable of "hanging out." They get together with friends around tasks—common activities that they can do together. While they are painting the little league bleachers or serving on the committee, they can relate to each other pretty well. When the task is done and there's nothing left to do but talk, the men start to slip away. This makes sense, since men do tend to be results oriented—more interested in product than process.

If this is true of you, you could try to combat this tendency by increasing your "hanging out" skills. That's probably a good idea. But in terms of enriching an existing friendship, why fight this tendency? One of the best ways to add new life to a friendship is to start an exciting project together. Build a boat, collaborate on a book, restore a car, start a newsletter, walk political precincts, set up a darkroom—together. In the space below, write three projects that you will propose to your friend.

4. Clean Up Old Business

Sometimes a friendship can stall because of unspoken conflicts. One of you may harbor resentment for some slight or betrayal in the past that is "over and done with," except that it stills preys on your mind. Do you still feel resentful of the time your friend seduced your girlfriend, wrecked your car, or insulted your wife? Are you still guilty about that money you never repaid, the promise you broke, or the time you lied to your friend? Are you still jealous of his athletic prowess or good looks? Does he still change the subject whenever you mention fights you have had in the past?

The way to resolve unspoken conflicts is to speak about them. Say, "I'd like to clear the air about something that has always bothered me."

Ventilate your feelings in a clear, nonblaming fashion. Ask for the forgiveness, the acknowledgment, the facts, the apology, or whatever it is you need to be able to clean up this old business. See chapter 10 on clarifying feelings, chapter 11 on expressing feelings, and chapter 13 on anger if you need pointers.

In the space below, write out an opening statement to your friend that would begin to clean up some of your old business.

5. Disclose Yourself

Look at your responses to the previous exercise in which you analyzed your closest friendship. What kinds of feelings and secrets about yourself do you withhold? What would happen if you disclosed these things? Friendship is nourished by sharing personal information, including embarrassing or upsetting secrets.

In the natural course of friendship, people become closer as they know more and more about each other. A lot of this knowledge comes from shared experience. But a significant amount of this knowledge, especially when you are making friends as an older man, comes from the stories you tell about yourself.

It starts slowly, as you chat about your preferences, dislikes, observations, and opinions. From there you can get into your personal history: parents, education, jobs, travel, and so forth. Once a basic level of trust is established, you start to reveal more significant information, such as your father's alcoholism, your experiments with drugs in school, sexual preferences, periods of angry outbursts or depression you have gone through, your struggles with addiction or compulsions or anxiety—whatever has been significant in your development and helped make you who you are today.

If you tend to reveal this sort of information slowly or not at all, you can shift a friendship into a higher gear by pressing through your discomfort and letting your friend glimpse a more complete picture of you. In the space below, write three important facts about yourself. The first one should be something that would be fairly easy to tell your friend, something that you are just about ready to share. The second item should be something that is more difficult to reveal. And the third should be something that you never plan to tell anyone (just to reassure yourself that there are some safe limits). You are not committing yourself to becoming an emotional, spiritual, or psychological flasher.

Ready to tell now:

Sometime soon:

Never:

6. *Enter into Contracts*

Enlist your friend's help in any self-improvement plan you may be considering. For example, if you want to lose weight, make a contract with your friend about how much you want to lose and how he can support you. You can use the same contract approach to get support in stopping smoking, stopping drinking, finishing reports on time, completing courses of study, jogging regularly, controlling anger, or sticking to a budget.

No matter what kind of change you are trying to make in your life, a friend can help by listening to you, giving advice, checking in with you periodically, charting your progress, calling you on your rationalizations, consoling you after setbacks, helping you set realistic goals, collecting fines for failures, congratulating you on successes, complimenting you on achievements, and so on.

It helps to put such contracts in writing, as strange as it may seem the first time you try it. Here is an example of how Tom and Greg contracted with each other about Tom's angry phone exchanges with his ex-wife:

> *I agree to speak slowly and softly when Diane calls me. If I'm short of time, I will let her know how long I can talk, and stick to it.*
>
> *I agree to listen carefully, to let her finish her sentences, and to paraphrase them back to her, instead of jumping in to defend myself and counterattack.*
>
> *I agree to make my points in three parts ("I think, I feel, I want") in order to slow myself down and give myself time to weed out the blaming statements.*
>
> *I agree to tell her I have to think about it and call her back whenever she asks for money or changes in the kids' visitation schedule.*
>
> *I agree to donate five bucks to the Catholic Missionary Fund every time I blow it and yell at Diane over the phone.*

> *Tom Ballen*

I agree to listen to you rant and rave about Diane (instead of you ranting and raving at her).

I agree to call you up weekly and pretend to be Diane hassling you about money or the kids, so that you can practice your active listening.

I agree to check in with you about how things are going. I agree to make sure you write the five dollar check to the Missionary Fund if you blow up at Diane.

Greg Cavaglio

In the space below, write out a contract that you could share with your friend.

———————————————
(Your signature)

———————————————
(His signature)

7. *Talk About Your Friendship*

In any relationship, the most intimate topic of conversation is the relationship itself. Gestalt therapists even have a special term for changing the subject to talk about the experience of relating: "content to process shift."

Tell your friend what you like about your friendship, what you get out of it, how much you appreciate being his friend. Brainstorm about ways you can improve and deepen the friendship. Admit the things that you don't like about the friendship and would like to change. Read this chapter together.

Relating on this level can be a difficult and scary experience. What you're really saying is "I love you" or "I like you." This kind of open expression of love or affection from one man to another is almost taboo in our culture. It marks you as gay, inappropriate, crazy, or all three. It makes you vulnerable to rejection or misunderstanding. If you have something negative to say about the friendship, that's also hard to express and hard for your friend to hear.

In the space below, write a note to your friend.

What I like about our friendship:

What I appreciate about you:

What I would like to do to change our friendship:

8. *Be Realistic*

Finally, you have to be realistic. Not every friend can be a soul mate. Some men will become close acquaintances, but not true friends. Some will just be tennis buddies, some will just be guys you nod at in the hall at work. That's okay. You have to learn to recognize when a friendship has gone as far as it can go and accept it.

The Story of Pat and Matt

Our friendship began in college days, now 25 years ago. We both wrote poetry, and were interested in the same young woman, Stephanie. So we found ourselves enrolled in a writers' workshop that she had organized. It was the days of Red Mountain wine, long hair, and tie-dyed clothes. Pat, with his beard and reams of stylish, cynical poetry, was well ahead on all measures of counterculture attainment. Matt still dressed in the unfortunate clothes his mother bought him and drove an old Cadillac— neither of which got high marks in the sixties.

Poetry and humor were the connection for a relationship that was not yet terribly personal, but it was enough to build on.

In the summer of '69, Matt organized a short-lived commune in an old house in Sausalito. Eight of us lived there, and seven remain friends today. It was in that old house, on a porch overlooking the midnight black waters of San Francisco Bay, that we had dozens of long talks. Funny and serious. Making plans and unbelievably sophomoric pronouncements about "the way things really work." Later we roomed together in a dump on Broderick Street in San Francisco—the kind of furnished apartment that had plastic covering the sofa. It was there we discovered that wine, poetry, science fiction novels, and narcissistic self-involvement are insufficient to nurture a friendship. We had a falling out. Pat moved into a storefront with his girlfriend; Matt moved into an old furniture truck that he and his dad had made into a funky rolling apartment. Pat's storefront was a response to his draft status—gothic letters in front declared it to be the "Free Conscience Church." Pat had paid his $15 to be a Universal Life minister. He even had a collar and black suit to help him dispense wine and advice to the curious and occasionally deranged citizens of the Haight-Ashbury.

Matt parked his truck a block away, using his time alone to learn how to cook and achieve some measure of independence from his family.

It was the bathroom that brought them together. Pat had one, and Matt didn't. When Pat's girlfriend moved out, Matt started spending long evenings again. We realized, though, that we needed more than wine and jokes and the companionable silence while we read. So we started a mimeographed poetry magazine called *Medusa*. And hitchhiked and hopped freights together around the country. We drifted and camped our way down part of the Mississippi. Ostensibly we were collecting material for writing; in truth we were just having a damn good time.

Another commune. Four of the original eight. This time in San Francisco—on the same block as a smack house and a funeral parlor. For a while a lovely feeling of fullness. The long conversations, the laughter of a hundred private jokes.

But again it wasn't enough. Matt was a slob, and Pat was careful about his environment. After a year, Pat moved out on his own; eventually marrying Leah. Matt felt abandoned and the friendship cooled. Matt eventually moved in with Martha and went to graduate school. It was the time for building careers and home life.

We did "couple things" together, but without the same intimacy and camaraderie we'd enjoyed earlier. We needed activities and projects as an excuse to get together—so we'd meet occasionally for lunch to plan them.

We bought a row boat and later an outboard for fishing trips to the Sacramento Delta.

We spent a night in a flop house to collect material for some short stories.

We printed and sold poetry broadsides.

We sponsored a weekly poetry reading at a local library.

We asked each other's help when we needed muscle or advice— moving, working on a car, and so on.

One day at lunch Pat showed up with the receipt for a post office box and a box of stationery with a letterhead reading "New Harbinger Publications." "Matt, you owe me ten bucks," he said. "For what?" "Your half of the stationery and post office box. We're starting a publishing company." And so we did. In Pat's spare bedroom.

Over the next few years we published a business manual and a children's book (by Matt's mom and dad). We had to see each other every week to take care of the business. In the process, we spent enough time together to get close again. To talk about real things. The consistency was important, and so was the opportunity for *private* conversation. Leah rarely intruded while we worked and talked.

In the fifteen years since we started publishing books, our lives have taken an oddly parallel course. Within a six-month period, Martha and Matt split up, and Pat's marriage to Leah ended. We were lonely. For the first time we cried together and totally dropped the emotional armor. We kept working at publishing (by now doing psychology self-help books) but spent a lot more time talking. We used the phone more. Pat got involved in personal growth experiences and groups, and brought some of what he learned back into our friendship. We made self-improvement contracts with each other about drinking habits, plans for socializing, and work-related issues.

The parallels continued. Within a six-month period, Matt met Jude, and Pat was introduced to Nancy, Jude's friend at work. A few years later, we married within a short time of each other and had sons who are only six months apart in age.

New Harbinger grew and moved out of Pat's bedroom. We began spending more of our work week at the publishing office. The lessons of previous years had impressed on us the need to have *regular* contact and always some shared activity. As a consequence we have religiously kept a weekly lunch date, and we have family dinners once every three or four weeks. Sometimes we take brief family vacations together. Mostly these days our shared activity is writing books like this one. Every six to eight weeks we take a room in Calistoga—just the two of us—and write. Intensely. But at meal times and breaks we talk. Sometimes random stuff, sometimes the business. We indulge in the old wry humor. But after a while, after we've settled in and have dispensed with the usual catching up, there are things said about what we really want or what's hurting. This is precious: two men sitting or walking comfortably in silence. Then the words coming, easy and direct.

That's not always true—the easy part. We've hit conflicts. "There's something I've had a hard time saying," Pat starts. And then we've got to see it through. There are still awkward attempts to put feelings into words. We fear being hurt. We fear letting anything harm this special love we have for each other.

The key for us—and for most male friendships—is time. Regular time, enough time. Time to circle around something that needs to be said. Time to *know* what needs to be said. Time for the growing of trust. Men need men. We are fortunate to have found and held onto each other.

7

Being Sexual:
Enjoying Responsible Sex

Does the combination of a fun word like "enjoying" with a grim word like "responsible" strike a sour chord for you? Does it sound like a contradiction in terms? Are you afraid that this chapter will be boring or contain some bad news you don't want to hear?

If that's your reaction, you're not alone. Every time we discussed this chapter, we cringed at the title. It expresses just what we want intellectually, but sounds "off" somehow. Perhaps the explanation is that the male sexual urge arises from a primitive part of the brain and glandular system that evolved over millions of years, operating under very simple rules: "have sex, make babies." The part of the brain that entertains abstractions such as "responsibility" is a fairly recent development in human evolution, and its exhortations to "do the right thing" are often drowned out by the glandular tumult from lower centers.

This chapter talks mostly about sex in the context of long-term relationships, for three reasons. First, most readers of this book are likely to be in a long-term sexual relationship. Second, those who are not in a long-term relationship probably hope to be in the future. Third, it is within long-term relationships that men encounter the most perplexing and chronic sexual problems.

This chapter is being written by two heterosexual men. Nevertheless, we have tried to use our imaginations, our reading, and our conversations with gay men to make the chapter applicable to all—straight, gay, or bisexual. We firmly believe that male sexuality can be legitimate, appropriate, joyous, and life-affirming whether a man is loving a woman or another man. If you are straight and reading about gay sexuality makes you uncomfortable, consider this chapter necessary practice in overcoming your homophobia. if you are bi or gay and find this chapter unsatisfactory, we're sorry. We did our best from our limited point of view.

Male Sexual Myths

Men struggle with a number of destructive sexual myths that serve to increase anxiety and reduce pleasure in all types of sexual contact. Put a check mark in the box next to each myth that strikes a familiar chord for you and may be influencing your sexual attitudes.

☐ **1. A man should always want and is always ready for sex.** This is macho nonsense. A man needs the right emotional climate, he needs to feel good physically, and he needs to find someone sexually stimulating before he can *want* sex. Male sexuality is not robotic, it is not a matter of pressing a button and the machinery all starts to work. A man needs a certain level of comfort and stimulation to be in the mood. Without it he will *not* be in the mood; he will lack the interest or ability to turn himself on.

☐ **2. A real man never loses his erection.** In porno movies a man's penis is always hard, he is always able to thrust inexhaustibly, and he has infinite staying power. He never loses his erection due to an untimely orgasm. But the truth is that every man has experienced some form of physical or emotional interference that made it hard to stay aroused; *every* man has experienced losing an erection. And there's hardly a man around who hasn't had an orgasm before he wanted to and before his partner wanted him to. Physical pain, worry, and a host of competing stimuli can drown out sexual feelings. It's something you should *expect* to happen from time to time. Your penis is affected by everything that is going on inside and outside of you. Its functioning greatly depends on how you feel.

☐ **3. A man's penis should be large.** A lot of men publicly claim that this doesn't matter. But in a magazine survey with over a thousand male respondents, there was almost universal concern about penis size. In spite of the fact that penises come in all sizes and that the medical literature indicates that size has little to do with pleasure, many men still cling to the belief that a large penis is necessary for really satisfying sex.

☐ **4. A man should always bring a partner to orgasm (preferably multiple orgasms).** Aside from the fact that 50 percent or more of women don't experience orgasm during intercourse and another percentage experience it infrequently, the greatest flaw in this myth is the assumption that good sex requires orgasm. Sex can be extremely satisfying *without* orgasm, and it's not a man's role to faithfully induce orgasm for a partner.

Many men are concerned about the quality of a partner's orgasm. If it isn't a socko, fireworks kind of orgasm, then he has failed to really turn a partner on. This focus on muscle contraction ignores the many functions sex has for (1) expressing tenderness, (2) holding and touching, (3) experiencing emotional closeness, (4) giving and receiving many varieties of physical pleasure, (5) getting reassurance, and so on. Orgasm is just one of many possible sexual experiences. You or your partner may not be interested in orgasm, or be able to have orgasm at a particular time. But you may be very interested in sex. The touching and holding feels good. The stimulation is satisfying. It's a nice way to make contact and to give to each other, but all of those sweet moments are denied to you if you're a believer in the orgasm myth.

☐ **5. Sex only involves intercourse followed by orgasm.** A lot of men feel that sex has to be a rigid progression that moves inevitably from kissing to foreplay to intercourse to orgasm. But a lot of satisfying sex involves masturbating or just fondling each other. It may involve oral-genital contact or just a sensuous back rub. Frequently, sex may not involve any progression at all. It may be a few moments of touching, a long delicious kiss; it may be an erotic movement or play acting. The more broadly you define sex, the more likely you are to enjoy its many possibilities without getting tethered to some stock formula.

☐ **6. A man always knows what to do in sex.** A man is supposed to know what a partner wants, even the secret, unspoken desires. A man is supposed to know exactly where the line falls between pleasure and discomfort. He is in charge. He choreographs the dance. It all depends on his knowledge and his skill because each step must be taken without any real help from a partner.

What an overwhelming task it is to have to figure it all out alone. Are men seers who can read a partner's mind and predict each sexual response? Are men supposed to have some innate knowledge of what feels good for every body they may touch? If a man is responsible for everything that happens during sex, for his partner's arousal and orgasm; if his job is to know automatically what a partner likes and needs, then sex becomes a daunting task.

☐ **7. A man should always be aggressive.** From the first kiss to the hard thrusting before orgasm, a man should wear, in the words of Bernie Zilbergeld in *The New Male Sexuality*, the "mask of aggressive sexuality, cool confidence, and stony silence." But what if you don't feel like initiating? What if you feel passive or vulnerable or scared? What if you need reassurance or support? What if it's a time when you're just not going to have an erection until your partner does something to turn you on?

It's fun, at times, to be aggressive. But it's fun to play other sexual roles as well. And it's rather exhausting to have to cook up macho dominance *every* time you want a hug or kiss or to be touched. The best sex is not always hard driving. The best sex is the sex that matches your mood, which could just as easily be sweet and tender as heavy and aggressive.

A corollary of myth 7 is that real men don't show feelings during sex. Showing vulnerability or fear or tenderness during sex feels disturbingly unmasculine. But since sex is an opportunity to communicate in a much deeper way than words, you're missing a chance to express a lot of what's inside you when you leave tender or vulnerable feelings out of sex. Both you and your partner lose a chance for deepening your intimacy.

☐ **8. All physical contact must lead to sex.** It's a rule for some: don't touch if you don't want sex. Hugging, holding, and kissing are only appropriate when building arousal. You're not allowed to touch if you're not ready to turn it into a big sexual production complete with mutual orgasm at the final moment of abandon. This myth really limits the way a man can nourish his partner. Making touching synonymous with sex takes away many ways you and a partner can comfort and support each other.

☐ **9. Sex has to be natural and spontaneous.** Good sex, as defined by this myth, is whatever you feel like doing at the moment. The trouble is that what you feel like doing may have almost nothing to do with the desires or feelings of your partner. This myth requires that you live without feedback and planning. You're really not supposed to use knowledge of a partner's feelings and preferences to act contrary to impulse. Nor would it be spontaneous to develop a mutual plan with your partner to try something new. This myth ties your hands and, in the name of spontaneity, makes sex monotonous.

☐ **10. Masturbation is an inferior form of sexuality.** Masturbation is seen by many men as something one is forced to do when "real" sex isn't available. The truth is that masturbation provides a very high-quality orgasm, sometimes much more pleasurable than intercourse. And masturbation, either alone or with a partner, can offer a special kind of gratification that can only come when the focus is all on you. You can be immersed in sensation without having to do anything or be anything for someone else.

Some men also view solo masturbation as a form of cheating their regular sexual partner out of some of their sexual energy. They agree with Chinese mystics who considered masturbation a dubious activity akin to "mating with ghosts." In actuality, nearly every man with a regular sexual partner also masturbates by himself regularly. It's natural and there's nothing wrong with it. Don't worry about masturbation unless it becomes your *only* form of sexual expression for an extended period of time, despite having a regular sexual partner available.

If you haven't marked the myths that pertain to you, do so now. But it's not enough merely to recognize that you've been influenced by a myth. You need to work on changing the behavior that is an outgrowth of the myth. The only practical way to change faulty attitudes is to change how you act in sexual situations. The following exercise will help you convert awareness into real behavior change.

Becoming Aware of Sexual Myths

1. For each myth affecting you, do the following:

a. Write down all the ways that this myth has caused problems or difficulties for you. Think of at least one specific example from your past that illustrates each problem.

b. Write down in your own words why the myth seems untrue. Think of the consequences for believing such a myth. Take some time with this. It's important to develop arguments *against* the myths that you can really believe.

2. Rewrite the myths that have affected you so they are true statements. Instead of the myth "Sex only involves intercourse," you might substitute the sentence "Sex involves all forms of pleasurable, intimate touching." Instead of the myth "A real man never loses his erection," you might substitute the sentence "Erections come and go depending on emotional and physical circumstances." Make sure your restatement of the myth feels true and accurate to you.

3. For each myth that's affected you, write down some corrective behaviors that will help you overcome the destructive effects of the myth. For example, consider the myth "Men don't show feelings during sex." New, corrective behaviors might include such things as:

"I'm going to mention it if I feel sad, like I often do, after I come."

"I'm going to try some tender kinds of touching and holding and really try to convey more than just being turned on."

"When I get the feeling that we're lost and not really connecting, I'm going to say something rather than just going on like nothing's happening.

4. Make a real effort to carry out the corrective behaviors as often as possible. Focus on the corrective behaviors related to one myth at a time. Trying to "shotgun" it and deal with all the myths simultaneously

will likely overwhelm and discourage you. When you feel that your new, corrective behaviors have made a significant shift in your thinking (in other words, the myth seems less believable), move your attention to the corrective behaviors associated with the next myth you want to work on.

Exercise adapted from Warwick Williams, *Rekindling Desire*.

Assessing Your Sex Life

Before you can determine where you want to go sexually, you need to know where you are now. On a separate piece of paper, write down a detailed description of your sex life. Take as much time as you need— even a couple of hours wouldn't be too much. You can write in complete sentences as in an essay or just make a list using single words or brief phrases. You can organize information under topical headings or just jot thoughts down at random as they occur to you.

However you describe your current sex life, make sure you answer these questions somewhere along the way:

What do you like about your current sex life? This is most important. Future improvements will be based on what you already know feels good.

What don't you like about your current sex life? What turns you off or fails to turn you on? What is uncomfortable? What problems occur that prevent you from experiencing the pleasure you want in sex?

What beliefs, fears, or myths about sex are contributing to the problems? Review the myths previously discussed and also record the thoughts that typically run through your mind while you are making love.

What external stressors may be complicating your current sex life? For example: finances, house guests, children, ill health, relationship conflicts other than sexual problems, work hassles.

Was there a time with your sexual partner when sex was more enjoyable? If so, what's different now? Why do you think things changed? What have you done or not done that influenced the change?

How are you dealing with problems in your current sex life? Avoiding sex, not talking about it, having more sex to prove nothing's wrong, or what?

What are your most common sexual fantasies? When you recall some of your wildest sexual daydreams, what themes recur? For example, oral sex, dominance or submission, group sex, violence, bondage, sex in public places, slow undressing. While you might not want to actually carry out some of these fantasies with your partner, they may give you an idea of how you might add excitement to your sex life if they were in a modified form.

Here are some excerpts from Andre's journal to give you an idea of how one man described his sex life.

I like:
Feeling really turned on
Exotic locations: beach, tents, outdoors, hotel rooms on vacation
Dim lights
When Betty wears her short nightie
When she grabs my cock unexpectedly, caresses it
Perfume
Gazing into her eyes while making love
Massage oil, lubricants
Light tickling with fingernails
Entering her when she's really wet and ready
When Betty initiates sex

I don't like:
Having to be the one who initiates all the time
How seldom we make love
Betty's drooping butt and thickening thighs
My own pot belly and skinny arms
Thinking "Maybe she wants to but I don't, so I'll pretend I'm sleepy."
Bright lights or total darkness
Long flannel nightgowns

Belief that isn't helping:
That we both have to be turned on, in the mood before anything starts

External stressors:
The kids! We can't make love in the mornings anymore because the kids come and crawl in bed before we're even awake.

When it was better:
First two years, before marriage and kids

How we deal with it:
Don't talk about it
Sometimes complain humorously, but don't do anything about it

Best fantasies:
Group sex with Betty and various other women
Being seduced by the stripper I saw when I was sixteen
Memories of Hawaii with Mary
Being held captive by amorous Amazons

Sensate Focus

In an ideal world, sex between two people would keep getting better and better and better. Each would learn more and more about what the other likes and doesn't like. Their lovemaking would become a virtuoso duet by two flawless performers.

Why doesn't it happen this way? Why is the more usual trend toward frustration, boredom, or conflict? Because most couples don't make a conscious effort to learn about each other's sexual preferences.

It's ironic, but you probably know a lot more about your partner's spending habits, political views, or taste in furniture than sexual preferences. This is the usual case for two reasons. First of all, it's difficult to describe the subtleties of sexual experience. Secondly, most people have been trained from childhood not to talk about their own sex life and not to ask about other peoples'.

Practicing "sensate focus" can help enormously by filling in some gaps in your mutual knowledge of each other. Three or four half-hour sessions with your partner can bring your sex life back to life. There are two parts to sensate focus: massage and sexual touching.

Massage

The goal of this exercise is to get practice in giving and receiving pleasure without any sexual "goals" such as reaching orgasm. Giving and receiving pleasure don't come naturally to all. Both are skills that you can learn and improve. Some people are better at one than another. You may feel comfortable giving your partner pleasure, but find it difficult to accept pleasure passively. Or vice versa.

Giving and receiving a nonsexual massage is a wonderful learning experience in how to be a generous giver and a willing taker. Massaging each other can bring you closer and make you more relaxed with each other.

Prepare by finding a half-hour when you won't be disturbed. Retire to your bedroom or living room or anywhere else that is warm and quiet, private and peaceful. Have some baby oil or massage lotion handy. A little oil reduces skin friction and makes the massage feel much better to both of you. Warm the oil in your palms, in a pan of hot water, or in a microwave oven.

Put an easily laundered spread over the bed or floor where you will do the massage. Have a towel handy for wiping off excess oil. A relaxing bath before starting is a good idea. Put on soft music, light incense, dim the lights or use a candle—whatever appeals to you.

Agree to take turns giving a fifteen-minute massage. The person to be massaged should undress. The massager can have clothes on or not, it doesn't matter. You can begin massaging anywhere. Most people especially like having their backs, faces, legs and feet massaged. At this point, don't massage or touch the genitals. This is sensuous practice, not a prelude to intercourse.

If you're receiving the massage, start by just lying there and enjoying it. Breathe slowly and deeply as your muscles are soothed into slackness. When you are somewhat relaxed, start giving your partner feedback. Say out loud what feels good and what doesn't. "A little harder...a bit lighter there...that feathery touch is great...pulling the skin feels good." It may seem awkward to talk while you're being massaged, but persist. At the beginning, it's important to tell each other as accurately and completely as possible what gives the most pleasure. The first couple of times you do this massage exercise, keep talking. Later you can let your "oohs and aahs" speak for you.

If you are giving the massage, concentrate on the fleshy parts of your partner's body and avoid the bony parts. Don't press directly on the spinal column, but massage the muscles on both sides of it. Start gently. As the muscles loosen and warm up, you can put more pressure on the larger muscles. Listen carefully to your partner's breathing and feedback about what feels good and not so good. Do more of what feels best. Although the person receiving the massage will probably have more to say, it's also important for the massager to comment on what it feels like to be giving the massage.

As a general guideline, you should start the massage with the full surface of both hands, fingers together. Do the same thing with each hand, in a symmetrical pattern. Keep your hands in contact with the body as much as possible, sliding over when you move to another area rather than lifting your hands off.

Be sure to tell your partner about anything that doesn't feel comfortable. If either of you becomes sexually excited, stop what you are doing and try something less stimulating. For the purposes of this exercise, intense sexual arousal is not the goal and should be avoided.

You can make the session longer than half an hour if you wish. The goal is to focus on both the giving and the receiving of pleasure, without stressing the fifty-fifty, even-steven nature of the exchange.

Sexual Touching

Think for a moment about the sexual rules you were taught to follow as you grew up. You were probably discouraged from touching your genitals as a child. You weren't supposed to play doctor with or expose yourself to the little girls. As an adolescent, you might have been warned that masturbation would grow hair on your palms, send you to hell, or make you blind, deaf, crazy, and so on. When you were a teenager, you weren't supposed to date until a certain age, and sex was discouraged until you were really "serious" about someone and ready to marry. As a boy, you actually had it a little easier than the girls. For them, the rules were probably even more strict, lest they be "ruined" by premature sex or early pregnancy.

With this kind of background, it's amazing that anyone achieves satisfying adult sexuality. Even those who rebel against the sexual rules they were taught and vow to be free of all hangups about sex find that a legacy of childhood remains. The sexual inhibition, fear, guilt, and uneasiness that most men have to some degree are leftover effects of childhood sexual rules.

The sexual touching exercise can remove some of this leftover fear, guilt, and inhibition by allowing you to return to a childlike sense of play. You finally have permission to play doctor. The idea is to take turns looking at, touching, and kissing each other's body, all over. Be especially sure to ask about, tell about, and try things that you know intellectually are okay, but still bother you a little emotionally. For example, if your partner thinks it's weird to have one's anus touched or toes kissed, be sure to do those things and talk about them.

Do the exercise in three half-hour practice sessions. Again, choose a place and time when you won't be disturbed or distracted. Start with clean bodies—after a relaxing bath is good. You can start undressed or undress each other at the beginning. When you both feel ready, begin caressing and kissing in some way that you have enjoyed in the past. But avoid any genital contact at first.

Pretend that you have never been intimate with each other. Pretend that you have never touched each other's genitals. Pretend further that you are both students, learning about human bodies for the first time.

Now take turns being the leader in "show and tell." Give your partner a guided visual tour of your body, explaining the function and sensations of every part. Then reverse roles. Pay special attention to breasts, buttocks, genitals, and anal area.

The goal is comfort rather than arousal. If any part of the examination makes you uncomfortable, tell your partner and talk about it. If any area is especially sensitive or tender, let each other know.

Once you are both comfortable looking, go on to touching. Again, give each other guided tours of your bodies, allowing the other to touch gently. Explain what feels good and what doesn't. Talk about the things that feel embarrassing or still forbidden. Pay attention to parts that feel very sensual that you may not usually think of as sexual: earlobes, inner thighs, backs of knees, and so on.

When you are comfortable with touching, take turns kissing each other all over. Start on the lips, French kissing. Eventually, kiss everywhere that you both agree is sensual. You can kiss each other's genitals or not, depending on how comfortable you feel about it. There's nothing wrong with oral sex, but it is not mandatory. Be open-minded, but if something really offends or bothers one of you, don't do it right now.

But also don't be surprised if you decide to try it later on. This exercise really does weaken inhibitions.

Don't go all the way to orgasm in this exercise. If you get really turned on, switch to something less stimulating and calm down. The goal here is greater openness, trust, knowledge, and comfort—not orgasm. It's more important to finish the exercise than to come.

Do this exercise three times, at least half an hour at a time. You can do it more often or for longer if you like. While you are learning about each other, remind yourself that a good lover isn't someone who already knows what to do, but rather someone who is always willing to learn more about his partner's needs and desires.

Andre and Betty tried this exercise before bed one night. Andre was surprised to learn three new things about Betty's body that he didn't know: she liked to have the backs of her knees rubbed lightly, she liked to have her eyelids kissed, and the most sensitive spot on her clitoris was not always in the same place—it moved around as he rubbed. Betty learned that Andre really liked light tickling with her fingernails, that he liked having the base of his testicles tickled almost as much as having his penis sucked, and that he was sensitive about his skinny arms and legs. About himself, Andre learned that he really enjoyed talking about sex once the subject was opened. Betty was relieved to find that Andre had been just as concerned about their dull sex life as she was. They managed to refrain from intercourse for a full 45 minutes, but then they declared the exercise over and made passionate love.

When Hormones Do Your Thinking

It feels great to be turned on. But who turns you on has almost nothing to do with who you like, who you could live with, who'd make a good partner.

A lot of men think that being turned on makes it right; that physical attraction is the main criterion for relationship choices. It's not. Over the years, a good many people may turn you on. Few of them, however, would you really like and enjoy as people. Even fewer could you ever feel close to.

If you want one-night sex, physical attraction is all you need. But people bond when they take off their clothes and touch. Not always, but often. And a lot of men bond into relationships where the only thing they have going is sex. There is little else in common: no shared values, lifestyle, or interests. Not much liking or appreciation or respect. This is the true meaning of the word "trapped."

For some gay men, the hormonal trap is particularly pernicious. Even in the age of AIDS, enough remains of the freewheeling bar scene and the greater gay acceptance of recreational sex to allow a gay man to drift from one purely physical encounter to another. He can fall into a pattern of love addiction in which he bonds over and over to inappropriate partners, so intoxicated by the early stages of attraction, flirtation, and romance that he can't exercise judgment about the long-term suitability of a potential partner. Add alcohol and drugs to this scenario and you have a trap that can swallow entire lives.

Because sex so often leads to relationship, it's advisable not to let your hormones do your thinking for you. The choices they make, as likely as not, will lead to a bit of temporary satisfaction, followed by months or years of big time incompatibility.

Before having sex with someone (assuming there's a chance for more than a single encounter), seriously ask yourself these six questions:

1. Would I be interested in this person as a friend?   In other words, is this someone you can like? Is this someone who has some of the basic qualities you seek in a friend?

2. Do I enjoy talking to this person?   Do you enjoy real conversation? Is it interesting? If all the talk was stripped of any sexual charge, would it still be interesting?

3. Do we share any interests in common?   The cliché is that opposites attract, but the truth is that people with important similarities are more likely to build a satisfying relationship. The more you have in common with this person, the better your chances for sharing things other than sex.

4. Do we share similar values and world views?   This is a real make-or-break in many relationships. Basic values are the foundation of a lot of life decisions. As a rule, the more divergent your values, the more conflict you can expect.

5. Do I like how this person relates to others?   Is the person generous to friends (children, family), basically kind, basically open? Are friendships long-standing or brief, supportive or conflicted? Are there *any* close friends? If not, there's usually a reason for this, and it doesn't bode well for a relationship with you.

6. Am I aware of serious turnoffs or danger signs?   Are there things you already know about this person that right now tell you it won't work? Consider past history, unpleasant habits, appearance, money issues, ways of talking or relating, and so on.

These questions create an opportunity to go beyond desire as you make sexual choices. The risks of bonding to the wrong person are just too great not to bring your *head* into the process.

Monogamy

This is a difficult issue for many men. Men and women have innately different drives and needs when it comes to multiple versus monogamous sex. Men are wired physiologically to turn on quickly to visual stimulation. Any attractive potential sex partner is going to trigger some level of desire. This basic programming tends to push men toward multiple pairings. Even a very satisfying relationship may, at times, feel constraining, and the desire to sexually encounter someone new grows to the level of preoccupation or obsession.

The problem for men is that the programming to pursue multiple partners runs head-on into basic realities about what works in relationships. With rare exceptions, non-monogamous sexual relationships remain emotionally stunted and structurally unstable. Two crucial building blocks for long-term satisfaction are usually missing: trust and a commitment to intimacy.

Trust. A body of research now suggests that bonding the process by which people build enduring relationships—is largely accomplished through touch. An open sexual contract between partners means that each must live with the risk that he or she will be abandoned if a partner develops a strong rival bond. Each time partners seek sexual intimacy outside the relationship, trust tends to diminish; there's a natural distancing, a protective psychological shield, that insulates against the possibility of hurt and loss.

Most damaging to trust is the discovered "affair." A partner suddenly learns that the relationship is not monogamous, that the promise of fidelity has not been kept. The overall effect is a crushing sense of having been deceived, a lost belief in the love and commitment of one's partner.

Trust is built on *safety* and *honesty*. Non-monogamous relationships have difficulty providing much of either. The fear of abandonment and loss, and the realization that a partner will likely share very little of his "other life" erodes the basic foundation of trust.

A commitment to intimacy. The reach for intimacy is a conscious choice. It is the decision to share the important feelings and experiences of your life. It is the decision to be seen, to let a partner into all the places where you are soft and vulnerable and sometimes afraid. And with that openness and vulnerability comes the highest payoff of partnership: the feeling of being accepted. You realize that someone has seen it all—the weakness, the uncertainty, the flaws—and still believes in you, still thinks you are fine. Acceptance is healing, and it acts as an armor against life's inevitable failures and losses.

Intimacy and acceptance are hard enough to achieve. But a non-monogamous relationship (either through contract or deceit) makes it far more difficult. How can you feel really known and accepted as long as a significant part of your life can't be shared?

It's a big deal having to hold things back, having to stay silent about important things you feel and do. It's a loss, and it drives a wedge between partners. We recommend that you think carefully about what you have to lose before looking for sex outside of your relationship.

Loving the One You're With

How do you stay turned on to the same person year after year? This is a tough question that actually has four answers.

First, in any long-term relationship, the frequency and quality of sexual pleasure may be an indicator of the health of the rest of the relationship. If you aren't turned on to your partner, think about the conflicts between you. Are there unspoken arguments, anger, withdrawal, resentment, jealousy, disagreement about money or child rearing, unhealed wounds from the past? Reading the rest of this book and working on sharing feelings, controlling anger, improving parenting skills, overcoming workaholism, and so on will go a long way toward restoring passion to the sexual side of your relationship.

Second, doing the sensate focus exercises in this chapter will help you expand the territory of your sexuality. You'll have more sensual practices that you enjoy doing together and greater knowledge of how to give and receive pleasure. This will help not only in bed, but outside it. Make a conscious effort to expand your notion of sexuality beyond orgasm to touching of all kinds: the kiss at the kitchen sink, the friendly squeeze in the garden, strolling hand in hand, or rubbing each other's feet while watching television. Stay in touch, literally.

Third, you need to develop selective focus. Instead of noticing that your partner's body is thickening and skin is dry, focus on the way the eyes still sparkle with mischief, the way a naked back curves when your lover bends over, the way freshly brushed hair shines and crackles with electricity. Ignore the parts that no longer turn you on. Instead of bemoaning lost youth, concentrate on the qualities of your partner that you still find attractive.

Fourth, make your fantasies work for you. Every man daydreams about sex with various partners and in various situations. Nearly every man masturbates while indulging these fantasies, regardless of how much actual intercourse he may also be enjoying with a real partner. And every man adds spice to his lovemaking by fantasizing about someone other than the one he's with. This isn't anything to be guilty about. It's normal. It's a survival skill.

Here's how to use your sexual fantasies to enhance your attraction to your partner: While you are masturbating to the accompaniment of your favorite sexual fantasy, replace the image of your fantasy lover at the last second with an image of your regular partner. Focusing on your partner just before orgasm will help reestablish a strong link between your partner and feelings of sexual excitement. Likewise, if you use fantasies of others or exotic situations while making love with your partner, switch focus to your partner right at the moment of orgasm. With practice, you will be able to switch to focusing on your partner earlier and earlier, making it possible to feel more strongly turned on to your partner *from the beginning*. This takes time, probably several months, but it's worth the effort.

HIV and AIDS

These days it's very difficult, especially when starting a new sexual relationship, to feel comfortable talking about AIDS. How much do you need to know about a potential partner? How should you ask? When and how should you volunteer information about your own health and sexual history?

One thing is clear: if you are HIV positive—a blood test has shown the HIV virus present in your body—you *must* tell any potential sexual partner. Secondly, if there is the remotest chance that you may have sex with a stranger, carry condoms at all times and use them. So far, only two things have been proven to prevent AIDS: the truth and condoms.

Special Problems

If you have erection problems or difficulty having or delaying orgasms, be assured that these are common problems for many men, problems that can be readily solved. We don't have room to go into the many causes and remedies for sexual disfunction. Besides, Bernie Zilbergeld has already covered the subject brilliantly. Get a copy of his *The New Male Sexuality* and read it.

8

Being Two:
Making Partnership Work

This is it. This is where any "new masculinity" must finally prove itself, by improving your long-term love relationships. Being a better man must also mean being a better partner.

This chapter is devoted to showing ways to get more love, more fulfillment, more fun, more support, and more satisfaction out of living with your partner. Your partner may be your girlfriend, wife, or another man. Again, if you are heterosexual and reading examples of two men in love makes you feel uncomfortable, please keep reading. For you, this chapter will provide a beneficial side effect in the form of practice in overcoming homophobia.

The Art of Listening

According to a recent study, the number one criterion for a happy relationship isn't sexual satisfaction, but rather the experience of being listened to and understood. The ability to hear your partner, and to acknowledge what you hear, forms a basic foundation of trust that supports and nourishes every aspect of your relationship.

For men, the expectations built into the traditional male role make listening hard. To fulfill that role, men have to know, to be the expert, to have the right answer. Men are supposed to solve things. But knowing and solving often get in the way of listening. You're so busy trying to fix things that you may not hear important aspects of what your partner feels and wants. If your job as a man is to protect your loved ones from pain, hearing that your partner hurts may trigger a sense of failure or self-blame. Your need to be the one who knows, who has the right answer, may leave you feeling threatened and resistant if your partner is asking *you* to change.

The art of listening is built on *intention*. At root, real listening is the intention to understand someone. Pure and simple. It's *not* about gathering ammunition to support your rebuttal argument. Or spacing out while waiting your turn. Or looking for evidence of your preconceptions. Or seeming attentive so that your partner will think you're interested. Or making the trade: I'll listen to you if you'll listen to me. Or listening just long enough to make sure that nothing really awful is happening and then checking out. Or looking for openings to deliver an opinion or judgment. Real listening has no ulterior agenda. It is an active process where your energy and intention are focused on a single objective: understanding your partner's experience, stepping behind your partner's eyes.

Blocks to Listening

The four largest blocks to listening for men are (1) judging, (2) advising, (3) sparring, and (4) being right. Ask yourself whether any of these sound familiar.

Judging. You attach a pejorative label to something your partner is saying or doing. "That's stupid...crazy...selfish...foolish...fucked up... incompetent...wasteful...driving us into bankruptcy...hypocritical... cruel" and so on. The judgment blocks any further understanding of your partner's feelings or behavior. Deliver one judgment and the rest of the conversation is likely to break down into an exchange of salvos. Your partner will experience the bitterness of being judged rather than the comfort of being acknowledged and understood. And you may be hurt by the counterattack. If you're going to make judgments, make sure that you do so after you have really listened.

Advising. You jump the gun with problem solving before you fully understand what your partner feels, why your partner feels that way, and what solutions your partner has already tried. Even if you understand the mechanics of a problem, it's important to hear the feelings and acknowledge your partner's pain before rushing to an answer. The rule is: listen first, solve later.

Sparring. You argue and debate, you take stands, you give opinions. "Marian, that class is a waste of time; why even worry about the paper?" "I know your show was preempted, but TV is just mind rot anyway." "When are you going to realize that I never get to rest? You're going to add a straw some day that will break the camel's back." "What's your problem, Rebecca? You always...."

Sparring is an excellent form of defense when your partner is saying something that threatens you. But the price is the erosion of trust—your partner's trust that you understand or even care what your partner feels.

Being right. You are determined to prove and justify your position. You filter from what your partner says only the part that might support your argument. What your partner feels and wants is less important than bolstering your beliefs and preconceptions. If you are criticized, the reflex is to start the artillery rather than hear the nature of your partner's distress.

Exercise. Think back over the last two significant conversations with your partner. See if you can identify any blocks to listening you may have used. Which blocks are most typical of you? Is there a block which you characteristically rely on when you feel threatened or hurt?

Active Listening

Listening isn't passive. It is not a mere shutting of the mouth. Listening is an active commitment to your *intention* to understand. Here are some ways to listen actively.

Paraphrasing. Your partner needs acknowledgment that you are hearing what's been said. Acknowledgment provides reassurance that you are being attentive and helps to verify that you're getting it right. You can paraphrase by using lead-ins such as "So basically how you feel is...In other words...What you're saying is...What happened was...Let me understand, what was going on for you was...Do you mean?..." After the lead-in, just say what you think your partner is conveying in your own words. Summarize, but try at least to mention each main point or element of what was expressed.

Exercise. Tell your partner that you are working on listening skills. Encourage your partner to tell you a story of some recent experience that felt important. Your job is to paraphrase, at intervals, what's just been said. Put in your own words what you've heard and then ask your partner if you're getting it right. Your partner should be encouraged to make corrections or additions to what you said, and you can incorporate those corrections in a new attempt at paraphrasing. Keep at it, paraphrasing and correcting, until your partner's satisfied that you heard it right.

Clarifying. This is an adjunct to paraphrasing and simply involves asking questions to fill out the picture. Since your intention is to understand, you may need more information or background to appreciate your partner's experience. "Were you at home when this happened?...What did it feel like to have him look at you like that?...Were you tired?... How long did it take you?...Were you disappointed?...Anxious?...Relieved?...Is that the statement that hurt your feelings?...Did you need more support from me?...Had you hoped that she'd help you?...What happened after you left?"

The purpose of clarifying questions is not to challenge, confront, discredit, or criticize. The sole purpose is to understand as fully as possible the events, feelings, or needs that your partner is conveying.

Feedback. The last step in active listening is to offer feedback. You've paraphrased and clarified. You have an understanding of what was said. Now, in a *nonjudgmental* way, you can share your reaction—what you thought or felt.

Feedback doesn't mean falling back into judging, advising, sparring, or proving you're right. Your feedback must be supportive—that is, it conveys a sense of concern and acceptance. Express any feelings as "I" statements. "I felt sad...hurt...excited...apprehensive." Put your thoughts into the form of nonthreatening conjecture:

"I was wondering if _____
might have been going on for you."

"I had the sense that you might also be _____."

"It might be possible that _____."

Notice how this kind of feedback leaves room for your partner to agree, disagree, or explore the issue without having to get defensive. You are merely offering another perspective, not making absolute judgments about reality.

Exercise. Preselect a topic that often leads to conflict with your partner. The next time that topic comes up, mention that you are still focusing on listening skills and are going to work on paraphrasing and clarifying what's being said. Explain that you will give feedback, if any, only after you really understand the issue, and that you are committed to give only *nonjudgmental* feedback. Ask your partner to remind you to paraphrase and ask clarifying questions if you forget to do it. New habits are built slowly, but this exercise can be an important step toward improved listening skills.

Handling Conflict

Every relationship starts with excitement and hope. There is a sense of mutual satisfaction, a joy in merely being in each other's company. But the time inevitably arrives when this symbiosis, this honeymoon sense of oneness, begins to break under the pressure of diverging needs. You cannot long sustain the illusion of two people as one self. Sooner or later separate needs emerge. How partners resolve the inescapable conflicts of a shared life ultimately determines the health and level of satisfaction in their relationship. *The amount of trust, pleasure, and nurturance you experience depends on how you deal with conflict.*

People who grow up in dysfunctional families learn strategies of conflict-resolution that depend on force and the threat of pain to manipulate a partner into giving up his or her needs. These techniques, called *aversive strategies*, are designed to distract or punish the other person from asserting wants and desires.

When your father belittled and denigrated your mother every time she discussed her concerns, you may have learned through modeling to handle conflicts in the same way. If your mother threatened or made people feel guilty when she didn't get her way, you may have learned to protect your needs in a similar fashion. Early modeling accounts for most of your training in problem-resolution skills. What your parents did is what you will tend to do.

Aversive Strategies

What follows is an exploration of the eight aversive strategies that are most frequently used to resolve conflict.

1. Discounting. You attempt to prove to your partner that her or his needs are invalid or somehow less compelling than your own. "I do hard physical labor all day, and you sit in a chair. I don't know why you're complaining about a little work around the house." "You used to live in a pig sty, and it didn't bother you. I don't know why all of a sudden that couch is so intolerable. If we're going to spend money, we should spend it on a rowing machine. My back's going to get nothing but worse if I don't strengthen those muscles." "You're always complaining about not having enough time together. It can't be that important or you'd turn off the TV. I'm here. I don't see you making much of an effort."

Notice that the partner's needs are always painted as minor or exaggerated. When the speaker acknowledges his own needs, they appear more important, more valid.

2. Withdrawal or abandonment. One of the most harmful ways to get what you want in a conflict is to withdraw emotionally from your partner. The effect is often so painful that she or he will tend to give in or give up some important desire. With this technique, a grudging statement like "Okay, okay, we'll go to the beach this year" is followed by pouting silence or worse, by a profound coldness or physical withdrawal. "I think I'll visit Ted tonight. Don't wait up." Or this example: One partner asks to explore something a little different, sexually. The response is a deep sigh, a grimace, a head shake, and finally an exit from the room. The message is clear: "Pressure me about sex, and you're on your own."

3. Threats. This strategy is self-explanatory. You let a partner know that you'll do something hurtful if you don't get what you want. "If you're going to buy that kind of stuff, I'm canceling your credit card."

"I'm going home, you can come with me or you can find somewhere else to live."

4. Blaming. Here the effort is to make someone feel bad for needing anything and specifically to suggest that their need is their own fault. "If you'd do more with your life, you wouldn't be so lonely all the time." "You wouldn't be so overwhelmed with the kids if you made regular time to spend with them." "It's your crazy mother that stresses you out and the fact that you can't say no to her, not my work schedule. Tell her to get off your back, don't hassle me."

5. Belittling or denigrating. You make the person feel stupid or inappropriate for wanting something you don't want. "Why do you need another car? Did you put too many dents in the old one?" "Why do you want seafood for the dinner? A little late to start healthy eating, isn't it?" "Why are we visiting Sarah? All the two of you do is complain about work. You could do that on the phone and not bore everybody."

6. Guilt tripping. Here the strategy is to make the person feel like a moral failure for not doing what you want. The basic message is that a partner is being unfair, inconsiderate, or bad for having different needs or not responding to yours. "I spent every night this week doing our bloody taxes, and you can't even give me a shoulder massage." "I watch the kids while you go to class, but you can't give me an hour to write one lousy letter to my sister." "We have sex always on your schedule, while I'm dead tired at night, but you never respond with the slightest interest when I'm awake and turned on in the morning. There's something a little self-centered about that."

7. Derailing. You respond to your partner's needs by shifting the focus of conversation. This is usually done with a provocative statement that effectively recenters attention on a different issue. "I know we only have two nights a week together, but I'll lose my fellowship if I don't take a full load. I think Bernhardt is trying to get rid of me anyway. He thinks I'm lazy. I have to do all this stupid research just so they'll think I'm useful to have around. Could you, by the way, type that Jung paper for me that's due Monday?" Notice how the partner's concern is soon obscured by a list of problems in graduate school. "Your father's health is a problem, but my mother's so batty that every day I expect she'll leave the gas on and blow herself up. Do you think I should get somebody in there to help her, or just let things limp along?"

8. Punishment. You let your partner know that you'll withdraw something she or he finds nurturing if you don't get what you want. "We don't have to go on vacation at all if we can't agree what to do." Consider the effect of "I'm not really in the mood" said coldly in response to a sexual overture hours after the partner asked for more help with the garden. Some punishment, as the above example indicates, takes a passive-aggressive form. Nothing is said directly, but the emotional tone suddenly turns arctic. Or there are excuses to avoid shared pleasures.

Four Principles of Healthy Conflict Resolution

The strategies listed above don't work in the long run. They can pay big dividends over a period of weeks or even months. But eventually people get inured to them. Coercion ceases to be compelling. So instead of getting what you want, you get resistance or resentment. Trust and satisfaction decline, and your relationship becomes a struggle of intimate adversaries.

There are four basic principles of conflict resolution that can help you steer away from established aversive patterns.

1. Acknowledge when you hear a need. Use active listening to uncover your partner's concern. Ask questions. Clarify. Keep probing till you understand what exactly is wanted.

You: *You're feeling a distance between us?* (Paraphrasing) *Do you feel we're not being emotionally close?* (Clarifying question)

Partner: *Maybe. I just feel sort of out there, sort of alone.*

You: *You're feeling by yourself. Like I'm not really with you.* (Active listening) *Does it feel like we're not spending enough time together?* (Clarifying question)

Partner: *No, that's not it. We're both here a lot.*

You: *Has something happened that set this feeling off or made it worse?* (Clarifying question)

Partner: *I guess. When you laughed at the idea of my starting to paint again.*

You: *I laughed? It felt like I was making fun of you?* (Clarifying question)

Partner: *Like it was a stupid idea or I'm not good enough at it.*

You: *So I hurt you by laughing.* (Paraphrasing) *And you've continued to feel hurt and shut down?* (Clarifying question)

Partner: *Yeah.*

You: *You don't trust me? It's hard to feel close?* (Clarifying question)

Partner: *Yeah.*

You: *What do you need from me about this? What can I do?*

Partner: *I need more support from you about my painting.*

Notice how the questioner never gets defensive, but stays always with the intention of understanding his partner. The effort has only one purpose: getting the problem and corresponding need into clearer focus. Knowing what your partner needs is a crucial starting place for further problem solving.

2. Pain, not blame. Your partner's needs are only half the conflict. You have important needs too, and you may feel a pressure to express them. Chapter 11, "Being Open: Expressing Your Feelings," and chapter 12, "Being Assertive: Asking for What You Want," can help with this. But the most important principle when expressing what hurts or bothers you is to keep the focus on *your* pain in the situation rather than blaming your partner. Fault finding creates resistance and over time blocks real communication. So talk about your needs only in terms of what *you* feel, not the flaws and failures of the other person.

Blame statement: *You never get home on time.*

Pain statement: *I miss you and feel pretty lonely here when you're late.*

Blame statement: *You give the kids ten times the attention you give to me.*

Pain statement: *There's a lot happening with the kids, but I miss the closeness between us.*

Blame statement: *The house looks like it was bombed. You've made a little Hiroshima.*

Pain statement: *I'm uncomfortable with the clutter. I think I'd feel more relaxed if we could maintain one room, like a sanctuary, that stayed in order.*

Blame statement: *You looked bored.* (said during sex)

Pain statement: *It didn't seem like we were connected, and I really miss that feeling with you.*

3. Principle of equally valid needs. This is an assumption that you have to make for problem solving to work. You *must* act from the position that you and your partner have *equally* legitimate and valid needs. The needs are different, perhaps even contradictory, but they are equally important. When you try to invalidate a partner's needs, using any of the aversive strategies, you are creating an impasse. Your partner will resist such discounting of her or his needs, and you, naturally, will resist any counterattack against your own.

The only way out is to rigidly adhere to the principle of equally valid needs. It protects both of you from aversive putdowns, and it paves the way for negotiated compromise.

4. Problem solving as partners, not adversaries. When you solve problems as adversaries, as individuals competing against each other for your needs, there can only be winners and losers. One or both of you will be defeated by the process and will have to give up what you want.

When you solve problems as partners, you acknowledge that you are in it together. A problem for one is a problem for both. A need for one is a need that requires the attention of both. The relationship serves each of you, and you are partners in the process of finding how you both can get some of what you need.

When you operate with the principle of equally valid needs, it allows you to join together in a mutual search for compromise alternatives. Here are some strategies that partners who are committed to solving problems together use to compromise.

- My way this time, your way next time.

- My way when I'm doing it, your way when you're doing it.

- If you do _____ for me, I'll do _____ for you.

- Part of what I want with part of what you want.

- Try it my way for a week and see. If you don't like it, we'll go back to the old way.

- We'll split the difference.

The main function of the compromise process is to ensure that each person gets part of what he or she needs without the adversarial outcomes of victory and defeat.

Exercise. Carefully review the last three episodes of conflict you have had with your partner. What aversive strategies did you use? (Focus on your own, not your partner's.) Now prepare to function differently in the next conflict situation. Write or type the following four steps on a piece of paper and put it on your shaving mirror. Review it each morning.

Step 1: Listen actively to understand my partner's need.

Step 2: State my need nonblamingly.

Step 3: Directly acknowledge that *both* our needs are valid and legitimate.

Step 4: Solve it as partners. Find a compromise where both of us get some of what we want.

Changing Negative Schemas

Partners always form mental pictures of each other. These pictures don't describe physical appearance, but instead summarize the personal qualities that influence the relationship. These mental pictures are called schemas, and they can be based on literally thousands of small events. Since no one can remember so much data, the events are sorted into categories (schemas). The more events there are supporting each schema, the more powerful its influence becomes.

Here's an example: Bob sees Suzanne as being self-centered. That's a schema. Every time she does something he labels as self-centered, the event gets sorted into that group of experiences. The more events Bob labels as "Suzanne's selfishness," the greater the influence of this schema will be. Bob reacts now with more and more irritation to Suzanne's "self-centered shit." His schema fast becomes the central focus of their conflicts.

Sandy and Richard play together in a local orchestra. Sandy works hard to practice new pieces he will play. At home, he notices that Richard hardly ever practices. Richard also does less than his share of the laundry, and he picks up only rarely. These and other experiences are lumped into the "Richard is lazy" schema. The more events Sandy categorizes in this way, the more enraged he becomes by Richard's "laziness."

You can also have schemas about your partner's motivations ("She's trying to avoid sex"), intentions ("He wants me to feel as defeated as he does"), feelings toward you ("She feels sorry for me"), and judgments about you ("She thinks I'm incompetent").

Your schemas about your partner's motivations, intentions, feelings, and judgments about you are extremely destructive. They are usually formed and supported by enormous quantities of mind reading. Basically, you take a button and sew a vest on it. You begin with some bit of ambiguous behavior you've observed and make a negative conclusion. Once the schema is formed ("She thinks I'm too passive"), all future ambiguous behavior tends to get labeled with the schema: "She's frowning, I'm not taking enough sexual initiative... She's quiet, she's gotten sick of initiating conversation...She's looking at the ceiling, she's disgusted because I didn't call any place for a reservation." Now you have an automatic boot with which to kick yourself. Every minor reaction from your partner triggers your assumption that your partner is once again passing judgment on your "passivity." It's a nightmare.

Perhaps the most malignant of all schemas is the belief that your partner doesn't really love you. "If he loved me, we would hug a lot more." "If she loved me, she'd skip some of those dance classes." "I'm a paycheck. That's all I'm here for."

The net result of negative schemas is a picture of your partner and the relationship that hurts, angers, or even frightens you. Yet for the most part schemas are built on conjecture, mere interpretations of behavior. Little effort is made to get confirmation for these assumptions from your partner.

Schemas and Calibrated Communication

Unconfirmed negative schemas create something called *calibrated communication*. It's the process by which false assumptions lead you to make inappropriate (often angry) responses, which in turn generate defensive (often angry) reactions from your partner. By calibrated increments, your exchanges move further and further from what was really going on. A lot of anger and hurt gets built on that first negative assumption.

Paul, for example, has a schema that Louise avoids anything unpleasant—particularly by using the excuse of tiredness. On parent-teacher night, she complains of exhaustion and stays home. Paul returns from the conference with a conviction that Louise has used the excuse to leave him with the job of hearing about their daughter's behavior problems in school. He's angry and acts cold and irritable for a while. Then he complains about the pile of wash. Louise, who's coming down with the flu, again says she's too tired to deal with it. Her response confirms Paul's schema. Now he's really steaming, and he says a few more provocative things until they finally have a fight about who should have called the dryer repairman. In calibrated steps, the real problem is obscured as conflict escalates.

Beating the Schema Trap

Breaking the hold of negative schemas is no small task, but it's vital to the health of your relationship. There are two things you can do.

1. Check it out. This means putting your assumption, your hidden schema, into words. The key here is to ask your question in a nonattacking way. Use a stock phrase like "Sometimes I wonder...Recently I had the thought...There have been moments when I found myself suspecting...Somehow I wondered if...." Notice that the opening phrase doesn't imply that you have a corner on truth and reality. It conveys the desire to know and understand, without beating the person up with your negative assumption.

Now comes the meat of the solution: finding a way to describe your schema that doesn't turn your partner into a bad person. This isn't so hard when you're checking out intentions, motivations, feelings, and judgments about you. "Sometimes I have the feeling that you kinda see me as lazy, like when I came home without picking up the lamb chops tonight." "I sense that you're angry at me in quite a few situations. Like when I got us lost today, or when I didn't want to go to that work party. Is there any truth in that?" "I've been imagining lately that sex isn't too interesting for you, or maybe even something you're avoiding. Have you felt anything like that?"

When the schema has to do with negative traits in your partner, the task is more delicate. Try to find neutral words that don't imply a value judgment. If a word or phrase sounds attacking, don't use it. Probably the best strategy is to write your questions out beforehand to make sure they don't carry a punch (or at least the smallest punch possible). "Sometimes," Sandy says to Richard, "I have the feeling that you tend to avoid things that are hard or unpleasant. For example, you practice a lot less than I do. But where it really gets hard for me is when you're less attentive to chores and things we have to do around the house. I imagine that you're just leaving it to me." Notice that Sandy never uses the pejorative term "lazy." He expresses his concern without directly attacking Richard. As it turns out, Richard acknowledges that he tends to avoid things that feel "like work." But he hadn't intended, or even noticed, that he was dumping extra work on Sandy. He expresses concern, and a desire to divide things more equitably. Sandy was right that Richard was avoiding tasks, but his negative assumption that Richard was happy to stick him with the work turned out to be far from the truth.

Bob needed to do some checking out with Suzanne. His task was to ask about her "selfishness" without using such a value-laden term. "Suzanne, there have been times when I've felt upset about something or expressed some need to you—like recently when I wanted you to go with me to visit my father. But you didn't express much concern or pay as much attention to my problem as I wanted. I kinda feel like when I express something that it's hard to get your focus off your concerns and onto me. I'm wondering if that's true, that you're kind of caught up in your own stuff, or whether I'm misperceiving it." Bob had to write out every word so he wouldn't slip into negative labels. He decided to behaviorally define what was happening ("not paying too much attention") rather than use words like "selfish." The result was a clear description of his negative schema, but not something so confrontive that Suzanne would be thrown into a defensive stance. Suzanne eventually acknowledged that she'd been preoccupied and had a hard time "cranking up" to respond to Bob. She reported that she had been increasingly depressed after a recent job change and felt "totally caught" in the stresses at work. Bob was right that Suzanne had not been paying attention, but his negative schema of selfishness had to be changed when he got the new information.

Exercise. Think back over the last half dozen conflicts you have had with your partner. Is there a negative schema that tends to fuel your anger, that runs like a thread through many of these confrontations? Look for negative traits that you use to label certain behavior, particularly things you think your partner should have some control over. Now commit yourself to checking it out. Script your questions in advance by first selecting a neutral opening phrase: "I've sensed recently...." Next find neutral words to describe the negative trait or schema. It usually helps simply to define the problem operationally, by describing the behavior that bothers you in a nonattacking way. Use Bob and Sandy as models. End by asking if your assumption is true. Keep working your script till it feels as supportive as possible, without losing focus on the basic question you need to ask. You might consider checking it with a friend to get more feedback.

2. Building accurate empathy. Here the focus is on reworking your negative assumption by changing how you look at your partner's problematic behavior. Accurate empathy starts with this basic conviction: Everyone is doing the very best he or she can. Here's a more complete way of saying it: Considering your partner's needs, fears, assumptions, history, skills, and perceived choices, she or he is doing the absolute best that can be done.

To build accurate empathy, you need to prove that this new assumption is true. You need to find the needs, fears, assumptions, history, skills (or lack of skills), and perceived choices that are making your partner behave exactly as she or he behaves. Your partner's total awareness, as it pertains to any given choice, is built on these six elements.

Exercise. To practice accurate empathy, select a recent choice made by your partner that you labeled with your negative schema. Now, to promote empathy rather than judgment, prove that your partner is doing her or his best. Using your knowledge of your partner's behavior and history, show how each of the six items below has influenced the choice.

1. Needs

2. Fears

3. Assumptions

4. History

5. Skills (or lack of skills)

6. Perceived choices

Example. Arthur had developed the schema that Wendy was often cruel. He saw many vaguely critical remarks she had made as evidence for this assumption. Arthur decided to use the accurate empathy exercise to build a different picture. By assuming that Wendy was doing her best, that her behavior was merely an effort to cope and survive, Arthur could begin letting go of his anger. To "prove" that Wendy was doing her best, Arthur attempted to show how the six elements were contributing to her critical behavior.

1. Needs
She wants me to be around more, do a lot more stuff with her. She wants us to be closer. She talks about feeling lonely.

2. Fears
Mainly, Wendy is afraid that she doesn't matter to me. She's afraid I'm going to split and say, "It was nice knowing you."

3. Assumption
I think she assumes that I really don't care that much, that I don't really want anything to grow between us. Maybe she thinks she can't ask me for anything, that I wouldn't do it if she asked directly. That sounds right: she assumes I wouldn't do things for her.

4. History
She was the one who was ignored in the family. Even when she got into a lot of trouble at school, nobody ever really paid attention. She sort of gave up expecting anybody would do anything for her.

5. Skills (or lack of skills)
She either doesn't know how or is afraid to ask for things. So she probably makes these cutting remarks hoping I get the point.

6. Perceived choices

She thinks she doesn't have a choice. If she asks anything, I won't do it, or maybe I'll leave. It's a no-win situation. She'll never get what she wants. So she just deals with it by making little digs. It really is the best she can do.

Knowing Your System

A system is a circular way couples relate so that problems never get solved. The whole process of dealing with conflicting needs starts and stops in the same place. Nothing moves. Nothing changes. The best way to understand couples' systems is to see an example of one. The most widely recognized couple system is called the *pursuer-distancer*:

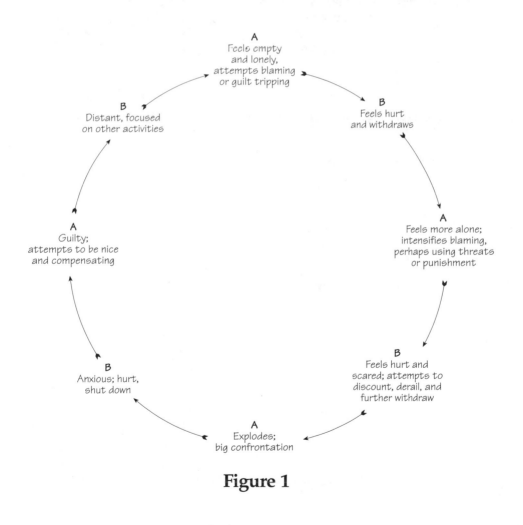

Figure 1

In the *pursuer-distancer* system, one partner makes demands (often in a blaming style), and the other partner placates or gets defensive and ultimately withdraws. Because systems always go in circles, you can see from the illustration that the system starts over exactly where it began.

Notice how the more B withdraws, the more A pursues and gets angry. And the more pressure and blame B feels from A, the more B withdraws. Each response triggers an intensification of the other's pathological attempt to solve the problem. B is trying to feel safe and get away from pressure and disapproval by pulling back emotionally. A is trying to stop the loneliness and get better connected by pushing, blaming, and pursuing. Both solutions only make things worse and keep the system going in its endless cycle.

Keep two things in mind. (1) No one is to blame for this circular trap. Both people contribute equally to the cycle's momentum. A wouldn't need to pursue and attack if B didn't withdraw. And B wouldn't need to withdraw if A didn't apply pressure and blame. (2) The cycle can change. If B stopped withdrawing and somehow acknowledged A's partner's need, the pattern would start to shift. If A stopped the aversive strategies and talked about her or his needs in a nonattacking way, there might be new opportunities for understanding and compromise. The point is that a painful system can be broken and both partners freed.

Another recognized system grows from the metaphor of the rebellious or irresponsible child who is controlled by the warden or caretaker. The more one partner stays out late, gets fired, drinks, gambles, has health problems, or creates uproar, the more the other partner tries to control, tame, and take care of her or his "wild child."

Every unhappy couple has their own system. Sometimes it's a variant on one of the above. Sometimes it's quite unique.

Mapping Your System

It's time now to map the sequence of events that keeps your relationship going in circles. Remember, by definition, a system always has to start and end in the same place. It's like a snake biting its own tail. You need to be able to show each step of how you and your partner go around the circle and get back to the beginning.

To get a full picture of the system, it's helpful to know (1) what happens (each partner's behavior—often played out as one of the aversive strategies), (2) what the feelings are (how you or your partner are reacting emotionally *at that point in the sequence*), and (3) the schema (how you see your partner or your partner sees you *at that point in the sequence*).

Try filling in as much of the following chart as you can. It might be a good idea to get your partner to help fill in his or her feelings and thoughts or give you feedback on how the sequence goes. Start the sequence at a point where things have not yet escalated. Remember, whoever you start with, you or your partner, that person isn't to blame. Each person is equally responsible for keeping the sequence going.

Partner A	Behavior: Feelings: Schema:
Partner B	Behavior: Feelings: Schema:
Partner A	Behavior: Feelings: Schema:
Partner B	Behavior: Feelings: Schema:
Partner A	Behavior: Feelings: Schema:
Partner B	Behavior: Feelings: Schema:
Partner A	Behavior: Feelings: Schema:
Partner B	Behavior: Feelings: Schema:
Partner A	Behavior: Feelings: Schema:
Partner B	Behavior: Feelings: Schema:

Arturo used the chart to map his system as follows.

Me: Behavior: *I get focused on some interest, kind of obsessed with it, like getting involved with the theatre company, rehearsing, hanging out.*

     Feelings: *Harried, excited, nervous that Rita's pissed.*

     Schema: *Rita's going to get jealous.*

Rita: Behavior: *Asks me about rehearsal schedule. Kind of scrutinizes what I'm doing. Her eyes are* on *me.*

     Feelings: *I think she's scared.*

     Schema: *That I'm wild and careless and stupid (which pisses me off).*

Me: Behavior: *Really get into it, go all out, make it a passion (like the nature photography and working with the El Salvador group and practicing the circus act).*

     Feelings: *Angry at Rita for watching me and being suspicious.*

     Schema: *She's anxious and trying to control me, and worried about any woman I come in contact with.*

Rita: Behavior: *Complaining about me being irresponsible. All pissed that I'm not doing this and that at home. Pissed if I take a day off work. Pissed if I'm home from rehearsal later than I said I would. Complaining about my smoking dope. Blah, blah, blah.*

     Feelings: *I don't really know. Angry??*

     Schema: *I'm wild and stupid and don't care.*

Me: Behavior: *Start kind of mentioning things that will probably piss her off. "So and so gives good stage kisses." "The cast is very tight, very intimate." To let her know I have a life. And it's not her fucking life.*

     Feelings: *Anger, resentment, wanting to get away.*

     Schema: *She's controlling me.*

Rita: Behavior: *Shows up during rehearsal to check up on me.*

     Feelings: *I don't know.*

     Schema: *I'm wild and stupid and don't care.*

Me: Behavior: *I ask Marilyn to go downtown and see* Long Day's Journey *with me. Just to be with someone who doesn't think I'm an asshole. Mention it to Rita.*

Feelings: *Angry, alone, wanting to get away.*

Schema: *Same as before.*

Rita: Behavior: *Sets some kind of curfew—I've got to be in by a certain time. I've got to do x, y, z at home. Or she's pulling the plug on our relationship.*

Feelings: *Don't know.*

Schema: *I'm wild, don't care. The same.*

Me: Behavior: *I try to go along with it. She's extremely serious. It's like we're on the edge of losing it.*

Feelings: *Scared, angry.*

Schema: *She could walk away, detach, and that would be it. She's very capable of that.*

Rita: Behavior: *Very distant and withdrawn. Cutting.*

Feelings: *Fuck it, who needs him.*

Schema: *He's an asshole, I'd be better off without him??*

Me: Behavior: *The play is over. I've cooled down my involvement (I always reach this stage with everything).*

Feelings: *Alone, angry. Still scared.*

Schema: *Same.*

Rita: Behavior: *Somewhat warmer. A kind of wary distance. Still somewhat cutting.*

Feelings: *??*

Schema: *The usual.*

Me: Behavior: *Trying to be good. Trying to soften her, jolly her up.*

Feelings: *Same.*

Schema: *She could walk away. She doesn't even really like me.*

Rita: Behavior: *Thawing out, laughing more (unless I say anything about things I want to do).*

Feelings: *More relaxed.*

Schema: *??*

Me: Behavior: *Something new comes along. Here we go again.*

Arturo drew a line from the last step to the first step in the sequence. He noticed two important things: (1) His schema that Rita was trying to control him had enormous influence on his reactions and his behavior. (2) He was rebelling. And the more he rebelled, the more Rita clamped down on him. Conversely, the more she clamped down, the more he wanted to rebel.

When you've filled in the last of your sequence, the one that leads back to where things start over, your map of the system is complete. Now, just draw an arrow from the last step right back to the first to form the circle. If you haven't already gotten feedback, this is a good time to take your map to your partner. Use the opportunity to correct some of your assumptions about your partner's thoughts and feelings, as well as your own schemas. Does your partner see steps in the sequence that you've missed? If you can agree, go ahead and add them. Emphasize to your partner that system analysis is the opposite of blame. It is an explanation of how *both* of you have gotten trapped in a pattern that's hurtful.

Intervening in Your System

Before attempting to intervene in your system, two important principles have to be emphasized.

1. The principle of personal responsibility. This is extremely simple, yet crucial to getting out of your system trap. You are responsible for fixing your own pain and meeting your own needs. Your partner is not responsible for changing so that you are in less pain or your needs are better met. That's your job. No one knows your needs better than you, no one is in a better position to appreciate how you feel than you are. Love and relationship do not obligate your partner to solve your problems.

A hard-to-face truth is that the amount of support, appreciation, and help you are now getting is all you can get, given the strategies you are now using. The only way you can get more support, appreciation, or help is to change what *you* are doing. In your relationship, by definition, you are getting everything you can get until *you* make some change in your approach and response to your partner.

2. The principle of 100 percent responsibility. Each person in a relationship is 100 percent responsible for the outcome of all interactions. If you don't like how an interaction is going, or how it typically turns out, you bear the entire responsibility for altering what you do so that both your behavior and the outcome can be different.

Here's how the two principles translate into actual practice. Walter and Jim are struggling with a pursuer-distancer system. Walter is a civil engineer, and he expects Jim to accompany him on weekends when he inspects buildings in progress. Walter expresses his need by accusing Jim of never spending time with him. The result is that Jim at first agrees and then ends up canceling at the last minute. This infuriates Walter, who attacks Jim for being irresponsible and not making their relationship a high enough priority.

The principle of personal responsibility suggests that Walter is entirely responsible for his own needs and feelings. If he's missing Jim and wants to spend more time with him, then he'll either have to schedule more interesting things for the weekend or ask Jim in a way that feels more inviting. The principle of 100 percent responsibility indicates that Walter really has the job of changing the outcome. Maybe Walter is going to have to do active listening to find out Jim's needs and wants in the relationship. Maybe Walter will have to include some of those desires in the weekend plan or negotiate a compromise. The specifics aren't important. What does matter is that Walter has to accept responsibility for how the weekends go for both of them.

Here are some beginning steps for the process of changing your system.

1. Use the active listening process to explore your partner's feelings and needs.

2. Write a brief script to check out any major schemas about your partner that are influencing your behavior. Show the map of your system to your partner to verify any judgments about you that you have projected onto her or him.

3. Do an exercise of accurate empathy to soften one or more of your negative schemas.

4. Now look at your schema map. Where can you intervene? Where is the place where it would be easiest to change your behavior? This is often toward the beginning of a cycle, before the pain has had much chance to escalate, or at the end when things are cooling down. In the pursuer-distancer example in figure 1, there are two places where partner B might try to intervene. One is early in the escalation sequence when B is first feeling hurt and starting to withdraw. There, an attempt at active listening and negotiation might be extremely helpful. A second point is after partner A is making guilty attempts to compensate for the rage. Here it might be possible for B to do an accurate empathy exercise to soften his judgments and then initiate a problem-solving conversation.

Returning for a moment to the case of Arturo, it's possible to analyze the system again for a place to intervene. Using the principle that it's easier to intervene toward the beginning or toward the end of a cycle, Arturo might consider trying one of the following.

1. At the point early on where he starts to rebel and "go all out" for his new interests, Arturo might initiate active listening to explore Rita's concerns. That process could lead to some form of compromise that takes account of both partners' needs. Arturo might also explore his perception that Rita is afraid with an accurate empathy exercise.

2. Arturo could refrain from baiting Rita with information designed to provoke her jealousy.

3. Arturo's "trying to be good" behavior is exactly what leads to the next round of compulsive involvements. He psychologically suffocates by attempting to be and do only what Rita wants and then overcorrects by finding an interesting new activity that also serves as a form of rebellion. An alternative would be to work out an arrangement with Rita where each of them plans time for independent activities. Arturo may also need to explore with Rita things he would like to change at home. Outside activities might be slightly less alluring if he could assert more directly some of his day-to-day needs with Rita (see chapter 12, "Being Assertive: Asking for What You Want").

Sometimes open communication isn't the answer in a systems problem. The caretaker of a wild child may need to set limits about his or her giving or allow the wild child to experience the consequences of his or her behavior. And, on the other side, a rebel may need to explore healthier ways of defining his or her autonomy, setting limits, and protecting his or her psychological territory.

The kind of intervention very much depends on what you're doing that doesn't work. Clearly, more of the same is merely adding fuel to the fire. The answer is a *new response* (but not another aversive strategy) that stimulates new responses on the part of your partner. If you're struggling to find a point of intervention or a new behavior to try, consult your partner. Ask her or him for help. Your partner, who may know as much about the system as you do, could be an excellent resource for making a design for change. If you're still stumped, it might be helpful to consult a family systems therapist who can offer some expert help in making systemic changes.

Reciprocal Reinforcement

Time has a tendency to erode levels of pleasure and satisfaction in even the best relationships. In the beginning it's exciting just to be together. Over the course of months or years, episodes of conflict, the scars of anger, and a natural entropy all conspire to leave partners less willing to give and nurture each other.

There is a way to reverse this process. *Reciprocal reinforcement* encourages each partner to give more of what he or she believes is rewarding to the other person. Tell your partner about this exercise, and suggest that you do it together. Here are the seven steps.

1. Independently (without consulting each other) refine a list of five things that you could do that would be rewarding or nurturing to your partner. Forget the grand gestures, the expensive jewelry, the custom kitchen cabinets. Choose small items—none of them should take you more than an hour to set up or be very expensive. But they should all be things that past experience has taught you feel good to your partner.

Try to make at least some of the items ones that you can repeat. You can only buy something once, but you can give a massage any number of times.

2. Don't tell each other what's on your respective lists. Just do them for one week. Try to do each item at least once. Avoid fanfare or calling attention to the fact that you're doing something nice. Be very low key. Try not to talk about it.

3. At the end of a week share your lists. Each of you can talk about your experience. Give feedback. Describe what felt good and mention (without blame) what may not have felt quite as rewarding.

4. Drop any items from the list that didn't work all that well. And get two to three suggestions from your partner for things that she or he finds nurturing and would like added to your list. Your partner should do the same.

5. Now continue the program for a second week. Do each item on your list at least once. Plan ahead. Make time for the things you've chosen to do.

6. At the beginning of the third week have another feedback session. Pay attention to the items your partner responded to most. These are *high-quality reinforcers*—for whatever reason, they are especially nurturing to your partner. Do these items have anything in common? Do they have to do with physical touch? Do they lessen the workload? Do they involve food? Some special recreation? Using what you've learned about the high-quality reinforcers, add two more items to your list and surprise your partner with them during the next week.

7. By the beginning of the fourth week you may start to notice a qualitative change in your relationship. Both of you may be more spontaneously affectionate, more open, and having more fun together. There may be less conflict and anger. The goal now is to maintain the program and the good feelings. Continue as you have been. Attempt to do at least four to five items from the list each week. Add one or two new items. And get new ideas from your partner, but only things *you* want to do. Don't allow yourself to feel pressure to do something that doesn't feel good. And try not to keep a ledger sheet—charting the relative amount each of you gives to the other. That way leads to hurt and bitterness. This isn't a matter of exact exchange. Rather, it is a process of building more giving and generosity into your relationship. When you measure the giving, it spoils the gift.

After discussing it with his wife, Bill decided to try the reciprocal reinforcement program. Here's what happened.

1. He started brainstorming things that Susan might appreciate. Here was Bill's list: Do the dishes, plant her tulips, neck and shoulder massage, affectionate hugs, expressing appreciation, going to one of her foreign movies, dangly earrings, drive out to the headlands where we

can hike, dinner at Solerno's, doing the bills myself, visiting her mother with her, encouraging her to go to dance class while I take care of kids, take care of kids while she has lunch with Sarah, let her take a break when I get home from work, bring home a fudge sundae from Bott's, suggest a walk, get one of those Italian salad bowls she's been talking about, flowers.

Bill discarded items that took excessive time or effort, and decided on the following five: massage, salad bowl, encouraging dance class, visiting her mother with her, expressing appreciation.

2. Bill was able to do each item except the salad bowl in the first week. He expressed an appreciation at least three or four times.

3. He and Susan shared their lists at the end of the week. He was surprised at one or two of the things Susan had selected and actually hadn't been aware of her doing some of them. To his further surprise, Susan had not really wanted him to accompany her to see her mother, but had been extremely delighted with Bill's support for taking dance class.

4. Bill dropped "visiting her mother" from his list, but added two suggestions from Susan: to get a reading light that won't keep her awake at night and give more hugs that weren't specifically sexual. Susan included some of Bill's suggestions on her own list.

5. For the second week, Bill stayed conscious of his list and made plans for when he would do several of the items, and he finally did get the Italian salad bowl.

6. At the start of the third week, Bill and Susan had another feedback session. When he later analyzed the items that Susan seemed to enjoy most, they appeared to involve either physical nurturing (massage, hugs) or helping her find time for her own pursuits. This gave him ideas for a couple of "surprise items": drawing her a hot bubble bath and getting the kids into bed while she relaxed.

7. Susan and Bill agreed that the whole tone of their relationship was changing. There was a new sense of cheerfulness and a higher than normal willingness to help, plus they were feeling more sexually open than they had since the children were born. Bill continued the program, adding and changing items over the weeks. He made a real effort to keep in mind his weekly plan and commitment to be more giving with Susan.

9

Being a Father: Raising Your Children

Adam had remained at work late preparing a brief. His boys were playing with Legos in their bedroom when he finally arrived home. He kissed them. He tickled Evan, his youngest, and held Ben upside down. In a moment he made his way to the kitchen for a highball. He said hello to his wife and carried the drink to the den, where he sank gratefully into the sofa. He scanned a few channels with the remote and settled in with a comedy special. An hour later he kissed the children in their beds and read them a story about trains.

Adam's parenting consisted of a total of fifteen minutes—four kisses, three tickles, one story, and a pretend bungie jump. How Adam fathers his kids isn't unusual. In fact, it's the norm. A major study found that fathers spend an average of seven minutes per day relating to each of their children. By and large, men spend more time showering and shaving than they do talking to their kids. Another study found that 52 percent of men are almost totally unavailable to their children. An estimated 60 percent of all children born since 1987 will not be living with or supported by their birth fathers by the time they reach adolescence. Incredibly, a majority of fathers give almost no time or emotional support. It's no wonder that so many people experience a profound father hunger and continue to crave, perhaps for a lifetime, the attention and approval of a caring male.

There are reasons why men spend so little time with their kids. Frankly, it is a low priority. Men enjoy challenges—achieving, striving, competing. They enjoy intense diversions and stimulating activities. For many men, kids are not a lot of fun. They require a slower pace of life; an appreciation of small, sweet moments punctuated with repetitive, mundane tasks. Children also need a lot of active giving and nurturance, something men in general get little training for. And to make the time at all interesting for the kids, you need an ability to invent creative play and problem-solving activities. Here again men have little practice with these skills.

If you find yourself pulled away from your children toward more compelling or less emotionally demanding activities, you're absolutely normal. It makes perfect sense. But the fact that it's normal doesn't make it any easier on your kids. They still need you—your time, your support, and your approval. Without you, they cannot possible grow to their full potential.

Life is a balancing act. You need to take care of yourself. And what nourishes you may take some time away from your children. But the same attention that you give to your own needs must be extended to theirs as well. In the same way that you schedule or carve time out for things you enjoy, you need to schedule time with them.

Exercise. For the next week, use the following grid to monitor how much time you spend in active involvement with your children. Make an entry in a time slot only when you are *actively* relating or playing with your child. Write the number of minutes the activity lasted, a brief description of what it was, and the child's name (if you have more than one). Here is an example, followed by an activity grid that you should fill out for each day of the coming week.

Hour	How long?	Activity
7:00 a.m.	15 minutes	Talking with Jordan and Bekah
8:00 a.m.	15 minutes	Talking in car with Bekah
9:00 a.m.		
10:00 a.m.		
11:00 a.m.		
12:00 noon		
1:00 p.m.		
2:00 p.m.		
3:00 p.m.		
4:00 p.m.		
5:00 p.m.	15 minutes	Playing ponies win Bekah
6:00 p.m.	15 minutes	Reading story to Bekah
7:00 p.m.	20 minutes	Bekah to bed, snuggling
8:00 p.m.	15 minutes	Legos with Jordan
9:00 p.m.	15 minutes	Good night talk with Jordan
10:00 p.m.		
11:00 p.m.		

Daily Activity Grid

Hour	How long?	Activity
7:00 a.m.		
8:00 a.m.		
9:00 a.m.		
10:00 a.m.		
11:00 a.m.		
12:00 noon		
1:00 p.m.		
2:00 p.m.		
3:00 p.m.		
4:00 p.m.		
5:00 p.m.		
6:00 p.m.		
7:00 p.m.		
8:00 p.m.		
9:00 p.m.		
10:00 p.m.		
11:00 p.m.		

Use the grid to analyze how much time and what activities you do with each of your children. You may notice some important things. In the case above, for example, more than twice as much private time was spent with Bekah than Jordan. If a pattern like this continues throughout the week, some adjustments might be in order. Notice if the week is uneven. Do you spend a lot of time with kids Wednesday, and then not again till Sunday? Adding a little time in between helps to maintain the sense of consistent attention. If you are a divorced father, this may be especially hard, but sometimes even a phone call or two during the week can help a lot.

Do you need more variety? Might you spend more time talking? Or less time talking while you develop new activities? Do you need more individual time with each child? Do you need to develop a particular shared interest with one or more of your children? Are you home and available when you are awake and active? Do you see your kids only on the weekends? Creating a balance of consistent attention and varied activities is especially hard for every-other-weekend dads.

After you've evaluated the week's child-centered activities, it's time to make a plan. Make copies of the weekly activity grid that follows and schedule time and activities for the next two weeks. This approach may seem mechanical, but scheduling is important. It gives your kids the same priority as all the other activities that you write down in your appointment book or calendar. As you did before, write the activity and the child's name in appropriate boxes on the week's grid. You don't need to indicate how long the activity will take, but it should last long enough to let your child really experience your attention and involvement. Spread activities as much as possible throughout the week. Remember, an activity can be anything from a brief conversation to a three-day fishing trip.

How To Give Your Children Attention

Here are some specific suggestions for giving your children the experience of an involved father.

Notice things. After each period of absence (i.e., when you get up in the morning or get home at night), take a close look at your child. See anything? New scrapes or bruises, a sad expression, nervousness, irritability, special enthusiasm or energy, a new project or involvement? Mention what you see and *ask* about it.

Ask real questions. A real question isn't "Anything new at school, dear?" "How's my girl today?" doesn't make it either. Real questions are specific and built on particular things you know about your child. "How did that pulling block you've been working on go in football practice today?" "How did you feel when it was your turn to read in the circle

Weekly Activity Grid

	Monday	Tuesday	Wednesday	Thursday	Friday	Saturday	Sunday
7:00 a.m.							
8:00 a.m.							
9:00 a.m.							
10:00 a.m.							
11:00 a.m.							
12:00 noon							
1:00 p.m.							
2:00 p.m.							
3:00 p.m.							
4:00 p.m.							
5:00 p.m.							
6:00 p.m.							
7:00 p.m.							
8:00 p.m.							
9:00 p.m.							
10:00 p.m.							
11:00 p.m.							

today?" "Did you and Barbara make a pretend picnic at nursery school today?" Notice that the questions are designed to start a conversation. Keep asking them. Little kids especially may need you to initiate new lines of conversation with new questions. It's work, but it builds closeness.

Listen actively. This means listening with your full attention—not making vague conversation while you're watching Sunday football, not half-listening while you plan your day tomorrow. As you read in chapter 8, "Being Two: Making Partnership Work," active listening involves paraphrasing what someone says. By saying it in your own words you acknowledge that you understand and are paying attention. If you don't fully grasp what your child is telling you, probe, ask questions. "Tell me more about that." "How did that work?" "What did Charlie mean when he said that?" "How did that make you feel?" "Can you describe how it looked?"

Respond to feelings. When your child tells you how he or she feels, that's a signal to pay special attention. Children need to know that their feelings are okay, and that how they feel matters to you. So ask questions about when the feeling started, what it's like, what person or event it seems connected to, how strong it is, and so on.

Don't immediately jump in to fix negative feelings: "Come on, Jim, you can get over that. It's no big deal." Trying to fix it before you really hear and understand the feeling conveys to your child that his or her emotions make you uncomfortable: "Dry those tears, where's that smiling face?" What you say might be sweet and well-intended, but the feeling still needs room to be expressed. So acknowledge the *when* and *what* and *how much* of a feeling before comforting, distracting, or smoothing things out.

Men are particularly prone to discounting feelings. When you discount your child's feelings, you either deny its reality, its validity, or its importance:

"You don't really feel angry at Nana, you're just tired, sweetie." (Denying reality)

"It's stupid to feel so bad about losing a fifty cent keychain." (Denying validity)

"How can you be so scared when I'm right here?" (Denying validity)

"It's a minor glitch. Don't worry. One college turning you down is no big deal." (Denying importance)

Pay attention to your own style of discounting. Nearly every man does it to some extent. What do you say when you're uncomfortable with a child's emotional response? Is there a way you immediately try to suppress or minimize it?

Respond appropriately to pain. Whether your child is in physical or emotional pain, it's the same drill. Assuming it's not a medical crisis, your first job is to soothe and support. You psychologically join your child in the pain (the act of empathy), and acknowledge how bad it feels. You rock, you caress, you reassure, you let your face show your concern.

The eagerness that men feel to fix and protect is natural and adaptive. But with your kids, the natural response isn't the best response. Hold back the impulse to fix it and make it right. Try to postpone problem solving until you've spent time soothing and acknowledging what hurts.

Include physical affection. So many people grow up with fathers who are physically remote. It's a great loss because physical affection is the most direct way to express love to a child. Children believe what a hug says far more than an easy "I love you."

Men tend to withdraw physically from their sons very early. They may continue to hug a daughter; but this, too, often stops in adolescence. There are appropriate ways to give physical affection to children of any age, male or female. It is strongly recommended that you continue to hug your son and hug your daughter, no matter how big they get. Keep the habit up. It only seems awkward when you stop doing it for a while.

Share yourself. More than half of all adults report the feeling that they never really knew their dad. It's nourishing to your children to get them some age-appropriate understanding of how you feel. "I've been feeling pretty sad that Grandma's sick." "I've been very excited and happy about the promotion at work. I'll be able to do more interesting things." "It hurts my feelings when you say, 'You're stupid,' Daddy." "It scares me when you climb that far off the ground. I like being here with you. It's fun for me when we do things together."

You can model openness for your children, particularly your sons, by allowing them a glimpse of your reactions. It's okay to tell kids in a straightforward way that something hurts or saddens you or that you're disappointed or thrilled or anything in between.

Attend to each child individually. If you have more than one child, you may find yourself relating to them as "the children," a fused group where each child's identity gets a little lost. Every child needs his or her own unique relationship to dad, and they each need time alone with you to develop that relationship. For this reason, it's recommended that you regularly schedule one-on-one experiences with each of your children.

Nightly Ritual

Decide which strategies for giving your children attention you wish to build into a nightly ritual with your children. Write them down on the left side of the grid that follows.

Nightly Ritual Activity Grid

Activity	Day 1	Day 2	Day 3	Day 4	Day 5	Day 6	Day 7

Now, over the next week, monitor how many of the items in your evening ritual you've remembered to do. Put a check mark in the box for each item you remembered to do on day one, day two, day three, and so on. By the end of the week, your communication ritual with your kids should be starting to get automatic. And that's the point: to make this new, richer form of communication habitual.

Bill, a divorced dad, had his son Thursday and Friday nights each week. He decided on the following evening ritual when his son stayed with him: (1) specific questions, (2) "spontaneous" hugs, (3) reading a story, and (4) "snuggling" for five or ten minutes while his son got sleepy. By the end of the second week, his ritual felt easy and automatic.

Building Self-Esteem

For a little while, you are the whole world to your kids, and everything they learn comes from you. You show them who they are. You are the mirror in which they see themselves. What they come to believe about themselves, whatever sense of worth and self-acceptance they attain, develops from the mirror of your reactions.

Because your children depend on you for healthy self-esteem, it makes sense for you to be both active and deliberate in building their sense of worth. The following eight suggestions can help you create a positive mirror to reflect back to your children their personal qualities.

1. Make a list of positive qualities for each of your children. Include all their abilities, talents, skills, interests, and so on. Choose items from each of the following areas:

- Physical appearance
- How he or she relates to others
- Personality
- Things he or she has learned to do
- Things he or she has learned to overcome
- Positive changes he or she has made
- Mental ability
- Physical ability
- Other things you really like about your child

This is an opportunity to focus on what a child does right instead of wrong. Check with your spouse, your child's grandparents, your friends, and even your child's friends, to find additional items for this list.

2. From the list of positive qualities, select at least three or four that you wish to praise frequently. Repetition, by itself, creates belief. What your child hears often from you will tend to sink in. Helpful rule: The

more specific you make your praise, the better. "You've showed a lot of hard work and staying power on that relief map you made from school," is much better praise then "You're a hard worker sometimes, Johnny."

Now resolve to find something on your list to praise *every day*. Add this to the nightly ritual you developed earlier. It's probably the biggest thing you can do to strengthen your child's self-worth.

3. Now make a list of the negative behavior patterns that you are aware of in your child. Write them below in the column on the left.

Now look at each negative item and analyze what need is being expressed by that behavior. How is your child trying to reduce his or her level of pain or get something positive with this behavior? Do some thinking about this. All behavior is an attempt to cope—to stop pain or increase feelings of well-being. That's the point of everything your child does. Write in the need that this negative behavior expresses in the appropriate box.

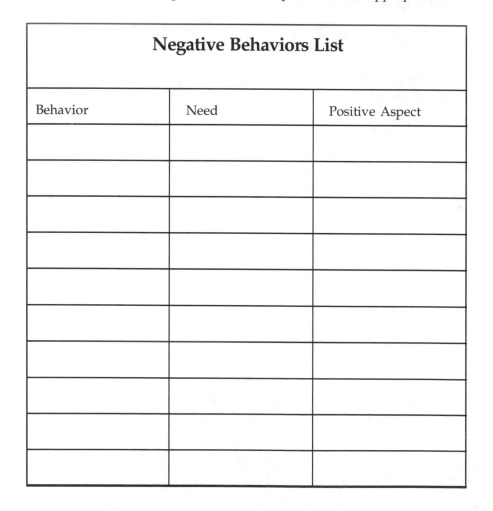

Negative Behaviors List		
Behavior	Need	Positive Aspect

Now look at the negative items from another angle. What positive aspect is being expressed by this behavior? Viewed from one perspective, your child's behavior may be stubborn, but from another, it shows a tenacity and strength of will. The latter is a positive attribute. Suppose you listed a negative behavior such as isolation—a child tends to withdraw to his or her room. The positive side here is that such a child has the capacity to entertain him or herself; there's a high level of independence. Almost every negative behavior has a corresponding positive aspect. Go ahead and write that aspect down in the space provided.

4. Select the two or three negative behaviors that occur most frequently. Every time you discipline or set limits regarding this specific behavior, resolve to mention its positive aspect. This way, disciplining doesn't have to be a wholly negative experience. Making a commitment to acknowledge the positive side of difficult behavior will also keep you from indulging in judgments and blame. "Your castle is creative and beautiful, and I know you don't want to clean it up. But it's all over the living room, Bill. It has to be put away now." "I know you're a good driver with good reflexes, but I don't want to see or hear of you speeding, ever. Are we clear about that, Jim?" "You've had a terrific time at the pajama party, Julie. I like how well you get along with your friends. But you need to consider us and quiet this down now."

5. Reinforce all positive behavior with praise. Never miss an opportunity to express appreciation for things your child does well. This is the best method for shaping desired behavior. Praise is a hundred times more effective than punishment, and it strengthens the father-child relationship, rather than straining it. What behaviors do you wish to increase and reinforce? List them on the grid that follows.

Each day over the next week make a check in the appropriate box if you are able to praise the positive behavior.

The flip side of this is to lay off of accusing and blaming when negative behavior occurs. Blaming usually tends to be in the form of an identity attack: "You always...You never...That's stupid...You're lazy...That's crazy." Notice that blame overgeneralizes the negative behavior and makes it sound like a basic flaw in character. What your child really hears is the message "You're bad, and I don't like you." This is devastating to self-esteem. The more you accuse and blame, the more you undermine your child's belief in his or her own worth.

6. Be there when your child shines. Your child needs a dad to witness his or her achievements. When your child has an opportunity to demonstrate a skill or ability, whatever it is, make sure you're there to see it. Then talk about it. Relive it. Appreciate it.

Simon spent most of each Saturday with his daughter. Then she'd usually stay the night. But he also took her to skating practice on Tuesday, and always attended the competitions. He was there when she fell down

Behaviors To Praise							
Behavior	Day 1	Day 2	Day 3	Day 4	Day 5	Day 6	Day 7

and when she won a bronze. They spent a lot of time talking about her performances.

7. It's also important for a dad to promote skill acquisition—taking your daughter to gym class, your son to softball practice. This kind of involvement tells a child that you're not just interested in the finished product, but support each step of learning and growing.

8. Support your children socially. Know their friends. Your children are proud of you and proud to have your attention when their friends are present. They want to show you off. Let them.

Teaching Values

One of your main tasks as a father is to communicate values and teach your children basic rules of survival in the world. Some men become so preoccupied with this task that it transcends the equally important job of providing nurturance and support. They're so busy enforcing standards of behavior that they fail to provide their children the approval and acceptance that they desperately need. You may get so focused on teaching your son the principles of hard work and striving that you fail to notice when he hurts or feels scared or just plain isn't cut out for the task you've set for him. It's another kind of balance that you have to work on: weighing the need for support with the need for discipline or achievement.

Positive feedback is the most effective way of reinforcing your values. When you convey your values and rules for living with the context of a close, healthy bond, your child wants to imitate you. Your behavior and values become a model for how to act and what to believe.

Values that are communicated and reinforced through fear and punishment very often never get integrated. Psychologists call it *introjection*— the process by which the values and beliefs of a parent become part of the child's own ethical system. A child who feels close to you wants to stand in your likeness. A child who is afraid of you acts appropriately only as long as you're there to watch. Compliance is skin-deep. Left alone he or she ignores or even rebels against the rules and values that mean so much to you.

Physical punishment, in particular, doesn't work to instill values. One researcher who studied the moral development of children found that children who feared physical punishment tended to have less guilt, were less willing to accept blame, were less resistant to temptation, and had fewer internal behavioral controls than children who were not physically punished. He concluded that corporeal punishment "may even prevent the development of internal controls." A child may actually feel that it's okay to misbehave so long as he or she is willing to take the consequences of being hit. The evidence is persuasive: don't rely on slapping or hitting to make a child adhere to your values and rules. It won't work. (Hoffman, D. "Moral Development," in *Carmichael's Manual of Child Psychology*).

Values Need To Be Flexible

What you want in terms of behavior and achievement has to fit the child you have. You're not going to make a hyperactive kid into a studious desk jockey. A shy, socially awkward child isn't going to be a take-charge leader. Some children are never going to achieve at sports. And some are rarely going to achieve at anything *but* sports. Some children are extremely spontaneous and impulsive; others are careful and compulsive. Your child's limits and potentials have a lot to do with innate wiring and basic constitutional tendencies. Don't push the river. Set standards and goals that are reasonable for *this* child's temperament and pattern of abilities.

The Narcissistic Father

The narcissistic dad requires that his children (particularly his sons) excel and stand out so that he can vicariously experience the son's excellence as his own. Conversely, the son's struggles and failures also become the father's own, so that he rejects the child in order to distance himself from sharing in failure.

Many men experience this tendency. Your children represent you, they reflect who you are and what you have given them. When they shine, they polish your image. When they screw up, they diminish your own sense of worth. If your son fails to achieve or even pursue something you want for him, a very natural response is to get angry and withdraw. He's breaking the rules, he's not the son you wanted, not the son you can show off and be proud of. He's someone you can't identify with, perhaps can't even understand. This is when you face one of the hardest tasks of a father—letting go of the ideal and facing the real.

Realistic Expectations

There are four steps to developing realistic expectations for your particular child.

1. Listen to his or her experience. Ask why following the rules is difficult. Find out what's getting in the way of a particular desired behavior. Identify his or her reluctance or difficulty with the goals you've set. Try to experience the problem from your child's perspective; see it through his or her eyes. When you really understand what happens at the moments when a child goes off track, when he or she blows it, you're in a much better position to develop realistic rules and expectations.

2. Find out who he or she is (versus who you want him or her to be). The next page is blank, with a line down the middle. On the left side write the ideal qualities and traits you want for your child. If your child was perfect, what would he or she do, how would he or she act? List as many things as you can think of. Now, on the right side of the line, describe the positive qualities of your own child. You can use the list you developed in the "Building Self-Esteem" section of this chapter. Add any new items you can think of. Now, take a look at both sides of the page. Are there any matches? Run a line between the matched qualities. Now look at the disparities. What positive qualities does your child have that you didn't list for the ideal? Finding a way to appreciate some of these qualities while letting go of the ideal traits not reflected in your child's character can be an incredibly difficult task. Try to choose at least two areas where you can modify some of your expectations to better align with the *real* abilities and limitations of the kid you have.

Consider the case of William. His daughter was boy crazy, spent most of her time in the mall, and was pulling Cs and an occasional D in her high school classes. William, who was a college professor, placed high value on academic achievement and had struggled for years with his daughter's boredom with school. When William looked at the real versus

"Qualities" Chart

Ideal Qualities	My Child's Positive Qualities

the ideal (see his "Qualities" chart), he recognized that his daughter had a strong interest in fashion and modeling. She even put on mini fashion shows at home with some of her friends. William decided to send her to modeling school and stop beating her up for thinking that Steinbeck is a cosmetic firm.

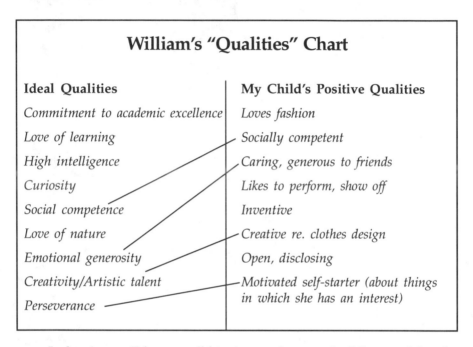

William's "Qualities" Chart

Ideal Qualities	My Child's Positive Qualities
Commitment to academic excellence	*Loves fashion*
Love of learning	*Socially competent*
High intelligence	*Caring, generous to friends*
Curiosity	*Likes to perform, show off*
Social competence	*Inventive*
Love of nature	*Creative re. clothes design*
Emotional generosity	*Open, disclosing*
Creativity/Artistic talent	*Motivated self-starter (about things*
Perseverance	*in which she has an interest)*

Joshua's son, Ed, spent all his time and money building model rockets. When Joshua was in high school, he had dates every night of the week and lettered in three different sports. He was a legendary defensive end for a team that eventually won a state championship. Not only was Ed disinterested in sports, but he was also something of a reclusive nerd who enjoyed tinkering a whole lot more than he enjoyed people. A lot of the qualities Joshua listed as ideal simply had to be thrown out when he realistically considered his boy's capabilities. Except competence. Joshua realized that Ed *was* competent, in science and engineering. In order to show that he valued what Ed did well, Joshua began spending time talking to his son about rockets, telemetry, aerodynamics, and so forth. He was still concerned about Ed's isolation, so he established a new, more realistic goal that his boy would join the science club at school. By letting go of the ideal, Joshua was able to make substantial changes in the way he related to Ed.

3. Share your new, more realistic expectations and secure agreement from your child. The main task here is to say what your new goals are, clearly and explicitly. Get some feedback. Find out if your child accepts your new expectations. If not, negotiate something that you both can live with.

4. Reinforce new expectations.   When your child moves in the desired direction, be certain to reward his efforts. "I'm really glad you checked in with the science club today. Even though no one was there, it was a first step." "I'm excited about your making an appointment at the modeling school. I'd like to help you buy an outfit so you'll feel really confident on your first day." Praise, attention, favors, and gifts are all highly rewarding.

Anger and Children

Anger harms children. It undermines their sense of worth and makes them afraid to express feelings and needs. Significant parental anger can stunt and cripple your children's emerging sense of self. Anger often conveys the message "You're bad, don't be you." And a child takes this message to heart.

A dad who is frequently angry tells his kids something about their basic identity. Each outburst adds to the perception that they are unacceptable and wrong. They have failed Dad, they are displeasing to him. And so grows the belief that they are flawed human beings who will always be unworthy in their father's eyes.

Don't kid yourself about the effects of male anger on children. It frightens. It inhibits. It *always* leaves scars.

Children as Stressors

Men are strong. Men carry the weight. That's what the culture says. Those are the rules most men go by.

But the rules of masculinity are a burden that create enormous stress. The tiredness at day's end has seeped into your pores. At times you feel the deep frustration of what you want to do but can't and the fear of a future that may be beyond your control. You come home with all of this, needing to put it down for a while and rest.

But it doesn't work that way. Now your children need you. They are clamoring for attention. They are fighting or sulking or not doing their chores or homework. The detritus of their lives clutters everything and leaves no space for you. You crave a moment's privacy, but there is none.

This is the point where many fathers start to blame and bark. They cope with the combined stress of work and kids by discharging it in the form of anger. They use anger-triggering thoughts, such as the following, to "let out steam."

- They're doing this deliberately.
- They don't care about anything but themselves.
- They're lazy...smart alecs...irresponsible...selfish...
- They should never...

The stress plus trigger thoughts ignite a lot of misdirected and damaging anger. There are two ways to stop it: (1) change your thinking about your children, and (2) change to more effective limit setting.

Trigger Thoughts

The first step is to identify what you tend to say to yourself when you're angry at your children. For one week, fill in the following log each time you find yourself angry with the kids.

Read through chapter 13, "Being Strong: Controlling Your Anger," particularly the sections on "Trigger Thoughts" and "Controlling Trigger Thoughts." Do you typically use blamers or shoulds? Do some of your trigger thoughts involve global labels ("She's lazy"), mind reading ("He's doing that deliberately to annoy me"), or magnification ("He never helps around the house, he's totally uninvolved")? Which types of trigger thoughts produce the most angry behavior on your part?

This is a good time to do some thinking about why children act the way they do. Your children's behavior has absolutely nothing to do with labels such as "bad," "lazy," "selfish," or any other global explanation. They behave the way they do because they have been rewarded and reinforced to act that way. They have literally been *taught* to do the annoying things that you want them to stop doing. *As a father, you are responsible for your children's behavior.* If you want it to change, you will have to develop ways to reward new, more appropriate behavior. And anger, as you probably already know, is a very ineffective way of influencing and shaping kids to change.

Now it's time to do some work on your trigger thoughts so you can take responsibility for what your kids do, rather than slipping into blame. The exercise on "Controlling Trigger Thoughts" in chapter 13 is designed to help you modify some of the thoughts that put you on the war path. Each time you feel angry during the next week, fill out a copy of the form in Chapter 13 "Analyzing Trigger Thoughts," filling in your trigger thought and rewriting it in such a way that it is absolutely accurate, without any form of exaggeration. Get rid of the global labels, the magnification, and any sort of unsubstantiated mind reading. Write down only what is unassailably true. Finally, write a brief statement describing your plan to reinforce new behavior in your child. What can *you* do to help your child act more appropriately?

If you do this exercise faithfully for a week, it is guaranteed to help you reduce your anger. Here's something else that may also help. Look

Trigger Thoughts Log

Trigger Sitatuion	Trigger Thoughts	My Behavior

at the list of coping thoughts below. Choose one or two that appeal to you and that you sense might be useful when you're starting to feel angry at your kids.

- _____ is doing the best he or she can.

- _____ is behaving exactly how he or she is being rewarded to behave. It's not his or her fault.

- I'm responsible for my child's behavior. I'll need to reinforce and reward the behavior I want.

- Instead of blowing up, I'm going to find out why he or she acts this way.

- I can set limits with real consequences and stick with them. I don't need to blow up.

- Anger is hurting my kids. I have the choice not to blow up.

- Kids do what they need to do, not what they should do.

- The kids will change only when they're reinforced to change. Anger isn't doing it.

- I'm not going to assume that I know why kids do things. I'll ask and check it out.

- Write the coping thought down, put it on your shaving or dresser mirror, and read it daily.

Effective Limit Setting

Supportive limit setting is far more effective than repeated anger episodes at influencing your children's behavior. There are five components to supportive limit setting. When all five are used in combination, they will greatly reduce conflicts with your kids.

1. Describe the behavior. Tell your child in a simple, nonpejorative way the behavior you want him to change or stop. "Billy, you're leaving a lot of heavy stereo components on the glass coffee table." "Martha, you're trying to make cupcakes while we're in the middle of putting dinner together." "Jim, you haven't been doing the dishes on your night." It's very important not to use language that conveys a putdown or in any way judges the child for the behavior.

2. State your reason for the behavior change. "There's a real possibility that glass table could break." "It's making it very hard to cook while you're doing the cupcakes." "The dishes are piling up, and we don't have enough for the next meal."

3. Acknowledge your child's feelings. Try to express your understanding of why your child is doing what he or she does. "I know it's a convenient space to put things." "I know the cupcakes are an exciting project and it's hard to wait till after dinner." "I know it's depressing to have to come in here and face this pile, particularly when you've spent so long on your homework tonight." By acknowledging your child's feelings, you make it clear that you empathize with and understand how he or she could act that way. Try not to skip this step. It transforms limit setting from a finger shaking, sometimes punitive exercise, into an opportunity to show your kids that you appreciate what it's like to be them.

4. Make a clear statement of what is expected. "Please keep anything heavy off the glass table." "We need you to wait till after dinner for a major baking project." "The dishes have to be done by bedtime on your night." The key here is to be specific and definite.

5. State the consequences. Ideally, you will develop both positive and negative consequences to reinforce the new behavior that you're asking for. "If you want, I'll move a shelf in here to put that stereo stuff on. But if you put heavy stuff on that table again, I'm going to dump it all on your bed." "Tell me about your next baking project, and we'll figure a good time for it. But if you interrupt dinner again, I'll take your stuff out of the oven, and we'll have to leave it half-baked." "I'm going to move a radio in here for you to listen to while you do the dishes. But if you skip your dish night, I think that warrants forfeiting half your allowance."

Prepare these steps in advance when you need to set a limit. Giving some thought to each component of what you'll say may help you to avoid hurtful comments. There's a good chance your kids will respond well to this approach. If they try to argue or resist your limit setting, it's suggested that you respond by telling them that the issue isn't open for discussion at the moment. If they want to suggest a specific alternative, they can discuss it with you at a later time.

For Fathers of Sons

Joseph Campbell, Robert Bly, and others have pointed out that a boy between the ages of twelve and eighteen goes through a spiritual or creative awakening, as well as a sexual awakening. Society acknowledges only the sexual awakening and frustrates both.

Many tribal societies mark the transition from boy to man with some kind of initiation ceremony. Pale reflections of these ceremonies survive today in a Jewish boy's bar mitzvah or the Catholic rite of confirmation.

If you have a son aged twelve to fourteen, consider having some sort of initiation ceremony for him to welcome him into the world of men. One way to do this is to have a small, select party of family and friends, including especially the important men in a boy's life: father, grandfathers, friends' fathers, uncles, older cousins, teachers, scout masters, coaches, and so on. Include only those men who understand the value of initiation and are willing to participate fully.

When everyone is assembled, the boy's mother or another significant woman in his life should say farewell and give him a parting gift. The idea is that he is leaving the world of women and children.

Then the men should take the boy to another place—a different room or better yet, a different building. There the boy should endure some kind of symbolic trial or task to prove that he is ready to be a man. This trial needn't be embarrassing or difficult, but it should be meaningful. You might lead him to the men's place blindfolded, requiring him to trust his fellow men. He might need to jump over a threshold or climb something or lift something heavy.

Then gather in a circle with the boy in the center. You might do something to symbolize togetherness, like holding hands, passing a candle, tying yarn from wrist to wrist, or getting in a huddle.

Each man gives the boy a gift. The gifts should be small, simple, symbolic, or natural: a polished stone, an arrowhead, a leatherbound diary, a hand-carved figure, a fountain pen, grandpa's watch, a poem, a treasured pocketknife, a special kind of hat, and so on. This is not the time for computers or motorbikes. It's nice if one of the gifts is something that can be worn throughout the rest of the party, as a sign that the boy is now a man.

As each man gives the boy his gift, he welcomes the boy to manhood, praises the boy for one of his good qualities, and gives him some advice about how to be a good man. For example, you might say, "I want you to have this watch as a symbol that you are grown up now and your time is more and more your own. I like how you figure out how to do things and how interested you are in how things work. My advice for being a man is to also figure out how things feel to others."

If your son is not completely overwhelmed at this point, he might say something to the men that he has prepared to say.

Then all the men rejoin the women and children. Throughout the rest of the party, your son is treated with honor and respect, like an adult man. He might sit at the head of the table, carve the turkey, cut the cake, be asked his opinion, play host as guests depart, and so on.

These are just suggestions. The important thing is to publicly acknowledge that your son is going through important changes, that he isn't a child anymore, that he is a man with the support of other men, and that being a man is a good and valuable thing to be.

IV

What Does It Feel Like?

This section covers emotional and physical health. Look here for basic techniques for:

Assessing and identifying your feelings
Expressing feelings clearly and accurately
Asking for what you want assertively and fairly
Controlling your anger
Taking care of your body

10

Being Aware: Clarifying Your Feelings

Do you feel your feelings?

What a stupid question!

It's a contradiction, isn't it? After all, if you're having a feeling, then it seems obvious that you must be feeling it.

But often it fails to work that way. Many feelings never reach the level of awareness. They exist in a psychological netherworld, somewhere outside your conscious experience.

This chapter is all about bringing these vague, unacknowledged feelings into fuller awareness. Knowing the full scope of what you feel is important because:

1. Feelings that you don't face can influence and even control you in hidden ways.

2. Feelings that you don't face can undermine your physical and emotional well-being.

3. The ability to experience and express negative feelings helps you keep your relationship healthy by identifying conflicts, promoting openness about things that hurt, and creating the opportunity for problem solving.

4. Having full awareness of your positive feelings gives you more ways to express your love.

Three Stories

John

John's son, Ronnie, was 15 and had become extremely preoccupied with skateboarding. John referred to Ronnie's friends as "skateboard bums" and set strict limits about how late he could stay out with them. When his boy skateboarded in the kitchen, doing flips, jumps, and wheelies, John found himself in a rage.

Anger is easy to feel. Sometimes, in fact, it was the only thing John could feel. He suspected there were other feelings underneath, but it was very difficult to experience what they were when the anger rushed so quickly to the surface.

Because John sensed that his relationship to Ronnie was deteriorating, he was motivated to do some work to explore his feelings. Using exercises that you will encounter later in this chapter, John discovered that below his anger lay four very powerful feelings that were affecting his behavior toward his son.

First, John became aware of sadness. He felt a sense of a lost camaraderie: it hurt to remember the years of affection and hugs and the easy way his son had once confided in him. Mixed in with the sadness was a sense of loneliness. John felt cast out of his son's life.

As John continued to think about his son, he also realized that he felt oddly anxious. Sitting in a room with Ronnie, he often experienced him as a stranger. The anxiety seemed to come from not understanding how to talk to a kid he no longer knew. And there was another kind of anxiety. He felt it knotting up his gut. It was a sense that his boy was going down the wrong road, heading for a life without discipline or goals.

John was also aware of guilt. Five years earlier he had become part owner of a tourist railroad, and the venture had taken a lot of time and energy. Maybe he had just not been there enough. The issue of the railroad also brought up feelings of hurt. Ronnie had condemned the railroad as a grown-up's toy. "It doesn't help anybody. People are starving out there, people are living in doorways in cardboard boxes, and you're playing with trains." His son's judgment felt like a punch in the stomach. And he realized that, more than anything, his anger at Ronnie had been an attempt to cover that hurt.

John's new awareness of his feelings made it possible to express a great deal more than anger at his son. Their next conversation went half the night and changed profoundly how they viewed each other.

A week after his conversation with Ronnie, John began to explore his feelings about his daughter. Enid was 12 and for the past several years had spent much time in her room doing computer games and math puzzles. When forced to interact, she was cooperative but remote. Always she was the first one excused from the table at dinner so she could slip away to the seclusion of her hiding place. As he walked by Enid's room, John often hesitated; he felt a sense that he should do or say something. But stopping in to say hello was an exercise in monosyllables. "Fine...I'm fine...Okay...Thanks...Yeah...Right...Fine...Bye."

As John started to pay attention to what he felt, the first thing that emerged was sadness. He missed Enid's sparkle and laughter. Just a few years ago she had seemed so much more open. With the sadness came strong feelings of love. He suddenly wanted to hug her and express how incredibly precious she was. He kept thinking about her, shut in the room, cut off from the family. The more he pictured her bent at her desk, absorbed in the puzzles, the more he felt a sense of alarm. Something felt wrong. Something had changed. He kept imagining her at the desk. She looked injured to him. And that awareness was really frightening.

John first took his feelings to his wife, and then the two of them sat down with Enid. She was initially resistant, but admitted that something was scaring her. It took more than two weeks of support and reassurance before Enid told her parents about a neighbor who was molesting her.

John's discovery of his own feelings was an important first step in changing his relationships to both of his children. And his awareness literally rescued his daughter from two years of terror and ongoing abuse.

Sid

Sid often responded with clipped irritation when his wife asked him to do something. She complained that he was "touchy as a pit bull with a toothache," defensive rather than helpful, and was hard to discuss or play with. While Sid knew he felt uncomfortable with his wife's requests, he wasn't sure what really was happening on an emotional level. Using the exercises in this chapter, he discovered some important things about his response to his wife.

Sid visualized a situation in which his wife asked him to mow the lawn. As he relived the scene, he was surprised to recognize feelings of shame. He had the strong sense that he was doing something wrong. The feeling was familiar, like an old wound that was continually reopened. Eventually he connected this feeling with memories of growing up. Both of his parents had been very critical, and just about everything he did had been labeled stupid, incompetent, and wrong.

In addition to shame, Sid was aware of an odd sense of being trapped—a feeling that he had no choice but to do whatever his wife wanted him to do. Denying her request felt like committing a sin or breaking a basic law of marriage.

There was also a layer of hurt: he sensed her disapproval. He imagined that she judged him as lazy, as not pulling his own weight. And alongside the hurt was sadness. Sid saw himself failing his wife and failing in his marriage because he wasn't cheerfully cooperative.

Sid's increased awareness of his feelings led to a discussion with his wife that was far more open than they had been in years. She learned something about the origin of his resistance. And she was also able to let Sid know that his projections about being lazy and failing her in the marriage were simply not true. She saw him as occasionally grumpy, but had none of the negative judgments he imagined.

By identifying his underlying feelings, Sid was able to expose the roots of a longtime source of conflict with his wife. Instead of reacting with an automatic anger, he could begin to think and talk about his shame and the confining sense of obligation. Instead of living with his negative assumptions, he was able to get corrective feedback that changed his perception of the relationship.

Emilio

Emilio did in-house employee training for a large aerospace firm. He was scheduled to provide a one-day seminar each week. The rest of his time was spent researching and developing new topics and doing employee assistance counseling. Emilio was also taking night classes toward a master's degree in psychology.

Although he told his friends that the job was everything he had ever wanted and that he felt extremely content, Emilio sensed that something was wrong. He found himself having the "Sunday dreads" as he contemplated the week ahead. He had difficulty sleeping, felt irritable, and had a hard time motivating himself to prepare the seminar materials.

In order to explore his feelings, Emilio imagined himself talking to his father. During his lifetime, Emilio's father had been a major source of support and encouragement. The words that he heard himself saying to his father were "There's no time for me." As he imagined saying this to his dad, several feelings became very clear: he felt depressed, and he also felt that he was living with a high level of stress. Between homework and going to classes and preparing the seminars, there wasn't a minute to relax. There were constant deadlines and a sense that he was always falling behind. The awareness of falling behind triggered another feeling: shame. Emilio knew that his seminars could be more carefully prepared and that he was sliding by in school. He sensed that his father would be less than approving of the "half-assed" approach he was taking to his work and studies.

Once his feelings were clear, it was possible for Emilio to see that his life was grossly overcommittted. There weren't enough hours in the day. His new awareness led to a decision. With some reluctance, he took a one-year leave of absence from school.

John and Sid and Emilio had one thing in common. Feelings that were hidden under anger or shoved to the edge of awareness were nonetheless crucial parts of their experience. They needed to know those feelings in order to:

- Change their behavior in a stagnant or blocked relationship
- Find out more about the feelings of others
- Make vital life decisions

But now comes an important question. If the awareness of feelings is so crucial, who do so many men have difficulty knowing or experiencing the full range of what they feel?

The Self System

One of the pioneers in psychological theory, Harry Stack Sullivan, described what he called the "self system." The self system is your total experience in the world—what your senses tell you, what you think and believe, what you desire, what you feel.

Stated this way, Sullivan's model makes it sound like each of us has an ability to shape our own awareness of the world. But there's a problem. While you develop, your parents and significant others influence you tremendously. They tell you what is okay to see, feel, and experience, and what you should never see, feel, or experience. They can scare you into denying, literally blocking out, part of your reality through what Sullivan called "forbidding gestures."

Forbidding gestures can have a singularly negative impact on a man's capacity to feel. Let's say your father was very uncomfortable with fear. Every time you cried and said you were afraid, he shook you and said, "Big boys don't whimper. Be strong! Stop that!" His forbidding gestures trained you never to express fear. In many cases, you might even block all awareness of fear. It's there, but you can't experience it. Instead of feeling fear when your wife says she's unhappy in the marriage, you get enraged. Instead of being afraid when your boss gives you a low performance evaluation, you get belligerent. You have to substitute some other *permissible* emotion for the fear.

Forbidding gestures train you to identify certain of your natural feelings and reactions as "not me." It's "not me" to be afraid. It's "not me" to be forgiving. It's "not me" to feel yearning. It's "not me" to feel hurt. "Not me" feelings and responses are disowned and banished from consciousness. They are kicked out of your awareness, but not your psyche. They remain as buried, hidden influences. They are important parts of your reality that you never get to act on and to know. Like John, you may sense that something is wrong, but have little idea what you really feel about it.

As the example shows, a father has enormous influence on a boy's self system. Your father's anger or disapproval may have led you to disown vast parts of who you are and what you feel. If your father had a "traditional" concept of male identity, he may have helped you disown "weak" feelings. It was okay to be sexual or angry; but not to be tender, sad, hurt, or fearful. Notice that John, Sid, and Emilio had each lost touch with his sadness. Feelings of shame, hurt, and fear had all also somehow been lost from awareness or covered over. These similarities are no accident. In childhood they had been taught not to feel those things. They had been trained to amputate essential parts of their emotional life.

Learning More About What You Feel

Is It Good or Bad?

Many times it's difficult to label a feeling. Something's going on. You're aware of having a reaction, but it's hard to attach words to it. The first step in identifying what you feel is to make the simple distinction: Is it pleasure or pain? Does it feel good or bad?

Try this exercise with a feeling that's too ephemeral or amorphous for you to know much about. Close your eyes and take at least three or four deep breaths. Focus on the feelings, or at least on the situation that tends to elicit the feeling. Just let your attention stay with the feeling. Does it feel good or bad when you stay with it? Does the feeling attract you or repel you? Do you want to linger with it, or would you prefer to shift your attention away?

Once you're clear which side of the pleasure-pain dichotomy the feeling belongs on, you're ready to explore further.

Where Do You Feel It? How Does It Feel?

Still with your eyes closed, take a few more deep breaths. Notice any tension in your body—in your arms and legs, your face and jaws, your shoulders, stomach, and chest. Take a few moments to relax this tension and make each part of your body comfortable. (See chapter 14, "Being Healthy: Taking Care of Your Body," for a variety of relaxation techniques you can use.)

Now return to the feeling you were focusing on earlier, the one you now recognize as painful or pleasurable. Notice where you feel that feeling in your body. In your stomach? Your forehead? Your jaw? Your hands? Your chest? Where is the feeling strongest inside of you? Now concentrate on that part of your body where the feeling seems to reside. Just notice the feeling and its location; that's all you need to think about. Don't analyze or judge it. You're an observer of yourself. You're watching without evaluating. Now imagine that the feeling has a shape. Just go ahead and give it a shape that seems to fit it. Is it a square? A triangle? A ball with a lot of spikes, like a mace? Whatever comes to mind, imagine your feeling is that shape.

Now, what size is it? Does the feeling feel big, small, middling? Is one part bigger than the other? Now give it a color. Let your mind do it spontaneously. Just experience the color that goes with the feeling. See the color and notice your reaction. Does it have a texture? Hard or soft?

Letting It Speak

Here's a technique that may seem odd but can be extremely helpful. What are the words that go with the feeling? Let it speak. Let the words come spontaneously, whatever they are. Feel it. See the shape and color. Hear the words.

When John tried this exercise on the anger he had toward his son, he noticed the feeling was a strange choking sensation in his throat. He imagined it to be the shape of a donut. The color, surprisingly, was silver. Very hard and smooth, like polished metal. The words that went with the feelings were difficult to hear. He tried imagining that the choking sensation was actually talking. After a minute or two of sticking with the image, John mentally heard the words, "He's gone." Immediately he knew that the words referred to his son, and a strange sense of loss broke through the layer of his irritation.

Feeling Into Action

What does this feeling make you want to do? What action does it call for? Does it make you want to hit? Shout? Run, sit motionless, buckle over like you've been punched? Do you want to shake someone? Caress someone? Hold tight? Turn away? Imagine yourself acting out the feeling. See your body moving spontaneously as it reacts to the emotion. You don't have to hold back your responses as you would do in the world. This is all in your mind, no one will know or be hurt.

If you are able to visualize yourself acting out the feeling, pay particular attention to anyone who becomes a target for your behavior. Whom do you want to hug, shout at, or turn away from? Is it someone in particular? Is it a whole group, like your family or colleagues at work? When you can see the action that your feeling elicits and the target at whom that action is directed, you may be much closer to understanding the scope and content of your emotion.

Old History

When in your life have you felt this feeling before? Let yourself drift back into the past, to a scene where you experienced a similar emotion.

See where you were and whom you were with. Try to get a sense of the circumstances, the context in which the feeling grows. What do the people there have to say?

Were your feelings in that situation long ago any clearer than they are now? Did you have one of the primary feelings (like primary colors)—sadness, anger, fear, joy? Or was the emotion more subtle—a hybrid or a softer hue? If you can identify your feeling in the past—by giving it a name or at least experiencing the circumstances or context—you are likely to notice strong similarities between it and your current experience.

When Sid looked back into his past for a feeling similar to what he experienced when his wife made requests, he immediately thought about his father. The man was a real Mr. Fixit who made a list of home improvement tasks for every weekend. But Dad could never do anything alone. Sid was his eternal go-for, his compliant but not very competent assistant. Sid had felt helpless. He would never have dreamed of saying, "Sorry, Dad. There's a ball game down at the park today." This connection to the feelings he had felt with his dad proved to be an important clue for getting at Sid's current feeling of being trapped.

Naming the Feeling

In a moment, you can look through the list of feelings in the next section to see if any of the terms describe your inner experience. But please keep in mind one thing: you're probably not looking for a single feeling. Most situations, as John, Sid, and Emilio can testify, evoke multiple feelings. Some of them may even be contradictory—loving and angry, frightened and strong, supportive and hurt. Feelings don't have to make sense. They don't have to be pure. They don't have to be consistent. The truth is that the feelings you experience in a particular situation or toward a particular person are rarely simple, rarely described by one neat label.

So go through the list slowly and put a check by any feeling that seems to apply.

The Feelings List

Positive Feelings

Accepted	Capable	Confident
Affectionate	Caring	Content
Alive	Cheerful	Courageous
Amused	Cherished	Curious
Beautiful	Comfortable	Delighted
Brave	Competent	Desirable
Calm	Concerned	Eager

Enthusiastic
Excited
Forgiving
Friendly
Fulfilled
Generous
Glad
Good
Grateful
Great
Happy
Hopeful
Humorous
Joyful
Loveable
Loved
Loving

Loyal
Passionate
Peaceful
Playful
Pleased
Powerful
Proud
Quiet
Relaxed
Relieved
Respected
Safe
Satisfied
Secure
Self-reliant
Sexy
Silly

Special
Strong
Supportive
Sympathetic
Tender
Thankful
Thrilled
Trusted
Understanding
Understood
Unique
Valuable
Warm
Witty
Wonderful
Worthwhile
Youthful

Negative Feelings

Afraid
Anxious
Apprehensive
Confused
Desperate
Distrustful
Fearful
Frantic

Helpless
Horrified
Inhibited
Out of control
Overwhelmed
Panicky
Pressured
Terrified

Threatened
Trapped
Troubled
Uncertain
Uneasy
Uptight
Vulnerable
Worried

If you checked one or more of the above negative feelings , it's likely that you are feeling in some kind of danger. You sense that something bad or painful or scary may happen. Try completing this sentence:

I am afraid_____will happen in the future.

Angry
Bitter
Bored
Contemptuous
Controlled
Disgusted
Exasperated
Frustrated

Furious
Hateful
Hostile
Impatient
Irritated
Outraged
Prejudiced
Provoked

Resentful
Stubborn
Touchy
Victimized
Violated
Unappreciated
Used

If you have marked one or more of these feelings, it is likely that you believe someone is causing you pain. You sense that they are choosing deliberately to hurt you and that their behavior is wrong and unjustified. Try filling in this sentence:

_____ chose to do _____and they
    (the person)   *(their action)*
were wrong to do it because_____.
                                          (your reason)

Bored	Helpless	Sad
Confused	Hopeless	Stuck
Defeated	Isolated	Tired
Dejected	Lonely	Trapped
Depressed	Melancholy	Troubled
Despairing	Miserable	Weary
Desperate	Muddled	Worn out
Devastated	Needy	Unfulfilled
Disappointed	Old	Useless
Discouraged	Overwhelmed	Yearning
Gloomy	Pessimistic	

If you checked feelings in this group, it is likely that you are experiencing a sense of loss. You have lost or feel yourself lacking something you need to feel nourished, satisfied, or happy. You may also sense that what is lost or lacking will be hard to replace or find. Try completing this sentence:

I have lost (am lacking)_____,

and I am_____about finding it (again).
                (your degree of certainty)

Awkward	Humiliated	Self-conscious
Embarrassed	Inhibited	Shy
Foolish	Insecure	Uncomfortable

If you marked any of these feelings, it is possible that you're experiencing a sense of being inadequate, inappropriate, or socially incompetent as seen by others. Try completing this sentence:

When I'm with_____
                (the person or people)
at_____
                (the situation)
I sense that they regard me as_____.
                (the negative trait they may observe in you)

| Apologetic | Regretful | Sorry |
| Guilty | Remorseful | Untrustworthy |

If you marked one of these feelings, it's likely that you have a sense of having done something wrong, of having broken your own rules or violated your own values. Try completing this sentence:

When I_____, it feels (felt) wrong because I know
            (*your action*)
I should always (never)_____.
                            (*your rule or value*)

| Devastated | Hurt | Rejected |
| Excluded | Ignored | Vulnerable |

If you checked any of these feelings, it's likely that you have a sense of being disapproved of or pushed away by others. Try completing this sentence:

_____don't like (disapprove of) me because I
(*the person or people*)

_____.
    (*your behavior, appearance, lifestyle, personality trait*)

| Craving | Envious | Left out |
| Deprived | Jealous | Yearning |

If you marked one of these, there's a strong probability you're desiring something possessed by others. Write down here what it is that you desire:

_____

_____.

Ashamed	Inferior	Unworthy
Inadequate	Stupid	Useless
Incompetent	Unattractive	Wrong

If you checked a feeling in this group, it's likely that you see yourself as somehow bad, wrong, or unworthy. Try completing this sentence:

There's something wrong with me because I_____.
                                            (*your perceived flaw*)

If you have trouble filling in something specific here, it's possible that these feelings reflect a part of your core identity, some deep wound from your childhood. Feeling from that source can often just seem true without reason, without specific content.

Right now you don't have to fix or change any of these feelings. Save that task for another time. Your main goal now is simply to know, experience, and if possible name the feelings you are having. Knowledge of your feelings comes first, because that knowledge gives you power. And the power that comes from awareness of your inner life is the power to change your life.

The Cover-Up

Getting at your feelings can seem daunting at times. Your self system may prohibit you from entering certain parts of your experience. But as you learn more about your feelings you may begin to recognize some of the strategies you have used to cover forbidden parts of your inner life. Many of these strategies may be down right dangerous to you and those you love.

To get a sense of how this works, look carefully at the "cover-up" chart on the next page.

Signal Feelings

Notice that signal feelings are very often pale reflections of the deeper, stronger feelings that as a man you may not be permitted to experience. The signal feelings can in themselves act as a barrier against deeper experience. Numbness, boredom, and irritation often function as a lid to clamp down on core emotions. But they can also act as a "red flag" that you are having feelings you need to explore.

Defenses

For many men, rage is a frequent companion. Whenever a core feeling threatens to come into consciousness, they find a reason to fight. There is always someone who has offended them, someone who's broken the rules, someone who has acted stupidly, someone who isn't driving right, someone who should know better, and so on. Rage is a good protection against core feelings because it is so intense that it tends to screen out everything else in awareness.

Some men use other forms of defense. The presence of compulsions (workaholism, compulsive sexuality, gambling, shopping, excessive use of diversions), addictions, avoidance, and denial indicate a massive effort to block awareness of core feelings. If you know that you use rage or

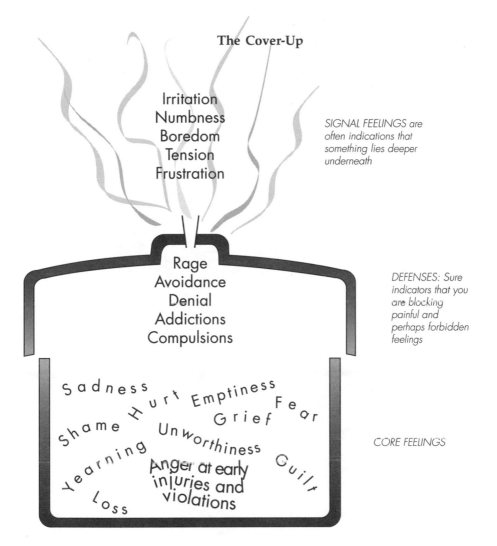

The Cover-Up

Irritation
Numbness
Boredom
Tension
Frustration

SIGNAL FEELINGS are often indications that something lies deeper underneath

Rage
Avoidance
Denial
Addictions
Compulsions

DEFENSES: Sure indicators that you are blocking painful and perhaps forbidden feelings

Sadness Shame Hurt Emptiness Fear Grief Yearning Unworthiness Guilt Anger at early injuries and violations Loss

CORE FEELINGS

other forms of defense with a high degree of regularity, you should seek professional help. This workbook will not be sufficient for you to make the changes that are necessary. If you use rage and other defenses rarely, then you may be able to use the following very simple exercise to begin learning more about your core feelings.

Feelings Diary

For the next two weeks, make an entry in a "feelings diary" for each occasion when you are aware of a signal feeling or a defense. Describe the signal feeling or defense as best you can, and then begin looking for any underlying feelings that you may be covering. Use the exercises outlined earlier in this chapter to identify and explore the core emotions that the signal feelings or defenses obscure.

Here's an example taken from Ralph's feelings diary.

Date	Signal Feelings	Defenses	Core Feelings
12/1	*Bored*		*Sad about my cat being killed*
12/4		*Compulsive eating and drinking all evening*	*Anxious about the new boss coming in next week, angry at not getting the promotion, a feeling of unworthiness that maybe I didn't deserve it*
12/5	*Susan didn't call; angry to an unusual degree about the low water pressure in the shower*		*Hurt that she probably isn't interested; empty feeling*
12/9	*Tension, very antsy around the house*		*Sort of empty, alone, wanting something to fill it up*
12/14		*Compulsive eating, avoiding people at cocktail reception for new boss*	*Very strong sense of unworthiness; a shameful feeling that my flaws are obvious to everyone*

Now go ahead and keep your own feelings diary. Find a notebook or pad that you can carry around with you. You can use the four-column approach that Ralph used or any other format that will let you focus on the process of covering up. This exercise is also a good way for you to practice the techniques you learned earlier in this chapter.

Once you have clarified important feelings, the next step is to express them in effective and appropriate ways. The next chapter will show you how.

11

Being Open:
Expressing Your Feelings

Telling someone how you really feel is a risk for everyone—man or woman. You could be misunderstood, criticized, ridiculed, rejected, or pitied.

Being a man means that the risk is greater for you, since our culture has taught you from infancy to keep silent about your inner experience. Consider the following points.

Most fathers talk to their sons about *things*. They discuss tasks, tools, machines, events—the objects of the world. A father rarely talks about what hurts, what he longs for, what scares or saddens him. And when his son talks about those things, a father may grow uncomfortably quiet, or he may retreat into making judgments to cover his anxiety. Or he may use humor to make light of the moments of his son's vulnerability. The lesson for the boy is that feelings have no place in the world of men. It is very rare for a boy to have access to other males who can show him how men talk about what is inside.

Male friendships are built around shared interests and tasks. Whether it's playing darts at the bar, rock climbing, or nature photography, men converse about what they *do*. If a man started talking about his loneliness or his fear of failure, an awkward silence would fall. Then there would be a joke, perhaps a suggestion to lighten up or buy another round. The society of men does not listen well to feelings. Emotions are a bringdown. Feelings remind men just how unacknowledged their inner lives are; they whisper of a vulnerability that most men are haunted by, yet desperate never to show.

Male self-esteem is based on performance. The rule is: Be cool, be competent, be strong, be in control, be the one who knows. Having feelings betrays a weakness that is the opposite of the classic male role. Having feelings is a threat to a sense of self that requires you to act and do, to push and accomplish, whatever the inner cost.

A man is never more at risk than when he shows his inner life. He is never more vulnerable to attack and loss of face. At that moment he is not strong, not cool, not in control. He may, in fact, be confused. He may understand precious little about what's happening inside of him. Now, as he begins to open up, any dig, any sarcasm, any judgment can hit him like a George Foreman punch.

So there are good reasons why talking about what you feel can take as much courage as it took to stand up to the bully when you were a kid or to face the rejections you've received when you've looked for work. Our culture doesn't give you much support. It takes a commitment on your part to push beyond the limits and strictures of the traditional male role.

Getting Ready

There are times when a situation requires an immediate, unrehearsed expression of your feelings. Mostly, however, life doesn't demand that kind of spontaneity. You usually have some time to think about the best way to say what you feel.

The assumption in this chapter is that you already have some sense of what you feel and a desire to express it. But like any important task, you need to plan how to do it.

"Getting ready" means figuring out the best *time*, *setting*, and *context* for an important communication. Think about when and where you'll be able to talk without interruption or distraction, without feelings of tiredness, hunger, or some other upset getting in the way. If you need privacy, arrange for it. If you need time to build up to or explain what you have to say, make sure that time is available. If you need to be relaxed first, make sure that you will be.

Context is also important. It helps if the other person has room to hear about you. If your girlfriend is in the middle of exam week, chances are she'll be less receptive than usual to your feelings of being cut off and your anger at not having enough time with her. It doesn't make sense to tell your son your feelings about his lousy grades while driving him to his big soccer match. Would you share your financial fears with your wife while touching and caressing in bed?

So do a little planning. It will make you feel safer, and the other person more receptive. Consider the case of Simon, who needed to think ahead about something he wanted to tell Mike. They had lived together in a committed gay partnership for eight years, and Simon had recently begun feeling a sense of entropy, almost stagnation. He wanted to spend less time in front of the TV and get more involved in creative or social activities. He was afraid this might be threatening to Mike, who had little interest in group involvements of any kind. Simon decided that the easiest way to bring it up would be during a restaurant dinner, probably Saturday night when they were both relaxed. He would have plenty of time to talk out and clarify his feelings, as well as hear Mike's reaction. They often felt close during a dinner out, and hopefully it would be easier to explain that Simon's boredom with TV didn't change his commitment to be with Mike.

The Key Feeling Word

It's easier to verbalize feeling if you can identify the *key feeling word*. That's the term which, better than any other, describes your emotional experience. Frequently this word is one of the primary feelings: sadness, anger, fear, joy, or love. If one of these isn't quite right, think about some of the hybrids or blends of the primary feelings: guilt, shame, hurt, jealousy, embarrassment, safety, acceptance. If you need more words to choose from, go back to the feeling list in the previous chapter.

Don't worry about trying to measure how intensely you experience the feeling. Right now the important thing is to be in the right ballpark. You just need a word that, in a general way, labels your emotion—a word that has at least some resonance with the feeling inside.

Embellishing

Often it isn't enough to just announce, "I'm sad...I'm hurt...I'm scared... I'm happy." Pronouncements like these leave a lot of information out, and the listener is forced to ask questions or fill in the gap by reading your mind. The listener may not know exactly what you mean by words like scared or happy (*definition*), how scared or happy you are (*intensity*), how long you've felt that way (*duration*), the triggering situation (*context*), or what the feeling reminds you of (*reference to similarity*).

Definition

People often have their own private meanings and definitions for words. One man says he feels "empty," and to him the word means *lonely* and *bored*. Another man uses the same word to mean *overwhelmed by a sense of loss*. Yet another describes periods of noncreativity as "empty."

The word "loving" can mean anything from *understanding* to *lustful*. Some men use the word "hurt" as a synonym for anger. Others use it to describe a feeling of shame or a sense of unworthiness.

Given the many meanings a simple word can have, it helps to find ways to define your terms. What do *you* mean by *angry, loving, hopeless, hurt,* and so on? Try not to compound the problem by using terms that are too general to help with the process of defining. "Upset" means nothing. "Overwhelmed" doesn't help much either.

Here's how Richard defined his feeling to his wife: "The thing I feel mostly is sad (*key feeling word*). It's a feeling of loss, distance. A feeling of separation between us. Missing you."

Raymond defined his feeling to his daughter in this way: "Jill, I feel hurt (*key feeling word*). I seem to give and give and very little comes back. It's a feeling almost of being used, taken for granted, and then pushed away. That's the part that hurts."

Notice how Richard and Raymond find terms that explain or expand the meaning of the key feeling word. Richard's sadness is really about separation and missing; Raymond's hurt stems from being taken for granted and pushed away. These few embellishments on the key feeling word increase the listener's understanding tremendously.

Intensity

How big is your feeling? Modifying words help to establish intensity. The following adverbs and phrases give a sense of whether a feeling is small, significant, or huge.

Small	*Significant*	*Huge*
A little	Quite	Incredibly
A touch	Rather	Overwhelmingly
Slightly	Somewhat	Terribly
A bit	Moderately	Unbelievably
Mildly	Fairly	Deeply
A brief wave of		Profoundly
A tinge of		Very

Obviously, "a bit" sad is less intense that "rather" sad, which is a level down from "profoundly" sad. It helps to think of the three levels of intensity and where among them your feelings seem to belong.

Another way to express intensity is to chose words that denote a very specific level of emotion. Here are some examples:

Small	Significant	Huge
Disappointed	Unhappy	Hopeless
Concerned	Scared	Terrified
Annoyed	Frustrated	Enraged
Foolish	Embarrassed	Humiliated
Stung	Hurt	Rejected
Sorry	Guilty	Ashamed
Affectionate	Loving	Passionate
Comfortable	Happy	Joyful

Duration

Try to give your feeling a time frame. Has it been going on an hour, all day, the last few years, since the beginning of your marriage, since your fourth birthday party when nobody came? It helps a listener to better understand your experience and assess its significance when you anchor things in time.

Context Versus Cause

Where does the feeling seem strongest? In what situation is it most often felt? If you experience the feeling frequently, is there a common theme or thread running through each trigger situation?

"Whenever I'm not busy, I notice this feeling of guilt, as if I'm doing something wrong."

"Whenever I'm with an attractive woman, I feel awkward and stupid."

"Whenever I'm in a situation where a lot is expected of me, I feel trapped and anxious."

Blame. Sometimes it's very tempting to blame something or someone for how you feel. The words "because" or "you make me" always assign blame. Phrases like these tend to make people defensive, and when people get defensive they stop listening.

"I feel worried because you're always taking these financial risks."

"I'm hurt because you spend the whole weekend working on the boat."

"You make me nervous when you're so critical."

It's safer to describe feelings in context—*where, when, with whom*, and *after what* the feeling occurs. Your statement will still link the feeling to the context, but the style is less accusing and doesn't seek to prove absolute causation. Here are some examples.

> "When we take long hikes, I often feel inadequate and a bit of an athletic failure."

Compare this *where* statement to a cause statement: "I feel inadequate and a failure because you always take those long hikes."

> "When I'm with you, I sometimes feel anxious and self-conscious."

Compare this *with whom* statement to the cause statements: "I'm anxious and self-conscious because of you" or "You make me anxious."

> "After you left I had a feeling of hopelessness."

Compare this *after what* statement to a cause statement: "You made me feel hopeless because you left."

> "When the church bells started ringing at noon, I thought of you and felt sad."

Compare this *when* statement to the cause statements: "I feel sad because I think of you" or "You make me sad."

Context really helps explain what's influencing your feeling. It roots the feeling in the situation that's affecting you emotionally, and this is often vital information to your listener.

Reference to Similarity

What does the feeling remind you of? Is there a situation in the past which is somehow analogous to the context of your current feeling? For example, you're disappointed, like the time the house deal fell through; or you're angry, like the time when Bill dented your car and didn't tell you. You're feeling close, like on that trip years ago to Mazatlan.

Perhaps there are metaphors that will help explain what you feel: "I'm as frustrated as a one-armed paperhanger." "I feel something between us, like there's a thick curtain, or a wall, and we can't touch each other." "I feel free with you, spontaneous, like I could shout 'I love you' in a crowd of strangers and you wouldn't mind." "I feel hopeless, like the last candle has gone out, and there's nothing to relight it." "When you said that, I felt as hurt as if you'd slapped me."

Putting It All Together

Here is a checklist for examining your feelings before expressing them.

Key word:

Definition (synonyms):

Intensity (small, significant, huge):

Duration (how long you have felt it):

Context (when, where, with whom, after what):

Reference to similarity (past situation, metaphor):

Heres's how Howard used the checklist when his brother didn't show up for Christmas dinner.

Key word: *Angry*

Definition: *Hurt, rejected, thrown away, didn't care enough to call or apologize*

Intensity: *Extremely angry and hurt*

Duration: *One day, but feeling of not being cared for is years old*

Context: *Whenever I ask for something or count on my brother, I get let down in some way*

Reference to similarity: *Like when we made plans to go fishing, rented the cabin, and he backed out at the last minute*

Guidelines for Expressing Feelings

Following these four specific guidelines for effectively verbalizing what you feel will assure that your message is heard as you intended it and that your listener stays receptive.

1. Take Responsibility for Your Feelings

When you take responsibility for your feelings, you accept that the feeling belongs to you. Nobody made you feel this way. It was *your* reaction, *your* emotional response to a situation.

The best way to acknowledge that your feelings belong to you is to make what are called "I" statements.

"I feel lost and alone since the breakup."

"I feel jealous of your new job."

"I felt hurt after you didn't come."

"I feel angry a lot at work."

Contrast the above "I" statements to "you" statements that blame and put all the responsibility for your feelings on others.

"Your leaving me made me feel completely lost and alone."

"Your new job makes me feel jealous."

"You hurt me by not coming."

"The lazy supervisors make me angry at work."

Notice in "you" statements that the offending party bears 100 percent responsibility for what you feel. It's all their fault. Your reactions aren't your own, based on your unique history, needs, beliefs, and patterns of coping. You're an emotional puppet whose responses are wholly determined.

"You" statements make others defensive and function as blocks to real communication. People feel accused and wrong. Then they tune you out while they work up a counterattack or rebuttal.

Here are some typical "you" statements that you are better off avoiding:

"You made me feel_____."

"When you_____,

it made me feel_____.

"You did_____

to me and made me feel_____."

"I feel that you_____."

This last "you" statement is a tricky one. It starts out like an "I" statement, but quickly turns into an accusation. It's a "you" statement in "I" clothing.

"I" messages may link feelings to a context, but they stop short of blaming.

Sam: "When you lost the tickets to the show, I felt irritated."

Notice that losing the tickets is *associated* with Sam's irritation, but the person who lost the tickets didn't *make* Sam irritated. Nobody makes you feel anything. You feel things as part of your reaction to another person's behavior. But five people could have five different reactions to the identical trigger situation. That's why each person must remain responsible for his *unique* reaction.

2. Be Direct

Try not to fog up your communications with vague terms and ambiguous statements. "I feel a little out of it" communicates almost nothing. "I feel weird" is even worse. Saying "I feel confused...strange...uncomfortable...crazy...a bit of a mess...kind of funny...the usual...whatever" doesn't make it as a direct use of language. The listener is either left without a clue or has to invent a meaning that may be miles off from what you intended to communicate.

Being direct is easier to achieve when you stick to your key feeling word: "I feel scared...sad...excited...hopeful...close and loving...irritated." The key word anchors the communication and allows you to refine the meaning through a variety of embellishments. Ask yourself a simple question: "Does the key feeling word I'm using denote an emotional state, or not?" If not, don't use it. Simple as that.

The second aspect of being direct involves the commitment to tell the truth. You talk about what you really feel, as opposed to what others expect you to feel or what feelings they are more likely to accept. You undermine your relationships if you say that you are uncomfortable when you're really angry, or express irritation when you're really scared, or say that you enjoy your girlfriend's family when the experience is worse than fingernails scraping a blackboard.

Some people describe their feelings in ways that are specifically designed to manipulate. A man whose wife was upset with his chronic lateness, told her he felt "hurt and unaccepted" in their marriage. She came to believe that her distress was actually harming him. His "feelings" caused her to back off and blocked further communication. A man told his lover, "I feel suffocated by your needs." "Suffocated" was a gross exaggeration. The effect was to stop his lover from expressing any needs at all.

Small deceits often feel safer at the time; they seem to protect you and may have some utility for influencing others. But you are cutting others off from knowing your true feelings. Cutting others off also cuts you off. Without the ability to express what's inside, you can end up feeling alone with your closest friends.

3. Be Clear

The key to being clear is to separate feelings from other types of messages. Actually, there are four basic types of communication.

1. Observations. This is a straight description of objective fact, a simple reporting of what the senses tell you. No speculation, conclusions, judgments, or opinions. As Sergeant Friday used to say, "Nothing but the facts."

"My old address was 469 Jersey Street."

"I dropped one of the new mugs this morning."

"You've worked ten extra hours this week."

2. Thoughts. These are your beliefs, theories, opinions, conclusions, and value judgments about what you've observed. They are an effort to synthesize what you've seen, heard, and read, so that you can understand why and how events occur. Thoughts may involve decisions about whether something is good or bad, right or wrong.

"Generosity is necessary to keep friends." (*Belief*)

"The ozone hole will soon expand to cover South America." (*Theory*)

"Rye bread is better than white." (*Opinion*)

"You were wrong to leave Susan." (*Value judgment*)

3. Feelings. Your emotional reaction without blame or judgments. A key feeling word plus any appropriate embellishments.

4. Needs. This is very often the bottom line of communication. After all is said and done, this is what you want. This is what needs to change in order for you to be satisfied. Relationships grow and strengthen when both people can clearly and supportively express what they need. Notice that statements of need don't involve value judgments or opinions.

"I'd love to go to a movie tonight. Are you up for it?"

"I need to visit Jim in the hospital. It would be good to have you there for support."

"I want to lay down and touch and hold each other."

"I want time to work this afternoon. Can you watch the kids?"

A feeling message stops being clear when you *contaminate* it with other kinds of communication. For example:

"I feel disgusted with your work."

Here the feeling is contaminated with a stated judgment and an unstated observation of some kind. Notice how the messages become much clearer when they're separated:

"Your reports have been consistently late, and you yourself were late three times this week." (*Observation*)

"This behavior creates problems with morale and delays production deadlines." (*Thought*)

"Frankly, I feel angry when I see the extent of this behavior." (*Feeling*)

Here's another contaminated message:

"I feel like I'm living with a child."

In this statement, feeling, need, and value judgment are all mixed into one blaming cocktail. They might be separated like this:

"I see you as basically focused on your own needs, your own pleasures." (*Opinion*)

"I feel angry. But a lot of it is feeling hurt, unimportant, left out." (*Feeling*)

"I need you to take the time to check in with me, ask what I'd like to do, what we could do together." (*Need*)

Situations become a lot clearer and kinder when feelings are separated from other messages. Here's an exercise for determining if your expression of feelings is contaminated with other messages.

1. Write out your feeling statement, just as you plan to say it (or have said it).

2. Does your statement contain any pejorative words that suggest a value judgment? Are there any blaming ("you") messages? If so, write your value judgment or opinion separately here. Try to make it as nonattacking as possible.

3. Have you left something out? Have you experienced something that is influencing your feeling? Write any observations here. Remember: only the facts, no opinions.

4. Is there a need embedded in your feeling? Is there something you're trying to influence the listener to do, or not do? Is there

something you want to see changed? Write your need or want here. Try to be specific.

If you've identified any additional messages that were woven into your feeling statement, rehearse expressing them separately, just as you've done in your exercise, before saying them out loud.

4. Be Congruent

Nothing is more confusing than when you are verbally saying one thing, but your tone of voice or body language is saying something else. The listener is being given a double message. You *say* you're hurt, but your voice *sounds* angry. You *say* you feel close, but your arms are folded and you're leaning away. You *say* you're sad, but your voice *sounds* loud, and you are frowning.

When your words and your tone or body language say different things, your message is *incongruent*. You're forcing the listener to choose which message to respond to. Studies show that in the vast majority of communications, people tend to believe body language and tone over verbal content. So if you want your feeling statement to be clear, your body (including facial expression) and voice have to match the words.

If you think that your body language may be incongruent, or if your feeling statements often seem to be taken wrong, here's what you can do: Rehearse a feeling statement while looking in a mirror, and tape-recording your voice.

Notice your posture. Are you leaning forward (indicating openness and availability) or leaning away (suggesting that you are feeling closed and distant)? Are your legs or arms crossed (defensive, possibly angry)? Are your hands balled up (angry, defensive) or open? Look at your facial expression. Does it seem angry, sad, scared, happy, loving? Is that expression consistent with the feeling you are trying to express?

You've watched yourself while you were talking. Now play the tape back and listen to your voice. If this were someone else talking to you, how would that person sound? Is the voice tone conveying any emotional content? Does the voice alone, separate from the words, say something about the feelings of the speaker? Are those feelings different from the verbal content?

If this exercise reveals incongruities, you have two choices:

1. Spend some time looking inside. Are the feelings communicated by your voice or body language authentic parts of you? Do they reflect aspects of your emotional experience that you have left out of the communication? If so, you now face the task of putting words to the new feelings and verbally including them in your feeling statement.

2. Practice. If, on the other hand, your tone or body language suggests feelings that you simply can't find after a period of self-examination, then you can use the mirror and tape recorder to practice changing your tone and posture to expressions that are consistent with the verbal content of your message.

Feeling Off the Cuff

Life isn't always gracious enough to allow a man the time to explore his feelings. Someone wants to know *right now*. A situation comes up that he has to react to. There's a conflict at home that requires him to express his side of the experience.

When you find yourself in an interaction that demands a feeling statement, there are three steps that can telescope the process of exploring and expressing.

1. Describe the context of your feeling in one nonpejorative sentence or phrase.

"When you ask me for money after a summer of not looking for work..."

2. Now add the key feeling word in an "I" statement. Look at the primary feelings first. Try each one in a sentence till one of them feels right. If you want, modify the feeling with "a little," "quite," or "extremely" to express intensity.

"I feel a little angry and worried about what's happening to you..."

3. Now you look for a simple embellishment that explains the feeling a little more. Something the feeling reminds you of, or a word that seems to make the feeling clearer.

"Sometimes I feel like I'm just a wallet, a source for things. I feel like I have to helplessly stand by watching you not do things I think you need to do."

Practice using this format with several situations from the past. Put the feelings into words as quickly as possible. Keep working at it until the format is familiar and relatively easy to use. If you want, practice with a tape recorder and check afterwards for clarity and congruity.

12

Being Assertive:
Asking for What You Want

You may be clear about your feelings and able to express them pretty well when you choose to, but still be miserable in an intimate relationship because you aren't able to come right out and ask for what you want. You may suffer in silence, wishing but not asking for certain expressions of support, loyalty, or warmth. You may endure sloppiness, boring sex, and irritating relatives rather than risk letting your partner know what bothers you. You may be dying for a vacation, a hug, or a change—and you'd *rather* die than ask for what you want.

Many men have difficulty expressing what they want—particularly in intimate relationships. Five codes of masculinity can literally force men into silence about their own needs.

Code 1: Men are strong. And truly strong people don't need things. Certainly not emotional support. If a man hurts, he is supposed to lick his wounds alone. He is supposed to provide for his own emotional nourishment, his own healing. When Salvador's girlfriend died in a boating accident, he found himself withdrawing form the very people he needed for support. Instead of letting anyone know that he needed to talk, or sometimes just needed company without talking, he went to the cemetery every day to be alone with his grief. The rule that a man must be strong blocked Salvador from letting anyone see how empty he was, how lost, how much he needed the comfort of friends.

Code 2: Men are stoic. Men are not supposed to acknowledge pain. They are expected to remain rock solid in the face of physical or emotional hurt. Consider Louis. His warehouse job involves heavy lifting. Over the last year he's endured increasing back pain, including spasms and sciatica. But he refuses to ask his wife's help with any of the heavy chores at home. He still lifts all the groceries, rearranges furniture, paints, washes walls, carries big bags of fertilizer, and so on. While he is frequently irritable, he never admits the extent of his pain. Nor does he try to share any of these tasks. Keith is another case. His sister occasionally makes critical comments about his job and earning capacity. He is particularly hurt by negative comparisons to her husband. Rather than acknowledge the hurt and ask her to stop, Keith is stoic. But some things even a stoic can't take. At a barbecue Keith hosted, his sister criticized him for not serving "butterball steaks like we do when you come over." Keith promptly kicked her out and hasn't spoken to her since.

Code 3: Men fix things themselves. Since a man should be strong and competent, he ought to be able to solve his own problems. A man should never depend on someone else to fix something. That's his job. And if he fails at it, if he turns to someone else for help he's admitting his own inadequacy. Bill was supporting his partner, Aaron, who was halfway through a Ph.D. program. They weren't making ends meet. Rather than asking Aaron to get a part-time job or seeking help from Aaron's parents, Bill simply got a second job. He solved the problem himself, but after a few 60-hour weeks, his ulcer began acting up.

Code 4: Men don't make mistakes. Asking for something means you've screwed up or are in some way deficient. A man anticipates. He's supposed to make decisions based on accurate predictions of the future. If he needs something, it's because he blew it. He didn't plan ahead adequately. Marty took an extended trip to Europe after graduating from college. He ran out of money in Barcelona. Wiring his dad for a loan felt like an admission of poor planning. Instead, Marty tried to panhandle on the street. Two days later he was picked up as an indigent and promptly deported.

Code 5: Men protect. You've seen the movies where the bullets start flying and the hero throws himself on top of the beautiful woman, protecting her with his body. She gets up and thanks him with a long kiss. It's a trite image, but the role of protector runs very deep. A man is supposed to put the ones he loves first. Their needs supersede his own. Their pain is more important than his own. Bart's seven-year-old son was hyperactive. His wife, Brooke, spent most of her time trying to control him and take care of the other two kids. Each night when Bart came home, Brooke looked exhausted. They settled in front of the TV, and she often fell asleep on the couch. Bart was aware of wanting more affection, more sexual contact, more real conversation. But instead of asking for what he wanted, he gave Brooke a back rub and listened to her stories of how overwhelming and out of control things were with their son. Bart's role of protector made it nearly impossible for him to acknowledge his own needs.

The Dilemma

The codes of masculinity create a vicious dilemma for many men. When you need something the codes say you shouldn't talk about, you have two choices:

1. Acknowledge your pain and your need. (But in doing so, you also tacitly admit your failure and inadequacy. You're not a real man.)

2. Keep silent about your needs. (But this is also dangerous. Without a way to ask for things, you get easily engulfed by the needs of others. Relationships feel out of control. It's like trying to drive a car with no brakes or steering wheel. You're helpless. You're getting taken for a ride.)

If you have been strongly influenced by some of the codes described above, chances are you wrestle with this dilemma often. Any significant need can trigger it. And there's no easy way out: you feel inadequate, that you're not a man, or you feel helpless and engulfed.

Many men stay trapped in this dilemma for a lifetime. To survive they often turn to one or more of the following *pseudo coping strategies*.

Pseudo Coping Strategies

Pseudo coping strategies reduce or control pain without solving the basic problem. You learn to cope with not having a voice, not having words for your needs. But you never learn to ask directly for what you want from another person.

Numbness.   Silence breeds a life of "quiet desperation." After a while the pain and yearning begin to burn out. The needs you were afraid to acknowledge gradually lose their urgency. You harden and shut down.

Anger and blame.   When the codes of masculinity forbid men to talk about their needs, many use anger as a cover and a substitute. Anger masks the pain of unmet needs, submerging it beneath a storm of surging emotions. If you just get angry enough, you won't feel how much you need to be touched, how much you need interest and attention. Not only does all the psychological intensity of anger mask pain, but it makes your pain someone else's fault. Now, instead of openly acknowledging your pain, you substitute a focus on the real or imagined flaws in others. The hidden assumption here is that if people were just caring, if they were just reasonably aware and attentive, you wouldn't have to ask for anything. People should recognize your wants long before you have to put them into words. In short, decent, smart people should save you from *the dilemma*.

Addictions. Since you can't ask for things you need, you don't get them. What's left in their place often feels like emptiness and longing. These feelings fill your awareness, and there seems nothing you can do about it. Addictions of all kinds provide a temporary solution. Overwork, overeating, drugs, alcohol, addictive recreations (like television), addictive sexuality and sexual conquest all have the capacity to numb pain. Addictions work reliably to shut off what you feel. Of course, you pay dearly for that anaesthesia.

Super-control. This is a common strategy for men. The idea is to keep so much control over every part of your life that you need never turn to anyone for help or support. There are men who construct the world exactly as they want it. They pay people to provide for them, they motivate and make deals, they are always in charge. But the structures that they build have one remarkable purpose: to make it so that they never have to ask for anything.

Pathological boundaries. If you can't say what you want and don't want, every close relationship is an exercise in powerlessness. Your needs can't be acknowledged, and so, by default, the other person has all the control. One solution is never to get close enough to feel the influence of someone else's wants. You keep a measured distance; don't let anyone in; don't make promises. Your personal boundaries thicken into impregnable walls. In another version of this strategy, you just keep looking in the mirror. You focus only on the parts of yourself that don't involve others—your preferences, your tastes, your desires. Rather than let the competing needs of others drown your unacknowledged wants, you psychologically erase the world and live without it.

Before You Ask

Recognize Your Rights

You have a right, even a responsibility, to ask for the things you need. You are the expert on you, the only one who knows what you feel. Before attempting to put your wants in words, it's important to remind yourself that you are a human being who is trying to survive. You feel pain; you feel desire. And you have a right to talk about those things out loud, you have a right to turn to someone else for help. The alternative is to gradually slip into one of the pseudo coping strategies, becoming more numb or angry or self-focused as the years go on.

Right now, make a commitment to yourself to squarely face some of the things you need, to put them into words, and to say those words out loud to someone who can help.

Recognize Your Limits

Everyone has the same responsibility you do. They are doing the best they can to take care of *their* own needs. That's their first and primary job—not to focus on and take care of your needs, but to provide for their *own* survival.

Because you need something from someone doesn't make you entitled to it. Their needs may be different or may actually conflict with your own. Both you and the person you are addressing have needs that are legitimate and equally important. Your right to express what you want is strengthened when you acknowledge the other person's right to want something else and to see the world through a very different lens than you do.

Identify What You Want

There are five rules for making an effective needs statement:

1. Be sure to deal with only one issue at a time.

2. Make your request specific.

3. Make your request behavioral.

4. Identify your alternatives.

5. Pre-script your request.

1. One thing at a time. You're going to overwhelm your wife if you ask her to be more careful about the budget, stop using scented shampoo, leave the window open for more air in the bedroom at night, give you a hand with the yard work, and stop wearing "grannie" nightgowns to bed. All of these issues may have some importance to you, but if you bring them up simultaneously, she is likely to feel overwhelmed and defensive. When you stick to one issue at a time, you increase the odds that the other person will listen receptively to your request.

2. Be specific. Generalities won't get you very far when it comes to making a needs statement. Instead of saying "I want things a little quieter around here," specify what you want by saying "I'd like a half-hour of quiet time when I get home from work." Instead of saying "We need to do something about the car," say "Do you have time to run the car down to the garage this morning?" If you want your child home at nine, it won't work to say "Be back soon, remember you have school tomorrow." Be specific about the time.

3. Ask for behavior change.   Don't ask people to change their attitudes, values, desires, or feelings. For one thing, you'll alienate them. But even worse, no change will occur. If your girlfriend likes to listen to heavy metal, there's not much point in telling her to broaden her taste in music. You can't ask your wife to *want* to go to the office party with you. Demanding that someone "be more considerate" or "care more" usually gets heard as an attack. No positive change comes from it.

The answer is to stick exclusively to behavioral requests. If you want someone to be more considerate, try to identify the behavior that would feel "considerate" to you. Considerate could mean not calling after ten o'clock at night, or not listening to your answering machine without permission, or letting you relax as a passenger when you've been driving all day. When you define being considerate as a particular thing the other person can do, it takes the guesswork out of the conversation. The other person can now say yes or no to your clear request.

James usually visited his good friend, Ted, on Wednesdays. They'd go out to dinner and then spend the evening playing pool. James was getting a little sick of mandatory pool each Wednesday. So he tried dropping hints. "Sometimes I need a little variety." This statement wasn't very specific, and Ted didn't get it. "Do you ever get tired of playing pool?" Ted said, no, he didn't. "Maybe we should do something a little more energetic tonight." But, again, James wasn't being specific, nor was he pinpointing a behavioral change. Finally, James proposed that they play racquetball in the early evening and have a late dinner. Ted wasn't enthusiastic, but he finally agreed to pool every other week and doing something more vigorous the rest of the time.

Bill wanted to have a child, but his wife, Winona, was ambivalent. While they had stopped using birth control two years before, nothing was happening. Bill wanted them both to get a fertility workup. Here's how he made his request: "You've got to really get behind this, Winona. You've got to *want* this. I need you to forget the uncertainties and really work with me on this." Unfortunately, Bill was asking Winona to change her attitudes and feelings. Nothing happened. Finally, Bill approached Winona in this way: "I'd like to make an appointment next week with a fertility specialist for us both to go and talk and schedule some preliminary tests. Are you willing?" Winona agreed. Once Bill started talking about specific behavior rather than feelings, Winona felt much less resistant. She was no longer expected to *be* a different person, she merely had to show up at a doctor's office.

4. Identify your self-care alternative.   This is your plan for how you'll solve the problem if the other person doesn't cooperate. For example, your girlfriend likes to eat out a lot. Most of the time you pick up the tab, and it's starting to feel like a lot of money. You want to propose eating at home more and taking turns doing the cooking. If she isn't happy with that proposal, your self-care alternative might be to go "dutch" on restaurant dinners. Your self-care alternative isn't intended to be punitive. It's merely an alternative plan whereby you can take care of your need if the other person doesn't agree with your proposed behavior change.

When making a request statement, don't introduce your self-care alternative right away. That's bringing in the big guns too early. Wait and see how the negotiations go before talking about your plan for independent action. Ron's brother always got "bombed" at family gatherings. He got loud and boorish, and finally, when he was too drunk to drive, Ron was expected to take him home. Ron decided to confront his brother about the drinking and ask that his brother "lay off the beers after dinner." His brother agreed, but at the very next gathering he opened a can of beer after dessert. It was time for Ron to tell his brother about his self-care alternative. "If you keep drinking, you're going to have to spend the night here. I'm not driving you home. It's up to you, but I'd appreciate it if you'd lay off the beer now."

5. Pre-script your request. Sometimes it helps to work out in advance what you want to say. A complete request statement has three parts: the situation, your feeling, and your want.

The situation is just the facts. No judgments, no putdowns, no value statements.

Your feeling is an "I" statement that doesn't blame or attack.

Your request is specific and behavioral.

Tom wanted his co-worker to refrain from smoking when they were driving together in the truck. Here's how he scripted the three elements of a request statement.

Situation: "When you smoke in the confined space of the truck..."

Feeling: "...I feel uncomfortable and a bit choked with all the smoke."

Request: "Could you hold on and smoke only after we get outside?"

Notice how Tom describes the situation without barbs or putdowns. It's a bare bones statement of the facts. His feeling is a nonblaming "I" statement about the physical effects of the smoke. His request identifies the exact behavior change that he wants. Tom also identified a self-care alternative which he didn't plan to talk about unless they failed to agree: "If we can't work this out, I guess I'll have to put in a request for a nonsmoking partner."

Here's a second example of pre-scripting. Tony had been going out with Marsha for about six weeks. She was oddly reticent about herself and tended to evade direct questions about past experiences. Tony was beginning to react to a kind of shallowness in their conversations. Everything was very surface, very here-and-now. He scripted his request statement in this way:

Situation: When I try to learn more about you—your family, things you've done in the past, what you've been through—I notice you change the subject.

Feeling: I feel disappointed that you don't tell me more about yourself. And a little hurt, like maybe you don't trust me.

Request: I'd love to know more about you. If I asked you some questions over dinner tonight, would you be willing to tell me more about yourself?

Notice that Tony doesn't put Marsha down as "closed" or "paranoid" for avoiding him. Those kinds of judgments will only make it harder to be close. He acknowledges that he's disappointed and hurt, but doesn't blame Marsha for it. Finally, he sets a specific time when he'd like to ask her some questions. Tony's ultimate self-care alternative is to stop dating Marsha. But there's no point in saying it at this point in the process.

Going For It

If asking for what you want is hard for you, then you need to commit yourself to making a change in your behavior now.

1. Right now, as you are reading this, identify something you have been reluctant to ask for, but are now willing to put into words. Write your script below:

Situation:

Feeling:

Request:

Self-care alternative:

2. Choose the right moment to make your request statement. Figure out a situation where you and the other person have the time and freedom to negotiate your request. It's probably best to choose a setting where you have some privacy and the full attention of the other person. Write down the setting where you plan to make your request:

3. Commit yourself to zero anger. Any amount of irritation or anger is going to undermine your request process, since it will just create resistance and defense. Make sure you speak in an even, nonhostile tone. If you aren't certain how to do this, just try to keep your voice flat, with very minimal inflection. Stay away from judgmental, value-laden words. Terms like *stupid, silly, crazy, a total waste, ugly,* and *ridiculous* are all no-nos.

If you don't trust yourself to maintain zero anger, record your request script on a cassette and see if you hear nuances of tone that betray a degree of anger or judgment. Keep recording and listening until all hints of anger are gone.

4. Have a plan to cope with resistance. Obviously, things aren't always going to go smoothly. The other person may have very different, even competing needs. *You have to assume that your request may not be entirely acceptable* to the other person. They do what they do for good reasons (to them). You want them to change. Getting what you want (or part of what you want) is likely to take some negotiation. Here's a sample plan for coping with resistance:

a. Do active listening to uncover and to clarify the other person's competing need. (See the "Active Listening" section in chapter 8, "Being Two: Making Partnership Work.")

b. Acknowledge the other person's needs and objections.

c. Make a new proposal incorporating both your needs. (See sample compromise structures in the problem-solving section of chapter 8.)

If resistance continues:

d. Encourage the other person to identify a solution that incorporates both your needs.

e. Build on the other person's solution to make your own counterproposal.

Saying No

One important part of asking for what you want is saying out loud what you *don't* want. Contrary to myth, many men have great difficulty saying no and setting limits. They end up feeling that they're denying something to the ones they love if they do, and engulfed if they don't. It's *the dilemma*.

The first step is to recognize that everyone has a responsibility to maintain his or her limits. Without limits you're just a doormat, something to walk on. Without limits, you invite others to abuse and take advantage of you. Saying no may feel ungenerous and may create tension and temporary discord, but it is a prerequisite for any healthy relationship.

Here's a simple structure for saying no in a way that will cause the minimum disturbance between yourself and others.

1. Start by acknowledging the other person's needs. This should be a simple, one-sentence statement that summarizes your understanding of the other person's position. The purpose of this step is to assure the other person that you hear and understand his or her wants.

2. State your position. Be direct and assertive. Don't apologize, don't put yourself down. Merely describe your preference, perspective, or feelings. "I'm tired right now. I have a project I'm finishing tonight." "This is more of a commitment than I want to take on right now." "I prefer having my own car."

3. Say no. Say it simply without elaboration: "No, thanks...I don't want to...I'd rather not...this is not for me...I've changed my mind...I won't be there."

Here are some examples of saying no using this three-step structure.

"I know you'd enjoy the opera (*acknowledgment*), but somehow I find the music irritating (*your position*). I prefer doing something else (*saying no*)."

"I know you'd love for us to go to Mazatlan, it's beautiful down there (*acknowledgment*). But I was sick with turista for half our trip last year (*your position*). I'd rather pass on Mexico (*saying no*)."

"The family gatherings are important to you (*acknowledgment*). But I always end up feeling insulted and put down by your sister and brother-in-law (*your position*). I'd rather visit just your parents (*saying no*)."

"I'm sorry you feel I'm being unfair (*acknowledgment*), but I don't see how I can afford private school for Luke (*your position*). I'd rather stay with the public school for now (*saying no*), but I'll help us find a better public school and try to arrange a transfer."

Try this structure and see how it works for you. You may find that it makes setting limits somewhat easier.

13

Being Strong: Controlling Your Anger

Men sometimes need anger. To defend their territory, to protect their families, to resist the many forms of oppression. Anger is an armor that can shield you from fear and doubt, a dark hormonal shove that keeps you pushing through pain and loss and frustration.

But for so many men, anger also is a trap. It is an all-too-frequent reflex that alienates friends and scars the closest relationships. Too many men rely on anger as a tool for problem solving, for expressing needs, and handling conflict. In the long run it rarely works. People back away, and then stay away. Marriages become mine fields. Conversations grow stilted. The faces of friends harden.

This chapter is a chance to understand your anger better, to explore its effect, and to develop tools for effective anger control.

Physiological Effects of Anger

Anger takes a toll on your health. There are at least a dozen studies which show that anger, whether you express it or hold it in, is linked to high blood pressure. A 25-year follow-up study of male physicians found that angry men had six times the incidence of coronary heart disease that their less hostile counterparts had. A study of almost 2,000 men at the Western Electric Company in Chicago revealed that men who scored high on a hostility scale were 1-1/2 times more likely to have a heart attack than men with lower scores.

Because anger increases stomach acidity, it is believed that angry men may be more vulnerable to gastritis, ulcers, and other gastrointestinal problems. Anger has also been implicated in the development of ulcerative colitis.

But anger may do far more than affect your circulatory system and digestion. A 25-year follow-up study of law students who had taken a test measuring hostility revealed a disturbing fact. Twenty percent of those who had scored in the top quarter on the hostility scale had died, in comparison to a death rate of only 5 percent for students who had low hostility scores. The study found that anger can damage many of your body systems and *increases the death rate from nearly every cause.*

Interpersonal Costs of Anger

Some people think that venting anger is a healthy coping mechanism. The idea is that anger is supposed to build up behind a "dam" of social inhibition until finally it breaks through to flood the system. So the healthy solution, according to this "hydraulic model" of anger, is to let the anger out whenever it's felt, leaving nothing to build in the reservoir.

Unfortunately, the facts don't support this common-sense idea. After summarizing the major research on anger in her book, *Anger: The Misunderstood Emotion*, Carol Tavris concluded that people who vent their rage tend to get angrier rather than less angry. She found in study after study that ventilation only served to "freeze" a hostile attitude or opinion. Whether the subjects were children, college students, or adults, research showed again and again that free expression of anger and hostility only seemed to *increase* angry and negative feelings.

Expressing anger serves to increase hostile feelings for one simple reason. When you get angry, you rehearse all your negative opinions about the target of your ire. All the faults, failings, violations, and wrongdoing are recounted. Each time you verbalize these negative perceptions, you make it easier to remember them and call them up at a moment's notice. In other words, anger hardens and strengthens an already negative opinion.

Anger Begets Anger

Since the ventilation of anger increases the likelihood that you will soon be angry again, each angry episode has a ripple effect. The occasion of one blowup sets in motion a process whereby you find yourself returning again and again to the sore point. And repeated anger leaves scars. The people you love become wary and less open. They're more likely to be hostile in return. Each angry episode changes the climate of your interpersonal life—by increments, relationships become colder and more distant.

Anger as a Defense

Anger always has a function. Its job is to protect you and keep you safe. These days, a man no longer needs anger to fight lions and wolves. You use it instead to protect yourself from painful feelings—hurt, fear, loss, or a sense of unworthiness. Many men have found that they can drive these feelings out of conscious awareness with a burst of anger. It works pretty well. The hurt or fear or sense of unworthiness disappears in the roiling waves of anger.

But defending yourself with anger has the effect of cutting others off. Chronic anger is a barrier to real listening, real problem solving, and real intimacy. It prevents understanding of the other person's experience. It destroys empathy.

So while anger may serve to protect you from feelings you would rather avoid, the cost is extremely high in the coin of interpersonal nurturance and support.

Consider the case of Terrence. Any kind of criticism triggered feelings of shame and worthlessness in him. To drive these feelings out of awareness, he attacked the source of the criticism. With enough anger, he was able to completely obscure his deep sense of inadequacy. But Terrence paid for his outbursts. He was denied a well-deserved promotion at work, and his wife retreated into her relationship with the children.

Isolation

Angry people tend to feel more lonely. Their sense of isolation has two causes. First, angry attitudes toward others tend to keep you from seeing the support that's available. The anger makes it hard to recognize when others are being loving, conciliatory, or reaching out. Secondly, chronically angry people tend to have high expectations of others. These expectations may make the support that's available seem worthless and lacking. A study of hostile people showed that while they have the same number of social contacts as people who are not hostile, they experience these contacts as being lower in quality and less satisfying (Tavris, 1989). So while isolation may not be an objective fact, the angry person *feels* cut off and isolated because no one ever seems to meet his high standards.

Problems on the Job

Dr. Meyer Friedman, the man who identified the Type A personality, reports that hostile, hard-driving people fail far more than they succeed in job settings. "Type A behavior, far from bringing about success in the factory, office, laboratory, or marketplace, is actually responsible for repeated disasters—careers and lives wrecked, whole businesses and large enterprises threatened with ruin." Friedman found that at work Type A's "simply burned themselves out in pointless struggle, impatience and anger."

Assessing Your Anger

It's time now to assess the effects of anger in your own life. The following inventory will provide an opportunity for you to ask yourself some serious questions. How does anger affect you and your relationships? Please fill out the following assessment as objectively as you can. The results will be very helpful as you begin to work on some of your more typical anger situations later in the chapter.

Anger Impact Inventory

0 = No effect
1 = Minor effect
2 = Moderate effect
3 = Very significant effect
4 = Major effect

Instructions: Using the five-point scale, rate the degree of impact your anger has on the following areas of your life.

	Rating
1. Relationships to authorities (teachers, bosses, police, government employees, and so on)	_____
2. Relationships to peers and colleagues at work	_____
3. Relationships to subordinates at work	_____
4. Relationships to customers, clients, business associates, and so on	_____
5. Relationships to children	_____
6. Relationships to children's school, other parents	_____
7. Relationships to spouse or lover	_____
8. Relationships to previous spouse or lover	_____
9. Relationships to in-laws	_____
10. Relationships to parents	_____

Rating

11. Relationships to other family members   _____

12. Relationships to current friends   _____

13. Relationships to former friends   _____

14. Relationships to neighbors   _____

15. The role of anger in lost relationships   _____

16. Relationships to recreational groups   _____
    or organizations

17. Relationships to religious groups   _____
    or organizations

18. Relationships to political and other groups _____

19. Impact of anger episodes on your health   _____

20. Effect of anger symptoms (rapid heart rate, _____
    tension, shoulder and neck pain, headache,
    irritableness, feeling of pressure, restless-
    ness, insomnia, brooding, and so on)

21. Time lost to angry feelings   _____

22. Effect of anger on relaxing or pleasurable   _____
    activities (sex, sports, hobbies, day in the
    country, vacations, and so on)

23. Effect of anger on drinking or drug use   _____

24. Effect of anger on creativity or productivity _____

25. Effect of anger on experience while driving _____

26. Accidents, errors, and mistakes   _____

From *When Anger Hurts* by M. McKay, P. Rogers, and J. McKay.

As you examine your inventory, see if any patterns emerge. Are you angrier at work or at home? With intimates or more distant relationships? Do you tend to feel angrier with authorities and parents, or with peers? Are your sexual relationships major battlegrounds? Have a significant number of relationships been lost to anger? This is a good time to identify one or two areas where controlling your anger would positively impact your life. You'll get a chance to focus on them later in the chapter.

How Anger Grows

Anger is a two-step process. To become angry you have to (1) feel stress, and (2) engage in *trigger thoughts* that function to ignite a hostile reaction. Both components are necessary before you can really *feel* angry. Angry thoughts without the presence of stress and physical arousal never reach the level of emotion. Physical or emotional stress without the hostile triggering thoughts remain just what they are—unpleasant but not angry feelings.

Consider the case of Rachel and Jim. Rachel is frustrated and disappointed because her vacation request was turned down at work. At the moment, she is taking a brisk hike with Jim, and an old back injury is beginning to ache. Both her emotional and physical stresses are combining to increase her tension and arousal. Now Rachel says to herself: "Why the hell is he walking so fast, he knows that aggravates my back problem." This trigger thought is all she needs to ignite feelings of anger, and a moment later she is upbraiding Jim for "having zero sensitivity to her needs" and being "totally uncaring."

This exchange now creates a stress reaction in Jim. Rachel's words trigger a deep sense of unworthiness, a feeling of being flawed and inadequate. It's an intolerable feeling, and Jim has learned to convert it into anger with trigger thoughts. He now says to himself, "She's never satisfied, she's a big bag of complaints. She expects too damned much." The trigger thought allows Jim's stressful feelings of unworthiness to be transformed into anger. He says in a low, hostile voice, "Fuck you too, Rachel." And now they're off to the races, using words as bludgeons to somehow discharge the pain and hurt.

Anger and Stress

Stress is the fuel of anger. The more stress you feel, the longer and hotter your anger burns. There are four kinds of stress that feed your anger.

1. Painful emotions.   As discussed before, anger helps you block and discharge painful feelings of fear, loss, hurt, shame, and unworthiness. Take guilt, for example. A man feels guilty about having given too little attention to his son. Guilt is a stress that he is strongly motivated to block or discharge. When his child dallies getting out of the car, the man says to himself, "He doesn't behave. He's defying me." That trigger thought is all he needs to turn the guilt into anger.

2. Painful sensations.   Stress is very often physical in origin. Rachel's bad back contributes to her arousal level. Any physical pain, even minor muscle tension, can be an underlying stressor that fuels angry feelings.

3. Frustrated drives. When you feel stuck, when you want something you can't have, when you're looking for something you can't find, your stress increases. Anger functions to vent high arousal levels that occur when your drives are frustrated.

4. Threats. Anything that threatens your physical or psychological well-being creates immediate arousal. That arousal makes you want to do something. It pushes you towards some protective stress reduction activity.

Stress of any kind sets off a psychological alarm mechanism that functions as a signal that things are not right. The more the arousal builds, the more you are motivated to do something about it. Anger is a form of discharge. It can give you temporary relief from building tension: a momentary shelter from feelings and sensations that have become uncomfortably strong.

In truth, anger is only one of many stress reduction strategies you could use. Here is a list of some of the things that people use *instead of anger* when they are stressed: crying, exercising, intense work activity, humor, writing the feelings down, relaxation exercises, verbalizing the distress, recreation, sex, problem-solving activities, problem-solving communications, pillow beating, listening to music, seeking a quiet place to rest. Every activity on this list is a tried and true stress reducer. Any one of them can be used in substitute for anger to reduce the stress you feel from painful feelings, painful sensations, frustrated drives, or threats.

The stress-reduction strategies you tend to use are largely a product of learning. You model what your parents did. If, when your father banged his finger with a hammer, he made a joke and took a little break from the task, you are likely to use that strategy when you feel physical pain. If he blamed you for not doing something right when he hit his finger, you learned to get angry when something hurts. If your mother shared her sadness with you when she lost a friend, you may have learned that verbalizing pain is a good way to relieve stress. If she picked a fight when she was sad, she was teaching you that anger is the best way to discharge emotional pain.

For the most part, men learn to get angry from their fathers. Your dad was your model for how a man should act in the world—how he copes, how he solves problems. It's a sad fact that many men rely on anger as a primary stress-reduction strategy. It is the first defense, the strategy of choice when dealing with pain of any kind. And the men who rely on anger teach their children the same methods of coping that they have used. And so it goes, from generation to generation, the legacy of male anger. The flashes of rage, passed from father to son, as men cope in the only ways they were taught.

Trigger Thoughts

Trigger thoughts are the flint that ignites angry feelings. There are two kinds of angry trigger thoughts: blaming statements and shoulds. Blaming statements label the offending person as wrong and bad. Here is the generic thought: "You deliberately did _____ to me." The key notion is that you have been intentionally harmed by the wrong behavior of another. Blaming statements are always built on the belief that *they* did it to you. Your pain was caused by someone else.

Blaming is done in a number of ways. Sometimes you may find yourself using *global labels*: someone is stupid, selfish, foolish, incompetent, careless, and so on. The label always carries the implication that the other person could do better, but has somehow been remiss. Sometimes blaming statements take the form of *assumed intent*. Essentially, this is mind reading. You come to the conclusion that someone has *deliberately* done something to hurt you. The assumption of deliberate harm is, in fact, the key element of assumed intent. It gives you the permission you need to punish the other person with your anger. A third form that blaming statements take is *magnifying*. Here you find yourself using words such as *terrible, awful, disgusting, horrendous*. Or you overgeneralize with words such as *always, all, every,* and *never*. These words tend to expand the perceived magnitude of the harm. They make you feel like more of a victim, and in the end they make you angrier.

Shoulds are also a major anger trigger. The generic thought is: "You should not have _____ but instead you should have _____." The implication is that the person should know how to act correctly, but has instead broken the rules of reasonable conduct. Once a person is seen as breaking the rules, he or she becomes bad, wrong, and deserving of punishment. Remember Rachel? When she said to herself that Jim ought to know that walking fast hurt her back, she used the should to make Jim bad, to see him as a wrongdoer who deserved an angry blast.

At the core of angry should statements is the *letting it out fallacy*. The basic concept here is that people who hurt you should be punished and deserve everything you dish out to them. The motto is: "They screwed up. Let 'em have it."

Another variant of shoulds is *the entitlement fallacy*. The underlying belief is that because you want something very much, you ought to have it. The problem with entitlement is that it confuses desire with obligation. It demands, "When I want something this much, you have no right to say no." Entitlement denies others the freedom to choose. It requires that they give up their limits, needs, or preferences for you. It says that your need must come first, and that when your needs are at stake, relationships must always serve you.

A third variant of shoulds is *the fallacy of fairness*. Here the assumption is that relationships can be governed by the same legal and contractual rules that apply in a court of law. There is some absolute standard of fair and correct behavior and a requirement that the emotional books in a relationship be kept strictly balanced. The problem with the demand for fairness is that in relationships there is no judge or jury to help you decide. No one can arbitrate what is a fair distribution of nourishment and support. And people end up defining fairness in such an arbitrary way. What you consider fair will always coincide with what you expect, need, or hope for from the other person. People can literally call anything fair or unfair, and the concept can be so conveniently self-serving that it loses any real usefulness in negotiating your wants.

The Anger Cycle

Anger is often perceived to have a life of its own. Here are the two ways an anger cycle can start. (1) Stress and arousal lead to trigger thoughts, which lead to anger, more trigger thoughts, more anger, more trigger thoughts, and so on in an escalating sequence. (2) Trigger thoughts create arousal, and together they ignite anger, more trigger thoughts, more anger, more trigger thoughts, and so on. However the cycle gets started, it tends to move in an upward spiral until you reach some kind of emotional denouement. Thoughts and angry feelings become a feedback loop. They can keep you simmering for hours or days. Even a blowup may not end it, since all the attacking things you say help you rehearse your trigger thoughts and strengthen their hold on you.

Anger Is a Choice

Because anger is more than pain and stress and frustration, because it depends on shoulds or blaming trigger thoughts, you have real choice about getting angry. You can literally decide whether to pull the trigger. When you feel stress, you can elect to use an alternative stress reduction strategy such as problem-solving communication, relaxation, or simply directing your energy into other activities. You can also change your thinking. You can change the blaming statements and shoulds into more accurate, more accepting perceptions. In later sections of this chapter you'll be given a plan for doing this. Right now it might be helpful to learn more about the role of stress and trigger thoughts in the situations where you typically get angry.

Analyzing Anger Situations

Choose three anger situations from the Anger Impact Inventory earlier in this chapter that you found were significantly affecting your life.

For each one, perform the following analysis.

1. Write down every stressor that contributed to your arousal.

   Painful emotion: _____

   Painful sensation: _____

   Frustrated drive: _____

   Threat: _____

2. Write the trigger thoughts that you typically experienced in this situation. If you have trouble remembering them, go back and visualize yourself in the scene. See the surroundings, reexperience the situation, hear the other person's voice, listen to their words. Now tune into your own thoughts. What are you saying to yourself? What are you thinking about the other person? How do you describe to yourself what is happening?

   Blaming statements: Try filling in the blanks in these sentences.

   They deliberately did _____ to me.

   They were wrong and behaved badly because _____

   _____.

   He or she is a_____ person.

   Shoulds: Try filling in these sentences.

   They should not have _____,

   but instead they should have _____.

   The basic rule of good conduct that they broke was _____

   _____.

   They deserve my anger because _____.

   Try to imagine the stress without the trigger thought, or the trigger thought without the stress. Could you have gotten really angry without both components?

Controlling Trigger Thoughts

The Principle of Personal Responsibility

A major antidote to angry trigger thoughts is recognizing the ways in which you are responsible for your own life. The principle of personal responsibility states that (1) *you are responsible for your own pain* and (2) *you are the one who must change your coping strategies to better meet your needs.*

If a situation is disturbing you, if something is painful or unpleasant, you are the one who must decide how to change it. There are four reasons for this.

1. You are the only one who really knows and understands your own needs. You are an authority on what feels good or bad to you. You have a lifetime of experience with your tastes, preferences, secret desires, hidden fears, aversions, and pleasures. Nobody else really knows you with the certainty with which you know yourself.

2. Other people, quite appropriately, focus on meeting their own needs. They know their own desires and fears, and they have full responsibility for nourishing and protecting themselves. It's not their job to take care of you. Even in the most intimate and loving relationships, each person is charged with a primary responsibility for his own needs. If anyone places your needs above their own, they have neglected their first responsibility of protecting and providing for themselves.

3. People's needs inevitability conflict.   There is no way two people can maintain perfect harmony. One person likes Bach, the other plays B. B. King. One person craves cool mountain glades, another seeks the hot, motionless air of a Baja beach. Everyone is seeking to get basic needs met, and unavoidably these needs collide. There is no way around it. Every relationship has to come to terms with a basic reality: the happiness of one will at times involve frustration or loss for the other. For many men and women, this conflict becomes a grim and bitter struggle.

4. Your overall life satisfaction depends on the effectiveness of your strategies for meeting needs and avoiding pain. *The amount of support, appreciation, and help you are now getting is all you can get, given the current strategies you are using.* The things you now do to generate nourishment and cooperation from others can't get you any more than you are receiving. To get more, you would have to use different strategies. For example, Salvador tries to make his daughter help around the house by getting angry and blaming her for the mess. He gets grudging cooperation for about three minutes, and then she slumps back to her favorite spot on the sofa. The amount of help Salvador gets *is all he can get*, given the blaming strategy he uses. He needs new methods of reinforcing helping behavior. Perhaps he should make her allowance contingent on certain tasks or permit her to have telephone time or trips to the mall only when she's done her jobs at home.

The principle of personal responsibility offers a way out of the anger and deadlock. It helps you overcome feelings of helplessness and victimization and accept full responsibility for solving the problem yourself. Consider Bill. He's trying to maintain a friendship with his ex-wife,

Sharon. Whenever they meet for lunch, Sharon is at least twenty minutes late. Bill is cold and angry when she finally sits down. He announces frostily that he's sick of having so little importance in her life that she can't make an effort to be on time. Bill's mind-set is that Sharon is responsible for the problem. As long as he maintains his angry, blaming position, he's helpless to solve things for himself. As soon as Bill took responsibility for his pain, he was able to see that he had a number of choices: he could pick Sharon up at her house or have her pick him up at home. He could bring a good book so he wouldn't mind waiting. He could arrange to arrive fifteen or twenty minutes late himself. Or he could arrange to meet Sharon in group settings so that he would have other people to enjoy when she was late.

Sandy had the same feelings of helplessness as Bill. His wife was in charge of paying the bills, but she was unbelievably forgetful. They frequently received late notices, paid overdue charges, and occasionally got calls from collectors. Sandy could never understand why his wife failed to keep track of the bills. Occasionally he'd blow up, calling her lazy and irresponsible. When Sandy applied the principle of personal responsibility to his situation, he saw new options. If he didn't like the late notices and extra fees, he could do the bills himself. Or he could provide reinforcement for his wife by setting deadlines and planning a weekend trip when she got them done. Or he could pay someone to balance the accounts and write the checks. All he'd have to do was sign them. There were a lot of possibilities, and Sandy realized that his anger had kept him from exploring any of them.

There are six ways you can take responsibility when you are unhappy with someone's behavior.

1. Develop more effective strategies for reinforcing others. Basically this means figuring out how to reward people for doing what you want—or how to make it unpleasant for them if they don't do what you want. The carrot or the stick. Ted found himself endlessly irritated with his assistant at work. His assistant collected bids from subcontractors so that Ted could assemble them into his general contractor's bid for a construction project. Ted frequently got angry, but the assistant realized that Ted was a paper tiger who really wouldn't do anything. Ted decided to use reinforcement to solve his problem. He informed his assistant that if the bids were in promptly, he would get four hours extra comp time. If they were in late, he would be suspended for a day without pay.

2. Take care of the need yourself. Jim found himself incensed because his children kept using his toothbrush, passing their colds and flu bugs on to him. For a while his anger kept him helpless. Then he decided to solve the problem by keeping his toothbrush in the drawer of his night table.

3. Develop new sources of support, nourishment, and apprecia-tion. The focus here is on going elsewhere for what you need, rather than continuing to expect support or help from someone who can't or won't give it to you. Sheldon's closest buddy had recently landed a new high-pressure job that was sucking a lot of time away from their friend-ship. There were cancellations and excuses and a whole lot less of the good times they had once shared. Initially Sheldon was angry. But at a certain point he began to recognize that he had put all of his eggs in one basket. Instead of sitting home, he joined a bike club and began participat-ing in group rides, picnics, and other social activities that allowed him to develop a whole new set of friends.

4. Set limits. A lot of men get angry when they are pressured into activities they would have preferred to avoid. Being willing to set limits is an important part of taking responsibility for the things that bother you. Walker's lover frequently galled him by borrowing his car for er-rands or when he was late to work. Walker fumed helplessly for a while, but finally decided that losing his car for a whole day was too much of an inconvenience. He told his lover that no matter how late he was, the car was no longer available for a work commute.

5. Negotiate assertively. This is the process of asking for what you want—directly, non-blamingly. When you and another person have con-flicting needs, you can generate compromises that include both sets of needs in the solution. See chapter 12, "Being Assertive: Asking for What You Want" for detailed suggestions about the process of negotiation.

6. Let go. There are two kinds of letting go. The first involves ac-cepting that the situation is not going to change and that ultimately you will have to live with it. Somehow you find a way to let go of the need for things to be different, the expectation that you will have what you want. Reuben had pressured his wife for some time to be warmer and more physically affectionate. When, as usual, she failed to give him a lavish greeting as he walked in at night, Reuben would say, "Thanks for the big hug." The sarcasm only had the effect of pushing her farther away. Reuben eventually came to terms with a basic reality: his wife was not the snuggly type. She was a fine woman who didn't happen to have that quality of strong physical responsiveness. Reuben's anger diminished, and his satisfaction with his marriage correspondingly increased when he let go of this expectation.

The second kind of letting go involves a recognition that certain sit-uations or relationships are so unrewarding or even toxic that they are not worth continuing. In this case, letting go requires an acceptance that the situation will not change and that it is costing you more than it is worth. This option can be frightening. There are often good reasons for staying in painful, unnourishing situations: someone depends on you, someone will be hurt, there would be a significant financial loss, and so on. At this point you may be unwilling to pay the price of letting go. But it's important for you to weigh the cost of letting go against the experience of helplessness and chronic anger that can take such an enormous toll on the quality of your life.

A Commitment to Accuracy

While the principle of personal responsibility can help you deal with trigger thoughts based on shoulds, accuracy is the main antidote for blaming statements. Global labels such as *selfish* and *stupid* are almost never accurate. They overgeneralize from certain behaviors to label someone as a whole. People may be selfish in some areas and generous in others. But rarely is any trait seen across the board. Accuracy is also important in the tendency to magnify. Your friend isn't late *every* time, he was late twice out of the last six meetings. Being accurate reduces the anger triggering effects of such a thought. The commitment to accuracy also forbids making assumptions about the motivations of others. Rather than assuming an intent to harm, you can do one of two things: (1) remind yourself that you have no certain knowledge of the forces that influence another person's behavior, or (2) open a dialogue with the other person to explore his or her motivations.

You need to commit yourself to avoiding all global labels (*stupid*, *incompetent*, *crazy*, *selfish*, *cold bitch*, and so on), mind reading ("He's trying to hurt my feelings, she just wants to show me up"), and magnifying (*all*, *every*, *everyone*, *nobody*, *totally*, *completely*, and so on). If you can banish these three forms of distorted thinking from your mental repertoire, you will have far fewer anger triggering thoughts. No matter how much stress you may feel, you'll be less likely to convert it into an angry response because you won't be as quick to push the blaming button.

Responding to Trigger Thoughts

This is an opportunity to get some practice responding to trigger thoughts. Make a copy of the following form. Each time you feel angry during the next week, fill it out. In the process you can analyze your trigger thoughts, and learn to rewrite them so they are less anger provoking.

Analyzing Trigger Thoughts

1. Trigger thought:

Shoulds:

_____

(person's name)

should not have _____

(what they did)

but instead he or she should have _____.

(the right thing to do)

Blaming statements:

_____

(the person)

deliberately did _____

(the offense)

to me.

Did your trigger statement include global labels? Which ones?

Did your trigger statement include mind reading? What did you imagine about the other person's intentions?

Did your trigger statement include magnifications? Which magnifying words did you use?

2. Rewrite your trigger statement without global labels, assumed intentions, or magnifiers. Try to make the statement absolutely accurate, without any form of exaggeration.

3. Applying the principle of personal responsibility to the anger provoking situation, which of the following do you need to do in order to take control of the situation?

☐ Develop more effective strategies for reinforcing others.

☐ Take care of the need myself.

☐ Develop new sources of support, nourishment, and appreciation.

☐ Set limits.

☐ Negotiate assertively.

☐ Let go.

4. Write a specific plan for how you will implement one or more of the six steps to responsibility listed earlier.

Coping with Provocation

Many anger evoking situations develop in a matter of a few moments. It's important to prepare yourself for provocation so that you can cope effectively, rather than roiling yourself into an angry attack. To do that, you'll need to develop skills in four areas:

1. Replacing trigger statements with healthy coping thoughts.

2. Learning a brief relaxation procedure to reduce your physical tension.

3. Replacing angry, blaming communications with assertive problem solving.

4. Learning the "time out" procedure.

Healthy Coping Thoughts

When you start to feel aroused and you're getting close to anger, you need to be able to say calming things to yourself. You need to literally instruct yourself to back off and cope some other way. Here are a list of coping thoughts that are designed to help you keep your cool when provoked. Not all of them will be useful. In fact, most of them probably won't feel right to you. Select two or three that you might be able to use and modify them so that they really feel right for you. Memorize them and make a commitment to yourself to try them out the next time you're starting to feel angry.

Coping with arousal.

- No one is right. No one is wrong. We just have different needs.
- No matter what is said, I know I'm a good person.
- Just as long as I keep my cool I'm in control.
- Just roll with the punches. Don't get bent out of shape.
- Stay away from blaming and judgments.
- Neutral words only.
- Calm and flat voice.
- No sarcasm, no attacks.
- Getting mad will cost me _____.
  (insert the negative consequences of anger in this situation)
- If I start to get mad, I'll just be banging my head against the wall, so I might as well relax.
- Getting upset won't help.
- It's not worth it to get so angry.
- I'm annoyed, but I can keep a lid on it.
- I'll stay rational. Anger won't solve anything.
- Anger is a signal of what I need to do. It's time to cope.
- Don't escalate. Cool it.
- There's nothing gained in getting mad.
- Easy does it. Remember to keep a sense of humor.
- If I'm stuck in a bad situation, I'll think about how to handle this in the future.

Coping with an angry person.

- I'll let him make a fool of himself.
- He'd probably like me to get real angry. Well, I'm going to disappoint him.
- I don't need to prove myself to him.
- I'm not going to let him get to me.
- It's really a shame that he has to act like this.
- For someone to be that irritable, he must be awfully unhappy.

- There's no need to doubt myself. What he says doesn't matter.

- I can't change him with anger. I'll just upset myself.

- Who cares what _____ thinks.

- This person doesn't know me. His opinion means nothing.

- I've acted this way in the past myself. I can give him some slack.

- Stay cool. Make no judgments about this person.

- I don't have to take shit. I'll simply withdraw from the conversation.

- I won't be manipulated into blowing up or losing my cool.

- Blowing up only gives them what they want.

From *When Anger Hurts,* by M. McKay, P. Rogers, and J. McKay.

One way to increase your commitment to using healthy coping thoughts is to write your selections down on a file card and carry it with you. Review the file card daily to remind yourself of the coping thoughts you'll need in the next anger evoking situation. While this approach may seem mechanical at first, the strategy of using coping thoughts has been shown again and again to greatly increase a man's control during times of stress. You have nothing to lose by experimenting for a week or two to see how well it will work for you.

Stress Control

Because stress provides the fuel for anger, it's important to develop relaxation skills that you can use quickly and effectively when faced with provocation. A simple procedure called cue-controlled relaxation will give you the capacity to relax almost instantly.

This is a combination of muscle scanning and breathing that allows you to relax very quickly, in two or three minutes. It's the recommended relaxation method for anger control or any other situation where you need to calm down quickly. The steps are simple:

1. Sit down and close your eyes. Scan your body from your forehead all the way down to your toes. Consciously relax any tight muscles you find. Let relaxation flood your body from head to toe.

    (If you have trouble with this "release only" method of body scanning, you may need to go forward to the next chapter, and learn progressive muscle relaxation, until you have fine-tuned your ability to distinguish between tense and relaxed muscles. In time, this scanning will take just a few seconds.)

2. Shift focus to your breathing, deep and slow. With each inhale, say to yourself, "Breathe in." With each exhale, say to yourself, "Relax." Whatever distractions come to mind, return to these words: "Breathe in...Relax...Breathe in...Relax...." Feel each breath bring peace and calm in and send anger and worry out. With practice, the words will become your cues to relax quickly and deeply.

Problem-Solving Communication

Perhaps the most important thing you need to remember in a provocative situation is what you want. The ability to express your wants and needs is a major key to overcoming the feeling of helplessness that so often leads to anger. Chapter 12, "Being Assertive: Asking for What You Want," offers specific suggestions for putting your needs into words, as well as clarifying the needs of the other person. This skill, more than anything else, may show you the way out of the anger trap.

Time Out

When you find yourself in a situation where you know from experience that your anger is going to escalate, you need a way to stop the interaction long enough to let things cool down. Perhaps the single most useful strategy in controlling the escalation of anger is a technique called "time out."

Time out requires prior agreement between two people who experience frequent conflict. The idea is that when either person notices the early warning signs of escalation, he or she can call a "time out." It's important to call the time out early, before both of you get really hot. The simplest way to do it is to make a T sign with your hands, just like the referees do. Once the T sign is made, all communication should stop. Both people, by prior agreement, are obligated to stop talking. There should be no last words, no parting shots.

The T sign is also a signal that it's time to separate for a while. Whoever calls the time out should leave for a predetermined length of time (one hour is usually a good cooling-off period). It's very important to return when the time is up so that the other person doesn't feel abandoned or punished. It's also important that the other person wait for your return so that both of you can try again with somewhat cooler heads.

While you're gone during a time out, try to do something physically challenging or relaxing. The idea is to work off some of the arousal so that you can return feeling less stressed. Don't rehearse the faults and failings of the other person—that will only make your anger burn hotter. Don't rehearse what you're going to say. And absolutely do not use drugs or alcohol during a time out separation.

When you get back, be certain to "check in:" Indicate whether you feel ready to return to a discussion of the conflict, and do so. If you're not ready, set a specific time when you both feel willing to resume an exploration of the issue. This helps to maintain trust and establishes your willingness to communicate.

The following is a time out contract that has been used extensively and successfully with partners who are struggling with anger.

Time Out Contract

When I realize that my (or my partner's) anger is rising, I will give a T signal for a time out and leave at once. I will not hit or kick anything, and I will not slam the door.

I will return in no later than one hour. I will take a walk, will use up the anger energy, and will not use alcohol or drugs while I'm away. I will try not to focus on resentments.

If my partner gives a T signal and leaves, I will return the sign and let my partner go without a hassle, no matter what is going on. I will not drink or use drugs while my partner is away and will avoid focusing on resentments.

Name: _____

Date: _____

Name: _____

Date: _____

Dress Rehearsal

Select a situation where you frequently feel anger. The following steps will help you develop and then rehearse a plan that may keep you from getting angry next time around.

1. Identify your trigger thoughts. Think back over similar situations in the past. What have you said to yourself to incite the anger? What blaming or should statements have you used?

2. Rewrite your trigger statements using the principles of accuracy and personal responsibility. See if you can turn the trigger statement into something milder and less attacking.

3. From the list of healthy coping thoughts, select two or three that feel appropriate for the situation. If you want, modify them till they feel right for you.

4. Write out a statement that identifies what you want or need in the situation in a direct, nonattacking style.

5. Now it's time to rehearse in advance your response to the anger provoking situation. Begin by writing out the anger provoking situation as a sequence—a series of things that you and the other person say back and forth while the anger escalates. Start out by describing the setting, what you're doing, and what the other person is doing. Now write the typical opening gambit, the thing that starts you feeling riled. What happens next? What do you say, and what does the other person say? But before the situation gets out of hand, write a statement in which you describe your needs or wants in the situation. The other person refuses to listen. So you ask about his or her needs to better understand the source of the conflict. The other person tells you what he or she wants, but no immediate solution or compromise presents itself. The other person remains provocative, and you eventually withdraw from the situation *without having exploded*.

Having written out a script of the scene, you can rehearse your new coping skills by visualizing it while using deep breathing and cue controlled relaxation to cope with arousal. You will also use your preselected healthy coping thoughts to help you resist the impulse to explode. If the old trigger thoughts start to surface, remind yourself of the rewritten versions that are more accurate and accept responsibility for resolving the problem.

Go ahead right now and visualize this scene, step by step, using relaxation and coping thoughts throughout whenever you feel a surge of anger. Do this "dress rehearsal" at least three times a day as you prepare for the next provocative situation. The relaxation skills and coping thoughts that you are using in the rehearsal will in time become part of your response to real-life provocations.

The case of Paul. Paul found himself getting extremely angry during his four-year-old daughter's bedtime. She had to be reminded three hundred times to get undressed. She would climb the stairs to her bedroom and then slide back down the bannister. She made faces in the mirror instead of brushing her teeth. Then she jumped up from the bed after Paul had tucked her in for another round of fun with her stuffed toys. Sooner or later, Paul would lose it and start screaming, his daughter would cry, and then he would have to spend fifteen minutes hugging and calming her down. He decided to apply the five steps of a dress rehearsal to his nightly nightmare.

For step one, he was able to identify a major trigger thought: "She doesn't care how much this upsets me, she just wants her way. She's willful."

For step two, Paul corrected his mind reading and the global label of "willful." He rewrote the trigger thought as follows: "She wants to do what she wants to do, and I'm not being effective at getting her to do what I want her to do."

Step three: Paul selected the following coping thoughts:

- Getting upset won't help.
- I'll stay rational. Anger won't solve anything.
- I can't change her with anger. I'll just hurt her and upset myself.

Paul wrote these healthy coping thoughts on a file card to help himself remember them.

Step four: Paul wrote out a clear statement of what he wanted from his child. He realized, as he analyzed his responsibility for the situation, that he was not properly reinforcing his daughter to move efficiently through the bedtime rituals. Paul chose this statement to tell her what he wanted and reinforce better compliance: "If you brush your teeth, go up the stairs, get into bed, and stay under the covers, I'll read you a bedtime story. Which one do you want?" Paul decided to repeat this statement at each point where his daughter began playing rather than moving toward bed.

Step five: Paul wrote out a script of the problem situation that included each of his daughter's typical procrastinations as he attempted to get her to bed. He included his request statement at each point where she veered off course. While imagining the scene during his dress rehearsal, Paul relaxed by using deep breathing and repeated healthy coping thoughts whenever he felt a surge of irritation. Once he caught himself labeling her as willful, but he changed it to: "She does what she wants to do, and I have to reinforce her to do what I want her to do." After a few days of dress rehearsals, Paul found the bedtime rituals becoming much less problematic. He felt in better control—both of his daughter's behavior and of his own angry response.

14

Being Healthy:
Taking Care of Your Body

Men's bodies are expendable. They just aren't as important as women's bodies because men can't have babies. From an evolutionary point of view, the human race must protect and tenderly care for individual women's bodies until they are well into their forties and have finished bearing young and caring for young children. On the other hand, the human race only needs a handful of young men to provide occasional squirts of sperm. Male bodies past their sexual prime are like clunker cars—not worth repairing or taking care of.

This is overstated to make a point, but not by much. The under-valuing of male life and health is an historical fact, clearly seen in war, in economics, in actuarial tables, and in patterns of health care utilization.

This chapter is not intended to tell you everything you need to know about your health. We don't have the space. Besides, basic self-care information is available in many other books and magazines. What this chapter does cover are the health issues that are of particular importance to you *as a man*:

- The fact that you have a body that deserves care
- How to relax and reduce stress in your life
- Diet and exercise to prevent high blood pressure and cholesterol
- Cancer of the prostate and testicles

Your Body Deserves Care

How long since you had a physical exam?

When did you last get your teeth cleaned?

Do you get enough sleep every night?

Do you take breaks to relax during the day?

Do you eat regular meals?

Do you eat a balanced diet?

Can you list the four basic food groups?

Do you get regular exercise?

How much do you weigh?

Are you reasonably fit for your age?

Do you smoke or drink or do drugs?

How much?

Do you drive drunk or drugged?

What are your chronic physical problems?

What should you be doing about them?

Do you need glasses but don't have any?

Do you drive fast or leave your seat belt off?

Do you use goggles, respirators, or other safety measures when appropriate?

Do you have a first aid kit in your home?

Do you practice safe sex?

The point of all these questions is not to remind you of your mother or induce guilt. The point is to uncover your attitude toward your body. Our culture considers men's bodies less valuable and less deserving of care than women's or children's bodies. If you have internalized this bias, you may feel that taking care of your body isn't very important.

Wrong. It's the only body you have. It deserves care. You deserve to take care of yourself, to make your one and only body as healthy, fit, and comfortable as you can.

This chapter will get you started. To begin, make an appointment for a physical exam if:

- You have some nagging symptoms that you were just hoping would go away.

- You are under forty and haven't had a checkup in three years.

- You are over forty and haven't had a checkup in over a year. (Make sure the checkup includes a rectal exam for prostate cancer.)

Relaxation and Stress Reduction

This is by far the longest part of this chapter, because it is the most important. Learning to relax is the single most important skill you can acquire to take care of your body. It's more crucial than even diet and exercise.

This section will cover the nature of stress, Progressive Muscle Relaxation, a breathing exercise, a visualization exercise, planning lifestyle changes for long-term stress reduction, and nurturing yourself.

Let's begin by examining the nature of that much overworked word, *stress*. You hear people talk about stress in many ways:

"I'm under a lot of stress."

"I don't handle stress well."

"I feel stressed-out."

"This is too stressful for me."

Stress is a confusing term because it means different things to different people. This is partly due to the origin of the word itself. Up until the 1950s, the term was used only in engineering and physics. It meant a force, usually the force of gravity, operating in a certain direction, on an object or a structure which resisted the force. This is the metaphorical meaning behind a statement such as "I'm under a lot of stress." It means "I feel like I've got sixteen tons of concrete on top of me."

The groundwork for the modern use of the word to describe a psychological problem was laid by Walter B. Cannon, a physiologist at Harvard around the turn of the century. He didn't use the term *stress*, but he was the first to describe the *fight or flight response*. The fight or flight response is a four-step process:

1. The conscious level of your brain perceives a situation as dangerous.

2. A message is sent from your higher brain levels to your brain stem.

3. Your brain stem excites the sympathetic half of your autonomic nervous system. These are the nerves that regulate your digestion, heart beat, glands, and the dilation of your blood vessels.

4. Your sympathetic nervous system speeds your breathing and heart rate. Your liver releases stored sugar to nourish your muscles. Your blood pressure rises. The blood vessels in your extrem-

ities and your digestive system contract so that your blood is concentrated in your heart and in the vessels serving your large voluntary muscles and your central nervous system. Your adrenal glands secrete adrenaline, plus epinephrin and norepinephrine. These are messenger hormones that make your body ready to move fast. Your pituitary gland releases endorphins. These are brain chemicals that block pain signals and have a slightly depressing effect on your immune system.

In other words, when you perceive danger, an automatic, complicated, and speedy reaction takes place to prepare you to fight or run away. Lately stress experts have been calling this reaction the fight, flight, or *freeze* response. In many modern situations, fighting and fleeing are not appropriate reactions. Often the best you can do is hunker down and endure—like a scared rabbit that freezes when danger approaches and waits tensely for the threat to go away.

Notice that the four steps of the fight, flight, or freeze reaction already suggest the way to fight stress: the whole response depends on your conscious assessment of danger. As soon as you decide that a situation is not dangerous, your higher brain levels stop sending panic messages to your brain stem, which in turn stops sending panic messages to your nervous system. The adrenaline and other hormones and chemicals that keep your body aroused are metabolized quickly. About three minutes after you stop sending your body danger messages, the fight, flight, or freeze response "burns out" and you return to normal.

In the 1950s Hans Selye was the first to use the word *stress* to describe what happens when you confront events that are not exactly dangerous, but which evoke the fight, flight, or freeze response anyway. Some examples are giving a speech, meeting strangers, being criticized, and driving in heavy traffic. What people, places, things, and events in your life do you find stressful?

Later, Thomas Holmes, a medical doctor at the University of Washington School of Medicine, showed that positive as well as negative events are stressful. Falling in love and getting married can demand just as much change, and thus be as stressful, as falling out of love and breaking up.

Holmes devised the "Schedule of Recent Experience," a checklist of stressful events, both positive and negative, that he used to predict your chances of getting sick from a stress-related illness.

On his schedule, major changes like getting married, losing your job, getting a divorce, or the death of a loved one are scored very high. Less stressful events like a change in the amount of exercise you get or going on vacation earn you a lower score. You add up the scores for all of the items on the list that have happened to you during the last two years. The higher your score, the more stress you are under, and the more likely you are to get sick.

In the last few years, researchers such as Richard Lazarus at the University of California have turned to studying the lesser, smaller disruptions of life. They have shown that the cumulative effects of all the minor, everyday stresses are more harmful than the major life changes on the Holmes schedule. The unscientific but very descriptive term commonly used for these minor irritations is "hassles." Hassles are the snubs, rebukes, bad weather, car problems, disappointments, tight schedules, red lights, spilled milk, and broken fingernails that everyone encounters and no one can entirely escape, however healthy, wealthy, or wise.

Whatever its source, stress causes illness in two ways. First, stress taxes nerves, muscles, and organs directly. For example, constant muscular tension from overactivation of the fight, flight, or freeze response can result in a chronically sore back. Or constant elevation of blood pressure can overwork your heart. The second way stress causes illness is by suppressing your immune system, making you more susceptible to infection and disease.

There are basically two ways to fight stress. One way is to focus on the *symptoms* of the fight, flight, or freeze response. The other way is to concentrate on the *causes* of the response. This chapter will help you fight stress in both ways.

Progressive Muscle Relaxation

Relaxation acts quickly and directly on the symptoms of stress, loosening chronically tight muscles. Relaxation training has been found helpful for the treatment of muscular tension, insomnia, fatigue, irritable bowel, muscle spasms, neck and back pain, and high blood pressure.

Relaxation also relieves painful emotions. While you are completely relaxed, it's impossible to feel emotions such as fear, anxiety, depression, or anger. All these emotions depend on a minimum level of physical arousal before they can be felt. This is the basis of relaxation's great calming effect. It returns you to a natural balance, a centered state of homeostasis in which your mind is at peace and your body can heal itself.

In 1929 a Chicago physician named Edmond Jacobson published a book entitled *Progressive Relaxation*. In it he described a simple procedure of deliberately tensing and releasing major muscle groups in sequence to achieve total body relaxation. Over sixty years later, Jacobson's methods are still the basis of nearly all relaxation training.

The procedure is easy. You start with your arms, tensing the various muscles, noticing what that feels like, then relaxing the muscles and noticing what relaxation feels like. You go on to do the same thing with the muscles associated with your head, then your torso, and finally your legs.

You do each muscle group at least twice, with more repetitions for especially tense areas.

Fifteen minutes, twice a day is the recommended schedule. In one or two weeks you should be able to reach deep levels of relaxation fairly quickly. You will come to know which muscles need more relaxation and you'll be very sensitive to the buildup of tension in your body. After you've mastered the basic procedure, you'll probably want to mostly use the shorthand version that is outlined later.

You can try to remember these instructions and follow them with your eyes closed. A better approach the first few times is to tape-record the instructions so that you can listen to them with your eyes closed. Speak slowly and clearly, in a calm voice. At a number of places throughout the script you will be instructed to pause for a count of five seconds before going on.

Progressive Muscle Relaxation Script

Lie down on your back on a couch, bed, or the floor. Find a comfortable position with your arms and legs uncrossed. You can put a pillow under your knees to take the strain off your lower back. Close your eyes gently.

Now clench your right fist, tighter and tighter, studying the tension as you hold your hand tightly in a fist. Keep it clenched and notice the tension in your fist, wrist, and forearm. Keep the muscles tight just a little longer... now relax. Feel the looseness in your right hand, and notice the contrast with the tension. Concentrate on the feeling of relaxation for a moment. (Pause five seconds.)

Try it again. Clench your right fist again, as tight as you can without hurting yourself. Study the feeling of muscular tension in your fist, your wrist, and your forearm... now relax. Feel the contrast as relaxation floods into your muscles. Notice the difference between tension and relaxation for a moment. (Pause five seconds.)

Now do the same thing with your left fist. Curl your left hand into a fist and hold it tightly. Keep it clenched and notice the tension in your hand, your wrist, and your forearm. Hold the tightness...hold it...and relax. Feel the looseness in your left hand now, notice how relaxation feels different from tension. Keep focused on the feeling in your left hand for another moment. (Pause five seconds).

Clench your left hand again, very tightly, but not so tight that it hurts. Study the feeling of tension in your forearm, your wrist, and your hand...now relax. Feel the contrast between the tension and the relaxation. Notice whether your muscles feel heavy, or warm, or tingling. Stay focused on the sensations of relaxation for a moment. (Pause five seconds.)

Now try it with both fists at once. Curl both hands into fists and clench them firmly. Hold the tension and notice how hard and tight they feel...now relax both fists at once. Feel the relaxation flow down your arms and into the muscles and joints of your forearms, your wrists, and your hands. Study this feeling of slack, loose relaxation for a moment. (Pause five seconds.)

Next, bend both your arms at the elbows and tense your biceps. Hold your upper arms as tightly flexed as you can. Notice what this feels like. Notice if it makes you feel paralyzed or nervous or like you are about to hit something. Now relax. Let the sensations of relaxation flood into the muscles of your arms, softening and warming your biceps. Study this delicious feeling of calm relaxation for a moment. (Pause five seconds.)

Now turn your attention to your head. Wrinkle your forehead as tightly as you can. Really frown and scowl and make the wrinkles as deep and hard as you can...now relax. Let yourself imagine your entire forehead and scalp becoming smooth as a baby's forehead. Concentrate on this feeling of smooth relaxation for a moment. (Pause five seconds.)

Wrinkle your forehead again. Try to make your whole scalp wrinkly too. Hold it tightly for just a little longer... and relax. Let the muscles go and let your forehead and scalp become as flat as a pool of perfectly still water. Really feel the contrast between a frowning and a relaxed brow. Tell yourself, "I'm letting go of all the tension." (Pause five seconds.)

Next, squint your eyes shut tightly. Look for the tension as you hold your eyes clenched tightly shut. Notice how your eyebrows come down and your cheeks go up to clamp your eyes shut. Now relax your eyes until they are just barely closed, just very lightly closed, your eyelids just lying softly over your eyes like rose petals. (Pause five seconds.)

Close your eyes tightly again. Really clamp them shut like you never intend to open them again. Study the feeling of tension. Then relax your eyes until they are barely shut. Notice the difference between the tension and the relaxation. Notice whether your eyelids or eyeballs twitch or feel warm or cool. (Pause five seconds.)

Now clench your jaw. Bite down hard, but not hard enough to crack a tooth. Press your teeth firmly together and notice the tension in your jaw. A lot of people grind or press their teeth together unconsciously, creating chronic tension in the jaw muscles. Now relax, letting your mouth open slightly. Feel the release of your jaw muscles as they relax. Let your jaw sag down and study the feeling of relaxation for a moment. (Pause five seconds.)

Try it again. Clench your jaw and really concentrate on the feeling of tension. Notice if it reminds you of feeling stubborn or hassled...then relax the tension and notice the contrast between muscular tension and relaxed muscles. Let yourself really appreciate the contrast between tension and relaxation. (Pause five seconds.)

Now press your tongue against the roof of your mouth. Feel the ache in the back of your mouth and down into your throat...relax your tongue and throat and feel the tension drain out of the muscles. Pay attention to the difference between the tension and the relaxation. (Pause five seconds.)

Once more, press your tongue up against the roof of your mouth. Press hard and feel the tension spread from the back of your mouth and down your throat. Study this tension and notice if it reminds you of crying or choking. Now relax the tension and observe the distinctions between tension and relaxation in your throat. (Pause five seconds.)

Press your lips forward now, pursing them into an "O." Hold your lips forward in a circle for a while, noticing the tension. Then relax your mouth and let it hang slightly open. Note the difference between the tension and the relaxation for a moment. (Pause five seconds.)

Try it again. Push your lips out into the shape of an "O" and hold it, concentrating on the sensations of tension. Then release the muscles and let your mouth relax. Focus on the sensations of calm relaxation. Tell yourself, "I'm allowing tension to flow away." (Pause five seconds.)

Next you'll tense and relax the muscles of your neck. A lot of people carry constant tension in their neck muscles. Start by pressing your head back as far as it can comfortably go and observing the tension in your neck. (Pause five seconds.)

Now roll your head to the right as far as you can, until you feel strain. Notice the changing location of stress in your muscles. (Pause five seconds.)

Then roll your head all the way to the left, as far as you can, and feel how the opposite muscles take up the tension. (Pause five seconds.)

Finally, straighten your head and bring it forward, pressing your chin against your chest as far as you can. Notice how this feels for a moment. (Pause five seconds.)

Now let your head fall gently back into repose, and relax all the muscles in your neck. Really study the sensations in your neck for another moment. (Pause five seconds.)

Repeat this procedure. Press your head back against the floor or bed you're lying on and hold the tension. (Pause five seconds.)

Now roll your head to the right and hold it tightly, noticing the tension. (Pause five seconds.)

Next roll your head all the way to the left and hold it there. See if the tension feels the same or slightly different from before. (Pause five seconds.)

Then raise your head and press your chin towards your chest and hold it up. (Pause five seconds.)

Relax, allowing your head to come back to a comfortable position. Study the contrast between the feelings of relaxation and the feelings of contracting and stretching your neck muscles. (Pause five seconds.)

Now shrug your shoulders. Keep the tension as you hunch your head down between your shoulders. A lot of tension can also be stored in your shoulders. Hold this pose for a bit, then relax. Allow your shoulders to sag down and feel the relaxation seeping through your shoulders, neck, and throat. (Pause five seconds.)

Shrug your shoulders again. Pull your head down between your shoulders and feel the pressure and tension as you hold the position for a little while. Now relax and let your shoulders go limp. Feel the warmth and heaviness as your shoulders and neck and throat relax. Study the difference in sensation between tension and relaxation. (Pause five seconds.)

Give your entire body a chance to relax. Breathe in and fill your lungs completely. Hold your breath and feel the tension in your chest. Now exhale and let your chest fall and become relaxed. Observe the difference in feeling between tension and relaxation in your chest. (Pause five seconds.)

Now inhale again and really fill your lungs to full capacity. Hold the breath and feel the stretching and strain all through your torso. Exhale with a sighing sound and feel relaxation steal over you. Explore the contrasts between the tension of the inhalation and the release of the exhalation. (Pause five seconds.)

Next, tighten your stomach muscles and hold them clenched as you focus your attention on the feeling of tension. Then release your stomach muscles and let the tension subside. Notice how it feels to create tension and then create relaxation. Say to yourself, "I am feeling calmer and more peaceful." (Pause five seconds.)

Try tensing your stomach again. Hold the tightness in your stomach and notice if it also makes your lower back feel tight. Relax your stomach muscles and shift your attention to the feelings of relaxation that flow throughout your stomach and lower back. (Pause five seconds.)

Now arch your back, without straining. If you have back trouble, skip the tensing part and just imagine draining any tension out of your back muscles. If you are arching your back, focus on the tension in your back muscles. Then relax your back and let it go flat again. This is another area where many people feel chronic muscular tension. Notice how your back feels when it is tense and when it is relaxed. (Pause five seconds.)

Now arch your back again. Hold the tension and study it carefully. Does your back feel like this often, when you are not consciously tensing the muscles? Now relax your muscles and let all the strain go away. Observe the contrast between tension and relaxation in your back. (Pause five seconds.)

Next, tighten your buttocks and thighs. Flex your thighs by pressing your heels downward as hard as you can. Hold this tension for a moment, then release it. Feel the relaxation flood into the large muscles of your buttocks and thighs. Concentrate on the subtle differences between tension and relaxation. (Pause five seconds.)

Tighten your buttocks and thighs one more time. Push your heels downward again as hard as you can. Hold this position while you study the tension in your muscles. Now relax and feel the large muscles relax. Pay attention to the differences between the tense and the loose muscles. (Pause five seconds.)

Now curl your toes downward to make your calf muscles tense. Do this gradually and stop if you start to get a cramp in the sole of your foot. Hold your toes down and study the sensation of muscular tension. Then uncurl your toes and release your calf muscles. See if you can perceive all the variations of pressure, stretching, temperature, and slight pain that mark the difference between tension and relaxation. (Pause five seconds.)

Try it again. Curl your toes downward and tense your calves. Hold the pose while you memorize the feelings of tension. Now relax and feel the sensations of relaxation take over. Try to catalog all the characteristics of relaxation. (Pause five seconds.)

Now bend your toes back toward your head, creating tension in your shins. Observe the feeling in your shins as you hold your toes in this position. Now relax and let your toes go back to a comfortable position. Notice the difference between the tension in your shins and the relaxation. (Pause five seconds.)

One more time, bend your toes back toward your head and hold the tension in your shins while you analyze the feelings associated with the contracted muscles. Then relax the muscles, let your feet down, and examine the new feeling of relaxation in your shins. Tell yourself, "The tension is melting away." (Pause five seconds.)

Lie still for a little while and enjoy the relaxation you have created in your body. You can create relaxation in your body just as naturally as you can create tension in your muscles.

In a moment you will open your eyes and get up. Remind yourself to take time during the next few hours to do your relaxation exercises. Now recall what your surroundings are like, open your eyes slowly, and get up when you are ready. Go about your routine feeling refreshed and relaxed.

Shorthand Procedure.   When you have gained some experience in relaxing your body, you may be able to use this shorthand procedure most of the time, instead of the full procedure.

To do the shorthand procedure, curl both your fists and tighten your biceps in a "Charles Atlas" pose. Hold this position and really concentrate on making your muscles as hard and tight as you can. Then relax, and let your arms fall to your sides. Feel the relaxation rush into the muscles as they go slack.

Next work on your head and neck. Wrinkle up your forehead in a frown, squint your eyes closed, purse your lips, and press your tongue up against the roof of your mouth. Try to wrinkle up your whole face like the meat of a walnut. At the same time, hunch up your shoulders. Reverse and roll your head around in the opposite direction. Then let everything relax and enjoy the warm feeling of relaxation as your face goes smooth and your neck loosens.

Then arch your back as you take a deep breath into your chest. Hold the breath and tense your stomach muscles. Keep holding the breath and focusing on the feelings of tension. Now flatten your back, exhale, and relax the tension in your stomach. Notice how very relaxing it is to breath out and relax like this.

Finally, tighten your buttocks and thighs. At the same time, curl your toes down to tighten your calves. Then pull your toes up toward your face. Hold this position for a moment and concentrate on what tension in your legs feels like. Then relax and switch to analyzing the feelings of relaxation.

Variations. There are other possibilities that you might want to try for altering the basic relaxation procedures. You can start at your feet and work upward for a little variety. You can try synchronizing your breathing with the tensing and relaxing, so that you breathe in while tensing, hold your breath while holding tension, and then exhale slowly while relaxing your muscles.

As you become more expert at relaxation, you will need less time to tense and relax all your muscles. Also, when you become an expert at noticing muscular tension, the deliberate tensing of your muscles will become less important. Begin using the "body awareness" or "release only" method, in which you systematically scan your body for tension and release it from your muscles without first tensing them. Follow the same sequence provided for the shorthand procedure. This method is not only faster, but is also preferable if you have sore or injured muscles that you don't want to aggravate by extra tension.

Try different relaxation sequences and methods until you find the ones that give you the best results.

Deep Breathing

Proper breathing is very important in stress reduction. If your breathing is shallow, with short breaths in a choppy or lazy rhythm, you may not get enough oxygen. Your complexion will be poor because your blood is dark and bluish instead of bright red. Your digestion will be bad, you'll get tired easily, you'll have trouble coping with daily hassles, and you'll tend to fall more easily into states of anxiety and depression. Full, deep, slow breathing corrects these tendencies by relaxing your body, oxygenating your blood, and removing waste from your circulatory system.

Although Westerners have only recently learned about the importance of breathing, Eastern cultures have used breathing exercises to relax the body and calm the mind for centuries.

Here is a script for a deep breathing exercise that you may want to tape-record for your own use.

Deep Breathing Script

Lie down, get comfortable, and close your eyes. Put your attention on your breathing. Place your hand on the spot that rises the most when you inhale. If this spot is on your chest, you are not using your full lung capacity. You're breathing mostly in the top of your lungs. Put your hand on your stomach and take full, deep breaths that make your stomach rise more than your chest.

Continue breathing slowly and deeply into your stomach. As you inhale, imagine that your nostrils are located in your heels. See your breath as a white cloud of steam or fog, very pure and cleansing. It comes in at your heels and sweeps up the back of your body, reaching your head as your lungs become full. The cloud picks up all impurities, tension, distractions, and fatigue as it passes through you. You can visualize these things as darkness, cinders, dust, or cloudiness.

As you exhale, imagine this white cloud swirling around, down the front of your body, picking up more impurities, and exiting through your toes. As your lungs are emptied, the cloud leaves your body entirely and is dissipated in space. It carries with it all the dark impurities, all the gritty tension, all the dusty fatigue, all the cloudy aches and pains.

Keep breathing slowly and deeply. Again, imagine the white cloud coming in at your heels, swirling around to fill every limb and digit, and carrying all the darkness out your toes. Your body gets brighter, cleaner, lighter with each breath.

If the traditional heel and toe imagery doesn't feel comfortable to you, change the entry and exit points to suit yourself. You could have your breath coming in your head and going out your feet, or in your nose and out your mouth, or whatever. Find the arrangement that feels the most logical and cleansing to you.

Visualization

In the cleansing breath exercise you used images of a white cloud and dust to enhance the relaxing effects of deep breathing. In this visualization exercise, you will explore your own personal imagery of tension and relaxation. You'll also work with your other senses—hearing, taste, smell, touch, and so on. This will help you create a vivid constellation of symbols for both tension and relaxation.

To do the visualization exercise, lie down, get comfortable, and let your mind go blank and quiet. Gradually become aware of a spot in your body where you normally feel soreness or tension. It might be your back, your neck, your shoulders, or your jaw.

If that part isn't sore or tense right now, deliberately tense it a little. While you are feeling that muscular tension, what images come up for you? What does your tension look like? What object or experience does it remind you of? What color is it? If you could listen to your tension, what would it sound like? Think of an unpleasant smell that could represent your tension. Is your tension hot or cold? Rough or smooth? Bitter or sour or salty?

Ideally, you should get at least one impression from each of your senses to represent tension: sight, hearing, taste, smell, and the various senses of touch. For example, a medical doctor associated muscular tension with twisted and knotted white cotton sheets, a blue-green color, steel-toed work shoes, resounding Chinese gongs, a high whistling sound, a metallic taste like tinfoil on silver dental fillings, the smell of ether, the feel of a wire brush, and cold wind on wet skin.

You may not get so many impressions. That's okay. The important thing is to get a few images or sensations that you associate strongly with muscular tension in your body.

It's even all right if you come up with no original images at all. You can choose a few from this list:

Tight twisted ropes
Hard, cold wax
The sound of jackhammers
Creaking hinges
The taste of lemon
The smell of hot metal
The feel of sandpaper
Cold wind
Hot, red muscles

Next, let the tension fade from your muscles. Concentrate on feeling warm, heavy, and completely relaxed. What images come to mind to represent total relaxation? These images may be logical extensions or transformations of your images of tension, or they may be new, unrelated images.

For example, the doctor saw the twisted sheets untwisting and becoming soft and smooth. The blue-green color faded to a pale, peachy yellow. The work shoes changed into fleecy bedroom slippers. The Chinese gong modulated into a soft piano sonata. The whistling sound faded into silence. The metallic taste and the smell of ether were replaced by the taste and smell of jasmine tea. The feel of the cold wind went away, to be replaced by warm sand and sun on the skin. He also associated relaxation with a picture he had once seen of lions sleeping, the sound of distant calliope music, and the sensations of getting a massage.

Once again, if you don't get any spontaneous sensations to represent relaxation, you can choose some from this list:

Twisted ropes untwist
Wax softens and melts
Jackhammers become distant woodpeckers
Hinges get oiled and become silent and smooth
The taste of lemon becomes the taste of your favorite dessert
The smell of hot metal becomes the smell of roses
Sandpaper becomes satin
Cold wind becomes warm sun
Hot, red muscles turn a cool green color

The images you choose for your first stress reduction visualizations are not too crucial. As you practice, you will be attracted to the right images for you, and new images will present themselves as you develop your skills.

When you want to work on relaxing a particular part of your body, first imagine your symbol for tension, located in that area of your body. For example, if you have chronic lower back pain, imagine that there are ropes in your lower back. They are twisted so tight that they are quivering with tension. Imagine the finest details: the color of the rope, the number of strands in each, the texture, the play of light and shadow over the ropes. Then bring in your personal symbol for relaxation. Imagine the ropes slackening. Watch them untwist. Feel them loosen their grip on your spine. See the ropes finally go limp and hang free, with no tension left at all.

Lifestyle Changes

The second way to fight stress is to go beyond symptoms and identify and change the *causes* of stress in your life. The only real way to beat stress once and for all is to change your stressful lifestyle and your stressful beliefs. This means changing your job and your relationships so that you no longer have punishing schedules and don't have to meet the demands of unreasonable people. It means getting off tobacco, alcohol, drugs, sugar, and so on to maximize your health. It means learning not to obsess about unfairness, failure, catastrophe, being perfect, and so on.

First of all, how about your schedule? What can you cut out? What wastes your time? How can you organize your time more effectively? When can you take a break each day to do your relaxation visualizations? What is the source of your greatest time pressure—your job? your studies?

your family? Something else? What kind of schedule do you want to have a year from now? In the space below, write down your goals regarding how you want to handle your schedule in the future.

Now think about your relationships with friends, family, lovers, colleagues, acquaintances, strangers. Who in your life contributes to your stress? Who makes demands on you? Who involves you in the same pointless arguments? Who criticizes you or interferes in your life? Whom do you get angry at all the time? Whom do wish you could avoid or say no to? Whom do you desperately try to please?

As you're thinking about other people, remember the unfortunate fact that they are unlikely to change to suit you. Think in terms of how you can change your own behavior to be more assertive, to avoid conflicts, to clear up misunderstandings, to deflect criticism, and so on. Use the space below to list changes you can make to avoid or improve the interactions that cause you stress. Other chapters in this book suggest specific strategies you can use to deal with anger and other feelings and to ask for what you want from others.

Next consider how your own beliefs and attitudes may be contributing to high stress levels. Do you tend to be judgmental about others? Do you see most issues in black and white? Do you dwell on your fears or worries and work yourself up into a state of panic? Do you fall into mind reading, assuming things about other people's motives and behavior for which you really don't have any evidence? Do you have unreasonably high expectations for yourself or others? Are you a perfectionist? Do you lack faith in your own ability to cope? Do you have any phobias? Do you need to feel in complete control at all times? Or do you feel like a victim of forces over which you have no control?

These are all habitual patterns of thought that create stress by an unnecessarily negative view of yourself, others, and the world. Persistent negative thought patterns can be difficult to change. If you suffer considerable mental stress of this kind and want to explore this promising avenue for improving your life, you should read our previous books: *Thoughts & Feelings* and *Prisoners of Belief,* both available from New Harbinger Publications at the address in the front of this book. You also might want to consult a cognitive therapist.

Self-Nurturing

The capacity to self-nurture is a major antidote for stress. Many men aren't taught how to nurture—either others or themselves. As a result they are not aware of how to give themselves experiences that are healing and calming.

Self-nurturing activities have the defining characteristic of leaving you feeling good when they're over. You're not exhausted, irritable, disappointed, empty, or strung out afterward. Self-nurturing activities are intrinsically pleasurable, *regardless of outcome.* An example is a sports activity that is really nurturing and feels good whether you win or lose. Self-nurturing activities leave you able to function more effectively rather than less effectively. You're better equipped to cope, relate, and take care of business.

Self-nurturing activities generally are not:

- Frenetic diversions. They don't take you for a ride and leave you flat.

- Numbing. They don't shut off or mask your feelings.

- Indulgent. They are not compulsive pleasures that help you evade family and work responsibilities.

Self-nurturing is an opportunity to give to yourself, to take some control in your life by doing the things that calm and relax you. It is a healthy discipline that leads to feelings of replenishment. The following are sixteen examples of self-nurturing activities. There are literally hundreds of ways to replenish yourself, but these will give you some ideas that might lead you to identify the kind of self-nurturing that will work for you.

1. Aerobics. This includes running, working out, swimming, speed walking, biking, and so forth. Many men experience aerobics as a high that melts away stress and replaces it with feelings of well-being.

2. Athletics. Tennis, golf, handball, racquetball; anything you really enjoy regardless of the score at the end of the game. Athletic activities that are nurturing rarely are highly competitive. To consistently enjoy a sport, you have to do it for the muscle joy, not as a confirmation of prowess or a bolster for your self-esteem.

3. Reading. It's lovely sometimes to enter the world of a book and take time off from ordinary existence.

4. Journal writing. Some men use a journal as a path to self-exploration and a way to increase awareness as they review the experiences of a day. Creative writing in any form can serve the same purpose. You can use material from your own experience as the foundation for a creative process. It's an opportunity to tune in to what you feel.

5. Listening to or playing music.

6. Taking time out for contemplation and quiet. This is the act of being your own companion, of drifting with your own thoughts, noticing your own feelings, and giving yourself a time to live in the here-and-now moment.

7. Meditation. Some men have found meditation to be of tremendous value for replenishing. The act of focusing and refocusing on your breath, a sound, or an image has a cleansing effect. You are literally washing your mind of stress.

8. Creating an aesthetic, calming environment. Some men make an effort to shape their living environment into something that pleases the eye and soothes the psyche. This may require nothing more than having a comfortable chair and reading lamp. Or it may involve creating an elaborate Japanese garden. Literally anything you do to enhance the sense of order and attractiveness in your surroundings may have a nurturing effect.

9. Eating. For many people, food is a reliable way of feeling good. Whether you carefully prepare your own meal or eat out where all that is done for you, eating is a good way of giving to yourself.

10. Taking walks. The evening stroll is an underrated pleasure. Many men build walking into their daily schedule as a way of relieving stress and slowing their pace.

11. Hot baths or showers. Heat is relaxing. Giving yourself time to enjoy hot water is a way of calming and replenishing yourself.

12. Calling someone. For this to be genuinely nourishing, the call can't be a task or obligation. The person you call has to be someone you feel good conversing with.

13. Getting a massage.

14. Pursuing a hobby. Whether it's darkroom photography, stamp collecting, or rebuilding musical instruments, a hobby has a way of focusing your energies onto a physical task. You forget everything, and live very much in the moment as you become absorbed in the process.

15. Gardening. The connection with the earth and the process of growing living things is very calming and life-affirming.

16. Finding projects. It could be building a sandbox for your kids, a bookshelf for your girlfriend, or a flower box for the bedroom window.

In the space provided, write three self-nurturing activities that you'd be willing to schedule into your life.

Consider this a commitment. Self-nurturing is something you may have gotten little training in, but it is a basic skill for living a satisfying life. Schedule one of your listed self-nurturing activities for each of the next seven days. Write it into your appointment calendar. Commit yourself to doing it, whether you feel like making the effort or not when the time comes. At the end of the week evaluate which activities were most satisfying, most relaxing. Keep scheduling those, but also add new items to your list so that you can expand your repertoire of self-giving.

Diet and Exercise

Diet and exercise are particularly important to you as a man because:

- Men are at higher risk than women for heart attacks and strokes.

- The way to prevent heart attack and stroke is to keep your blood pressure and your blood cholesterol levels low.

- The best way to keep blood pressure and cholesterol down is to *eat right and stay active.*

Blood Pressure. When you go for that physical exam, take this book and write down your blood pressure before you forget it:

Date_____   Blood pressure _____

_____

The top number is your systolic pressure. This is the highest pressure reached each time your heart beats, the maximum force exerted by your heart on the walls of your arteries. Systolic pressure varies greatly throughout the day and night, going down when you sleep or rest and going up when you exercise or experience strong emotions like anger or fear. Systolic pressure tends to increase with age. When this top number consistently measures above 140, it's time to start worrying and taking measures to decrease your blood pressure.

The bottom number is your diastolic pressure. Your circulatory system is under pressure at all times, even between heartbeats. At the point when your heart is its most relaxed, a baseline amount of pressure is still present. This is the diastolic pressure. It tends to increase slightly with age, but it is much more stable than the systolic pressure from moment to moment. In terms of health, the diastolic pressure is the most important, since it represents the constant, inescapable pressure that your circulatory system must withstand all the time. When your diastolic pressure gets much over 80, it's time to make some changes in your diet and exercise.

Cholesterol.   When you get your physical exam, make sure they take blood and test it for cholesterol levels. Cholesterol is a substance contained in animal fat and certain other foods. If there is too much in your blood, it is deposited on the walls of your blood vessels, narrowing them, increasing your blood pressure, and putting you in higher danger of heart attack.

There are different kinds of cholesterol reported on blood tests. The crucial measurement is your serum cholesterol level (measured in milligrams per deciliter). Your doctor is sure to point out which number that is. Write the number down here:

Date_____   Serum cholesterol_____mpd

If your cholesterol count is over 200 mpd, it's too high, and again you need to make changes in your diet and get more exercise.

Diet.   There are hundreds of books and magazine articles about nutrition. You could easily make a life study about it. If you're interested you can read up on nutrition, buy cookbooks, browse in health food stores, and become an expert on what you should and shouldn't eat.

But if a poor diet has got you into trouble, you're probably not very interested in nutrition and unlikely to devote a lot of time to study. Ask your doctor for some dietary guidelines to follow. Doctors usually have photocopied food lists and menus to hand out. If not, here are the basics:

- Eat a variety of foods, including something every day from the basic food groups:

   Vegetables and fruits—four servings
   Bread, cereals, grains—four servings
   Meat, poultry, fish, beans, peas—two servings
   Milk, cheese, yogurt—two servings

- Reduce fat, especially animal fat in red meat, gravy, eggs.

- Reduce sodium (salt), especially hidden salt in processed foods.

- Reduce sugar.

- Increase whole foods instead of highly processed foods.

- Avoid alcohol.

Exercise. Again, you can buy books, subscribe to magazines, join a health club, and become an expert on exercise. But if lack of exercise is a long-term problem, you also probably have long-term lack of interest. So here are the basics:

- The only kind of exercise that will strengthen your heart and lower your blood pressure is aerobic exercise.

- For an activity to be aerobic, it must get your heart and breathing going fast and keep it elevated for at least twenty minutes.

- Very fast walking, jogging, and swimming are the best aerobic exercises. Stationary bikes, treadmills, stair-steppers, and rowing machines are possible substitutes.

- Whatever you choose to do, do it at least three times a week and keep your heart rate up for twenty minutes each time.

- Start slowly. You don't want to bring on the heart attack you are supposed to be preventing. If you can't carry on a conversation while exercising, you are going at it too hard.

Prostate Cancer

If you're over forty, your annual physical checkup should include a rectal prostate exam. You lie on your side with your knees pulled up to your chest. The doctor inserts a gloved, lubricated finger about an inch and a half into your rectum and feels the base of the prostate gland. The illustration shows where the prostate lies at the base of the bladder.

If your prostate feels enlarged, irregular, or abnormally firm, it could be a sign of trouble. Prostate trouble can be a cancerous tumor, an infec-

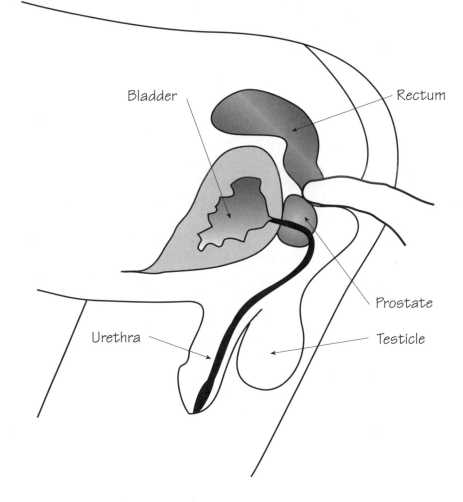

Bladder

Rectum

Prostate

Urethra

Testicle

tion, or a relatively harmless enlargement known as *benign prostatic hypertrophy*. Only the rectal exam can detect a tumor early. In the early stages of prostate cancer, you feel no symptoms. By the time prostate cancer becomes painful or starts to interfere with urination, it is well established and your chances of cure are worse. Given the way your body is constructed, you can't check your own prostate, so you have to have the doctor do it for you.

If you do have symptoms—it's hard to urinate, it's hard to stop urinating, you have to urinate frequently, it burns, or there's blood in your urine—don't panic. It's probably a benign enlargement of your prostate and not a tumor. But get examined right away and find out for sure.

Prostate cancer occurs most often around age 55. It kills about 30,000 men each year. By comparison, breast cancer kills about 50,000 women each year.

Testicular Cancer

Testicular cancer is one of the few cancers that affects younger men more than older men. It occurs most often between the ages of fifteen and thirty-five. It almost always affects one testicle, not both. The symptoms are a heavy feeling in the testicle, sometimes pain, and a small, pea-sized lump on the surface of the testicle. Treatment consists of surgery to remove the affected testicle, with chemotherapy and radiation if the cancer has spread to other parts of the body. Removal of one testicle still leaves you with enough sperm and hormones for a normal sex life.

Discovered early, the cure rate for testicular cancer is nearly 100 percent. Discovered late, your chances of cure drop to 70 percent. So it's wise to check yourself regularly, at least every month or two. It's very easy: after a shower or bath, when the skin on your scrotum is loose and soft, roll each testicle gently between thumb and forefinger. You're looking for anything that feels different from last time—a lump on the surface, an enlarged testicle, or any unusual hard spots. You can expect to find a small firm area near the rear of each testicle, and a cord leading up from the top. Those features are normal.

If you find any lumps or hard spots, or if one testicle gets bigger, you should see a doctor. It doesn't automatically mean that you have cancer. There are three or four kinds of relatively harmless infections or benign masses that can cause similar changes in your testicles—but only a doctor's exam and an ultrasound test can rule out cancer.

References

Bolles, R. *What Color is Your Parachute?* Berkeley, CA: Ten Speed Press, 1992.

Friedman, M., and D. Ulmer. *Type A Behavior and Your Heart.* New York: Alfred A. Knopf, 1984.

Harp, D. *The New Three Minute Meditator.* Oakland, CA: New Harbinger Publications, 1990.

Hite, S. *Hite Report: A Study of Male Sexuality.* New York: Ballantine, 1987.

Hoffman, D. "Moral Development." *Carmichael's Manual of Child Psychology,* edited by P. Mussen. New York: Wiley Publications, 1970.

Jacobson, E. *Progressive Relaxation.* Chicago: The University of Chicago Press, Midway Reprint, 1974.

Keen, S. *Fire in the Belly.* New York: Bantam Books, 1992.

Kipnis, A.R. *Knights Without Armor: A Practical Guide for Men in Quest of Masculine Soul.* Los Angeles: J.P. Tarcher, 1991.

Lee, J. *At My Father's Wedding: Men Coming to Terms With Their Father's and Themselves.* New York: Bantam, 1992.

_____ *The Flying Boy: Healing the Wounded Man.* Austin, TX: New Men's Press, 1987.

McKay, M., and P. Fanning. *Prisoners of Belief.* Oakland, CA: New Harbinger Publications, 1991.

McKay, M., and P. Fanning. *Thoughts & Feelings.* Oakland, CA: New Harbinger Publications, 1981.

McKay, M., P. Rogers, and J. McKay. *When Anger Hurts.* Oakland, CA: New Harbinger Publications, 1989.

Tavris, C. *Anger: The Misunderstood Emotion.* New York: Simon & Schuster, 1989.

The Whole Work Catalog. Boulder, CO: The New Careers Center.

Williams, W., *Rekindling Desire.* Oakland, CA: New Harbinger Publications, 1988.

Zilbergeld, B. *The New Male Sexuality.* New York: Bantam Books, 1992.

Other New Harbinger Self-Help Titles

Last Touch: Preparing for a Parents Death, $11.95
Consuming Passions: Help for Compulsive Shoppers, $11.95
Self-Esteem, Second Edition, $12.95
Depression & Anxiety Mangement: An audio tape for managing emotional problems, $11.95
I Can't Get Over It, A Handbook for Trauma Survivors, $12.95
Concerned Intervention, When Your Loved One Won't Quit Alcohol or Drugs, $11.95
Redefining Mr. Right, $11.95
Dying of Embarrassment: Help for Social Anxiety and Social Phobia, $11.95
The Depression Workbook: Living With Depression and Manic Depression, $13.95
Risk-Taking for Personal Growth: A Step-by-Step Workbook, $11.95
The Marriage Bed: Renewing Love, Friendship, Trust, and Romance, $11.95
Focal Group Psychotherapy: For Mental Health Professionals, $44.95
Hot Water Therapy: Save Your Back, Neck & Shoulders in 10 Minutes a Day $11.95
Older & Wiser: A Workbook for Coping With Aging, $12.95
Prisoners of Belief: Exposing & Changing Beliefs that Control Your Life, $10.95
Be Sick Well: A Healthy Approach to Chronic Illness, $11.95
Men & Grief: A Guide for Men Surviving the Death of a Loved One., $11.95
When the Bough Breaks: A Guide for Parents of Sexually Abused Childern, $11.95
Love Addiction: A Guide to Emotional Independence, $11.95
When Once Is Not Enough. Help for Obsessive Compulsives, $11.95
The New Three Minute Meditator, $9.95
Getting to Sleep, $10.95
The Relaxation & Stress Reduction Workbook, 3rd Edition, $13.95
Leader's Guide to the Relaxation & Stress Reduction Workbook, $19.95
Beyond Grief: A Guide for Recovering from the Death of a Loved One, $10.95
Thoughts & Feelings: The Art of Cognitive Stress Intervention, $13.95
Messages: The Communication Skills Book, $12.95
The Divorce Book, $11.95
Hypnosis for Change: A Manual of Proven Techniques, 2nd Edition, $12.95
The Deadly Diet: Recovering from Anorexia & Bulimia, $11.95
Chronic Pain Control Workbook, $13.95
Rekindling Desire: Bringing Your Sexual Relationship Back to Life, $12.95
Life Without Fear: Anxiety and Its Cure, $10.95
Visualization for Change, $12.95
Guideposts to Meaning: Discovering What Really Matters, $11.95
Videotape: Clinical Hypnosis for Stress & Anxiety Reduction, $24.95
Starting Out Right: Essential Parenting Skills for Your Child's First Seven Years, $12.95
Big Kids: A Parent's Guide to Weight Control for Children, $11.95
My Parent's Keeper: Adult Children of the Emotionally Disturbed, $11.95
When Anger Hurts, $12.95
Free of the Shadows: Recovering from Sexual Violence, $12.95
Resolving Conflict With Others and Within Yourself, $12.95
Lifetime Weight Control, $11.95
The Anxiety & Phobia Workbook, $13.95
Love and Renewal: A Couple's Guide to Commitment, $12.95
The Habit Control Workbook, $12.95

Call **toll free, 1-800-748-6273**, to order books. Have your Visa or Mastercard number ready. Or send a check for the titles you want to New Harbinger Publications, 5674 Shattuck Avenue, Oakland, CA 94609. Include $2.00 for the first book and 50¢ for each additional book, to cover shipping and handling. (California residents please include appropriate sales tax.) Allow four to six weeks for delivery.

Prices subject to change without notice.